THE RELIGIOUS DIMENSIONS OF PERSONALITY

THE
RELIGIOUS DIMENSIONS
OF PERSONALITY

WAYNE E. OATES

ASSOCIATION PRESS, NEW YORK

THE RELIGIOUS DIMENSIONS OF PERSONALITY

Library of Congress catalog card number: 57-11600

55

Printed in the United States of America
American Book–Stratford Press, Inc., New York

To
William Wayne Oates
and
Charles Edwin Oates

". . . for I say unto you, that in heaven their angels do always behold the face of my Father who is in heaven" (Matthew 18:10).

PREFACE

PERSONALITY THEORY IS AT THE CROSSROADS today. Both theologians and psychologists stand at the intersection. Their interests converge and separate at the point of identifying the religious dimensions of personality.

Let me be very clear as to what I mean by "the religious dimensions of personality." Implicit within this definition are the main themes of the following pages. In the first place, when I say "religious dimensions of personality," I am *not* proposing a facet-view of religion and personality. Religion is not just one facet of a many-facet reality known as personality. It refers to the total personality, and the following discussion will consistently emphasize a psychological holism which is really a modern re-affirmation of the vital holism of personality set forth in the Old and New Testaments. There are many subordinate themes in this book, but they all stand in relation and subordinate to this theme.

In the second place, when I say that there are religious dimensions of personality, I mean that personality not only has length of years, breadth of sensory contact, and depth of unconscious motivation. It also has height of aspiration and meaningful purpose which extends beyond that which is seen into the unseen realities of life. In other words, the dimension of ultimate concern and perception is necessary for any true interpretation of personality.

In the third place, the words "religious dimensions of personality" have more than just an allegorical use such as has just been stated. They refer also to *the interpretation of personality from a religious point of view or perspective*. The word "dimension" comes from a Latin word meaning "to measure." Modern conceptions of personality are measurings or interpretations of the phenomena of man's observation of himself and his fellows. They are points of view, perspectives, measurings of man as man. This book frankly interprets personality from a religious point of view.

In the fourth place, the dimensional understanding of personality set forth here refers to the specific nature of man's relatedness as a person. The whole point of view here is an interpersonal interpretation of personality. However, this interpersonal situation is multidimensional. Man is not just in a soliloquy with himself. He is in dialogue with his fellows. The dialogue itself has an ultimate dimension: man as an individual and as a race exists before and encounters God. When we use the words "religious dimensions of personality," therefore, we are underscoring the God-man relationship.

However, the very word "religious" itself needs explicit attention. It is used ambidextrously in this book. In one sense, it is used "right-handedly" to refer to man's ultimate concerns, to the spiritual interpretation of man's nature and destiny, and to his encounter with God. On the other hand, frank recognition is given to the fact that "religion" is an omnibus term which does not spell out the uniqueness of the Christian faith. Therefore, the term "religion" is used "left-handedly" at times in the same way that the apostle Paul used it in Acts 18, to refer to the rituals, idolatries, and the like that kept people from the knowledge of the Living God in Christ.

Therefore, this book is set forth from the vantage point of the Christian faith. This has been done because more general works of great merit are already in print, because the main questions of Christians are often overlooked in more general approaches, and because of my own personal commitment to the Christian faith. I have frankly and, I hope, articulately sought to set forth a Christian statement, examining scientific materials from this perspective with no apologies.

A word needs to be said about my method of inquiry. I am convinced that empirical observation which is existential, participant, and scientific is indispensable for the religious man who chooses to describe the nature of interpersonal processes. However, I am equally convinced that the theologian's contribution to psychology lies in the clues to the meaning of these processes which he by his discipline can give. His real function is to raise questions that need to be asked because of their importance and not just because a neat method has already been devised for "answering" them. He must have the courage to ask the imponderable questions.

As to my method of inquiry, I have appealed to many witnesses and quoted them extensively. One reason for this is that I am following William James' method of letting the autobiography of persons speak for them rather than "rehashing" their utterances with my meaning. Another reason is that I would like the book to be a real guide to the reader in becoming acquainted with the storehouse of literature in this rich area as well as with my own point of view. Careful attention to the interpretative analyses at the end of each chapter will give the reader a clear continuity of my own line of thought.

I could hope that this book will be of most help to the Christian who is hesitating to take psychology with full seriousness lest it remove his faith. Likewise, I could hope that what has been written here will be helpful in pointing out where contemporary psychological material needs correction through Christian insights. The conclusions drawn here are expressed with a depth of commitment but also with an openness of mind to the reader, be he minister or layman, Christian or non-Christian, who would join me in this search for an understanding of the religious dimensions of personality.

Acknowledgment of sources is made at the end of each chapter. However, I must express my indebtedness to James Rietmulder and Roland Burdick of Association Press for having helped me to develop this manuscript from the start to the finish. Their precision and care in the processes of editorial work make the life of an author a fellowship of creative work with his publishers. Professor Seward Hiltner of the University of Chicago read carefully this manuscript and made invaluable suggestions for its clarity. Likewise, I owe more than I can say to two classes in a course in the psychology of religion at the Southern Baptist Theological Seminary. They have been the willing discussants as I have taught this material. They have been my constant conversationalists as we have developed these ideas together. Miss Clara McCartt has prepared the final manuscript for publication, and my gratitude to her is deep and sincere for her having typed these pages in off-hours from a very responsible position.

Writing a technical manuscript is a tedious and lonely task. One foregoes many social occasions and "bull sessions" with his friends and colleagues. I am grateful for my two sons, Bill and Charles, however, who interrupted me often enough to remind me that writing a book is a secondary task to that of inscribing my love for them on the "fleshy tablets of their hearts." Likewise, my wife's gentle serenity has so nourished all three of our needs for earthly understanding that work is an adventure rather than a duty.

WAYNE E. OATES

The Southern Baptist Theological Seminary
Louisville, Kentucky

CONTENTS

CHAPTER I

————————— ◆ —————————

THE RELIGIOUS UNDERSTANDING
OF PERSONALITY IN TRANSITION

AT THE TIME OF THE WRITING OF THESE WORDS, a prominent Protestant preacher is leading a fabulously well-attended series of
religious meetings in the author's city of Louisville, Kentucky.
He is quoted in the morning paper as having said that the religious decisions of his audiences are not "emotional decisions, but
matters of the intellect and will." He is also reported to have said
that "the personality is a part of the soul; that part that lives on
after you die is the soul." *

Another minister reports that his laymen are asking him to
preach a sermon on "loving the Lord our God with all our *minds.*"
He is in a dilemma as to whether the mind is a separate part of
the person. If not, just how is he to preach on this subject re-
quested of him? Obviously, then, the problem of personality is
a "live" issue in the religious thinking of people. This is not just
a classroom exercise and object of research for scholars and
students. These two references alone reflect the importance of
defining the specifically religious dimensions of personality.

An orderly presentation of theological and other types of scien-

* Notes and credits for this chapter are found on page 29.

15

tific research on the nature of personality will help to form such a working hypothesis of the religious dimensions of personality. The concept of personality provides a comprehensive, organizing principle for a systematic psychology of religion. Likewise, such a psychology of religion is essentially a venture in Christian apologetics. In a very real way the psychology of personality is a rallying point at one and the same time for a secularization of the doctrine of man and an awakened religious concern among contemporary psychologists of personality.

Contemporary research persons in the field of personality are asking ultimate questions about the nature of personality. Gardner Murphy has expressed it in this way:

> In a future psychology of personality there will surely be a place for directly grappling with the question of man's response to the cosmos, his sense of unity with it, the nature of his esthetic demands upon it, and his feelings of loneliness or of consummation in his contemplation of it. There may be a touch of neurotic phobia in the persistence with which the modern study of man has evaded the question of his need in some way to come to terms with the cosmos as a whole. Whenever people have stopped the dizzying round of earning a living or the fascinating task of taking one another to pieces physically or metaphorically . . . they have felt incomplete as human beings except as they have endeavored to understand the filial relations of man to the cosmos which has begotten him. . . . It would, of course, be inexcusable dogmatism to insist that this or that is the psychological reason for such experiences, whether they derive from Oedipus complexes, from the fear of "too-bigness" of life, or from a primitive intellectual need for integration of experience. No one knows how adequate these guesses may be or what other factors may be involved. But our study of man must include the study of his response to the cosmos of which he is a reflection.[1]

The "dizzying round of earning a living" and "taking folks apart" has also been the part of the theologian as well as the psychologist. Both from the point of view of the theologian and from that of the psychologist, then, it is my fond hope that this book will be a stimulus to serious thinking as to the religious dimensions of personality. Contemporary psychologists of personality have expressed this need, and the need must be met by theologians. Contemporary preaching, religious education, systematic and biblical theology, and philosophical theology all have much at stake in the kind of conception of personality that becomes the controlling motif of modern man's image of himself. We need to mark well an awareness on man's part of the inescapable religious dimensions of his personality.

Several philosophical themes or motifs run through contemporary thinking on the religious dimensions of personality. These themes will appear persistently throughout the following chapters. Some understanding of them at the outset will give coherence and direction to the detailed studies that will follow. At times these themes appear quite distinct from each other; at others they are a veritable cacophony of confused voices. But they must be kept in mind. As Zunini, the Italian psychologist, has observed, "Too radical a separation of personality research from philosophy is both questionable and dangerous." [2] These philosophical frames of reference are greatly necessary for distinguishing the main components of an essentially Christian view of personality to be set forth in the concluding chapter.

DESCRIPTIVE OBJECTIVITY

The first theme is the *descriptive motif* that threads its way through all the research on personality. The passion for non-participant or objective observation, however much of an unrealized hypothesis it may be, has resulted in the accumulation of a residual body of fact about human personality. This body of fact is that to which Emil Brunner refers when he says that "there *is* a psychology which, at least in part, is not unaffected either by faith or unbelief, a knowledge of facts about man which the Christian must weave into his picture of man like anyone else, if his picture is to be true." [3] And, in the words of Karl Barth, this knowledge, as such, can "not be an enemy of the Christian confession of faith." [4]

However, this science thinks of man as a phenomenon, not of man himself as a person. It overlooks the fact which Harry Stack Sullivan noted about all observation: it is a participant observation, involving the selfhood of the observer in such a way as to change the reality of that person who is being observed. As Hendrik Kraemer has said, this attempt to be objective, to avoid judgments of value and truth, aims to understand religion and personality "according to its own intention and structure" in such a way that they can "speak for themselves." This is phenomenology, the aim of which is "to attain the highest possible objectivity." Yet, Kraemer is in accord with Sullivan at this point when he says that such understanding which

> cannot be accomplished with real divination and congeniality, without a *Verstehende Personlichkeit* (an understanding mind), shows already that the total being of a scholar, which includes his subjectivity, is called into action. The *Verstehende Personlichkeit*, by his particular being and structure, codetermines partly every phenomenology. . . .[5]

NATURALISTIC PERSONALITY THEORY

The second theme is a philosophical variation of the descriptive one which might be called *a naturalistic theme*. Naturalistic research persons make description a philosophical end in itself. They take the supposedly amoral, a-religious facts to which reference has just been made and make a closed system of naturalistic phenomena of them. Much of the research in psychology of religion, for instance, has been done on the moving assumption that religion is a naturalistic epiphenomenon but not a reality in and of itself. Man is perceived as a finite being with finite problems pursuing finite ends. He is both his own salvation and his own destruction. The highest refinement of this is humanism as a way of life. Nature is God, as Diderot has nature to say to man:

> In vain, O slave of superstition, do you seek your happiness beyond the limits of the world in which I have placed you. Have the courage to free yourself from the yoke of religion, my haughty rival which does not recognize my prerogatives. Cast out the Gods who have usurped my power, and return to my laws. Return to nature from which you have fled; she will console you and dispel all those fears which now oppress you. Submit to nature, to humanity, and to yourself again; and you will find flowers strewn all along the pathway of your life.[6]

This was largely the path cut out for man by the age of the Enlightenment, according to Cassirer. It led to a highly refined attitude of enlightened self-interest. But, as Cassirer also says, we cannot call this a basically irreligious attitude or an attitude inimical to religion. A religion of the finite is made an end in itself. The religion of reason fits well into it, and the ground of extreme forms of Protestant liberalism was well laid in this enlightened naturalism.

SUPERNATURALISM IN PERSONALITY PERSPECTIVES

Reactions against naturalistic personality orientations have produced supernaturalistic interpretations of personality throughout history. This has been particularly true among conservative religious thinkers concerning personality. In their attempts to conserve the claims of pietistic and conventionally popular religion, they often have taken views of personality that are alien to a Christian understanding of man. They have forcefully adopted an essentially pagan dualism of "body" and "spirit," natural and supernatural, and so on.

Put in the crudest terms, the supernaturalistic understanding of personality makes man's body "natural" and his soul "supernatural." The laws of nature control his body and are the un-rivaled province of medicine, psychology, and science in general. In fact, if watered-down reinterpretations of Thomas Aquinas are followed, a whole "natural theology" can be devised to cover this sphere of demarcated existence. The laws of the supernatural God apply to the soul of man; and man is perceived as "having" a soul which is the unrivaled province of religion, the working ground of the priest; and theology becomes an amputated "province" of human life. The archfundamentalist and/or supernaturalist, whether he is Protestant or Catholic, who takes such a position draws heavily upon Greek rather than Hebrew assumptions about personality. To quote Hendrik Kraemer, this is a

> tendency to treat the Biblical message and doctrine, not as *kerygma,* and their unpurified psychology [takes] *intellectus* (understanding) and *voluntas* (will) as *facultates animae* which were *diversi modi in eadem substantia* (faculties of the mind which were differing forms in the same substance). This represents Aristotelian and not Biblical psychology.[7]

It can be added, also, that the main source of this kind of thinking, which has been taken lock, stock, and barrel by Protestant fundamentalism is the Catholic theologian, Thomas Aquinas, and not Luther, Calvin, Knox, nor the Anabaptists.

Much of the warfare between science and religion has moved upon the presuppositions of a supernaturalist-naturalist controversy. To this controversy may be attributed much of heavy secularism in the field of psychology and psychotherapy today. Such either-or thinking about man, based upon presuppositions which were both unfamiliar to and rejected by the Hebrew-Christian writers of the primary documents of the Christian faith, has laid the groundwork for the secularization not only of science but also of religion. Therefore, one of the persistent ideas running throughout the following pages is that of pointing up the radical difference between what is commonly called "religion" and what is not so commonly known as the Christian faith. For, as Fosdick is quoted as having said, what many contemporary psychologists call religion, the New Testament and the eighth-century (B.C.) prophets call sin!

THE REVELATIONAL APPROACH TO PERSONALITY

This negation calls for a quick affirmation of another motif in personality research. This is a reaffirmation of the Hebrew view of the vitality and totality of personality as seen from the point of view of revelational theology. Such an approach to personality sees man in terms of the wholeness of the self as a creature standing *in relation* before God as the Creator. Nevertheless, this relationship is a disrupted relationship, made so by sin, accomplished through man's freedom. Man, through sin, is ambiguously and destructively related to himself, to his fellows, and to his Creator, and stands before God in need of reconciliation, redemption, and restoration of freedom, having been bound by his own rebellion, or sin. God actively engages man in self-encounter, interpersonal encounter, and in dialogue with himself.

This experience is both revelation and reconciliation, conviction and redemption. Through conviction or self-acceptance man knows himself in relation to God as a sinner. Through revelation and atonement man knows God as redeemer. He thrusts himself by faith upon the grace of God as he is revealed partially through the law and the prophets and fully in Jesus Christ. This experience reveals man's nature as being a self, or an I, to himself and lays upon him the responsibility of *becoming* the self that in creation and redemption he has been given the grace and power to become.

Contemporary theologians are exceptionally productive in developing a biblical theology that "spells out" the nature of personality in its religious dimension. Notable among these are Emil Brunner, in his book *The Doctrine of Creation and Redemp-*

tion; Surjit Singh, in his monograph *A Preface to Personality;*
Rudolph Bultmann, in his two-volume work *New Testament
Theology;* Reinhold Niebuhr, in his book *The Self and the
Dramas of History;* A. R. Johnson, in his monograph *The Vitality
of the Individual in the Thought of Ancient Israel;* J. A. T. Robinson, in *The Body: A Study in Pauline Theology;* Martin Buber,
in all his many works, but especially in *I and Thou* and *Between
Man and Man;* Hendrik Kraemer, in *Religion and the Christian
Faith.* Of course, the work of Søren Kierkegaard is a treasury of
insight on the nature of personality from a revelational point of
view. In Christian history probably the most influential writer
was Augustine. His understanding of personality has been carefully studied by John H. McClanahan in an unpublished doctoral thesis at the Southern Baptist Theological Seminary entitled *The Psychology of the Self in the Writings of Augustine*
(1957).

This particular theme of personality understanding shared
emphasis upon the totality and being-in-relation in common
with continental theories of psychology, such as Stern's person-
alism, Wertheimer's application of the Gestalt concept to personality, and Spranger's *Verstehen* attempt to "grasp events as
fraught with significance in relation as a totality." [8] However, the
distinctively redemptive aspects of this kind of psychology are
dealt with best by theologically oriented psychologists of personality.

This revelational or redemptional theme of the understanding
of the religious dimensions of personality will be progressively
developed throughout the rest of this treatise and consummated
in the last chapter on "The Christian Understanding of Personality." This position is not taken out of disdain for persons who
would take other positions. Rather it is taken from the standpoint
of the importance of a distinctly Hebrew-Christian view of personality for a clear understanding of a personality theory which
has long suffered from neglect in American psychology because

this position has not been frankly, clearly, and unashamedly spelled out in detail. Nor is this an easy task because the several perspectives of personality set forth in the foregoing discussion are intricately interwoven with one another in the fabric of the Western Christian tradition. One is naïve indeed if he does not recognize that insistence upon the "distinctly Hebrew-Christian" view of personality is in itself a cry for release from the bondage of much that is a part of him by reason of his having been born into an Occidental culture which has overlaid even his own understanding of the Hebrew-Christian view of personality with many extraneous accretions.

PERSONALITY THEORY IN TRANSITION

The very need to redefine and reaffirm the Hebrew-Christian conception of personality, however, suggests that the personality theory is undergoing a transition and that this redefinition and reaffirmation is timely indeed. Gardner Murphy, as he closes his monumental work on personality after having reviewed all the significant research at the time of his writing, says that two or three generations hence all that he recorded would be inadequate, fragmentary, and "temporally oriented." He intimates that the whole field of personality research is undergoing a "pulverization" and that the ultimate dimensions of man's personhood will be the direction of the reshaping of personality perspectives.

If, as theologians, we do our work well, we can participate meaningfully and—I hope—humbly in this redefinition of the personality in terms of its religious dimensions. To use Murphy's phrase in his remarks quoted at the outset of this chapter, this psychology of personality has room for "directly grappling" with these issues, questions, and concerns.

The Christian theologian cannot let the fear of being charged with a "Christian bias" keep him out of this grappling. Neither can he sit safely within the areas of the recorded sayings of the Scriptures and the church fathers who spoke the "language of Zion" without at the same time trying to learn the language of his fellow grapplers, the psychologists, psychiatrists, and psychoanalysts. He cannot do it for the very reason that these other research men are at this identical moment facing some of the same questions about man and his destiny with which the writers of Scripture and the documents of classical Christianity grappled. They are reformulating answers to these problems which often, as Richard Niebuhr says, use the classical concepts of redemption, atonement, reconciliation, and the like with little or no knowledge or regard for the historical meaning of the Christian faith.

Therefore, the task we have at hand in this treatise, in addition to being a systematization of the psychology of religion, actually goes beyond the province of the psychology of religion as such and enters the arena of Christian apologetics. The midcentury task of the psychologist of religion is not simply a descriptive one, as was true at the turn of the century in which the phenomena of the religious consciousness were recorded. Nor is it in essence a deification of the processes of the smooth continuities of the natural sciences, as has been true more recently. Even less, the task of the psychologist of religion is not to "retread" the weak places in Catholic and Protestant supernaturalist authoritarianism with a few patches of evidence made synthetically from the descriptive data of psychology and psychotherapy.

The task of midcentury psychology of religion as taught by a Christian theologian is to bring the witness of Reformation theology to bear upon the presuppositions, the conclusions, and the therapeutic methodology of contemporary psychology of personality. At the same time, the Christian theologian cannot take too immediate a recourse to the theological reality behind scientific psychology and psychotherapy. We agree with Hendrik

Kraemer that to do so "is a damaging simplification and a cause of complete breakdown of communications between Christian thinkers and the world. As in all things, one must be theological at the right moment, and not at every moment, which is a great art." [9]

The Christian theologian must hear the scientific research men in the field of personality theory until they have finished what they have to say. He must then stay "open" to them in the event that the very act of his listening to them has brought new light to them, and with the sure knowledge that they, too, are persons for whom Christ died, whether they know it or not. It is the theologian's task not only to bear witness to Christian truth, but to do so in such a way as to persuade even the psychologist to be reconciled to God in Christ. Furthermore, the psychologists are not going to quit their lifework just because he happens to be a theologian. They are going to continue their research, and through them even more light will come to help the theologian in his task. This will be true especially if they, too, are Christians.

However, the Christian theologian must not relegate his concern for personality just because psychologists do not become Christian and develop secular views of man, sin, and salvation. The Christian theologian must have the depth of perception to grasp the religious dimensions of personality running through their conversations, whether they recognize them or not. His theological science must rank first as he searches for disguised manifestations of religious concern and uncovers the hidden roots of phenomena reported by the psychologists of personality.

This task of the contemporary theologian as a participant in the personality-in-transition theory, psychology of religion, and the theological doctrine of man is imbued with a vivid sense of urgency in the light of the world situation today. Contemporary psychotherapy and psychologies of personality are in a subtle way preparing the Western mind for an easier acceptance of the humanistic, mystical religions of the East as over against the redemptive religious faith of Christianity. This is being done both consciously and unintentionally.

The great concern of the outstanding psychotherapists for religion, and their nonchalance and even hostility to the Christian faith, as such, is a case in point. And, as Kraemer says of the archetypal psychology of Jung, this type of psychology "concurs with that of primitive and esoteric Buddhism and with forms of esoteric Hinduism." [10] The fact that Karen Horney embraced Hinduism as her own faith before her death also speaks mutely to the involvement of psychotherapists with a religion that shapes itself around human needs rather than calling for a transformation of human nature into a new creation. Further evidence may be found in Gardner Murphy's work on personality when he speaks of "the fundamental unity of that ocean of which individual personalities are droplets." [11] When he speaks of psychologists of personality integrating their findings "with older insights of an intuitive or poetic sort," we wonder to what kind of sources he is referring.

College students particularly are being culturally conditioned for a depersonalized kind of religious syncretism. This is no one's "fault" so much as it is everyone's responsibility. The combined force of the negation by silence created by the effects of the separation of church and state upon religious teaching in schools, plus the ease with which religions other than Judaism and Christianity can be taught without opposition, does much to turn our whole culture in a distinctly non-Christian direction for religious insight.

The ease with which Buddhism, Hinduism, and the religious cults of the upper-middle, lower-upper, and upper-upper classes can be taught through courses in anthropology, psychology, and other diciplines also makes these beliefs to be "marks of distinction" for those who are "upwardly mobile" because of education recently achieved. Education is one of the main means of improving one's social status. Traditional religious beliefs held by a person's parental family are often sloughed off with other symbols of their "backwardness" and lack of sophistication. Too often social class problems become so interwoven with religious issues of life that they are hardly distinguishable from each other. Likewise, this interest is further re-enforced by the need to rebel against conventional forms of the Christian faith. These, too often, are caricatures taken for the real thing by a community of learning which is highly informed about everything except the primary sources of literature out of which their whole religious culture emerged, namely, the Old and New Testaments.

The main threat, however, is the secularization of religion into the historically rootless thought forms of the specialties of the various helping professions. This is vividly apparent in the way in which theological students, trained in public schools and universities, get their guiding image of the helping ministries from psychologists, psychiatrists, social workers, business administrators of human relations and so on. Through the influence of their churches they enter the Christian ministry, but the distinctly secular image of the private practitioner prevails.

For the student of psychology in college and in professional school, a forthright confrontation of the religious dimensions of personality is imperative. Probably in no field are more so-called "final" answers being given than to problems of the nature of personality and its religious dimensions. Students are, in too many instances, given one set of psychological "orthodoxies." They may be kept in the dark as to what the other psychologists of different persuasions have said about the same problems. Thankfully we can say that this is less true now than formerly. Also, the results of scientific research in the psychology of personality are often an unexplored continent for teachers of religion and their students. Yet, no systematic survey of this voluminous literature is easily accessible to their reach, and very few "maps" have been made of this "continent."

It must be emphasized that the confrontation and exploration of the religious dimensions of personality are necessary because the validity of the Christian claims is being "brushed off" too often by blasé remarks that "psychology says" that they are not to be taken seriously. Sophomoric handling of both religion and psychology can be effectively offset only by a serious study of what "psychology" and "religion" really say about the religious dimensions of personality. Therefore, the hope to be of real aid to college students, professors, and pastors in the wrestlings of the spirit that the study of psychology creates for growing minds is one of the main motives of this writing. The more I have studied in the field, the more secure my religious convictions have become. I could hope that this will enable others to define that goal also.

The crisis transition which contemporary psychological perspectives of personality are undergoing, then, has both an apologetic and a pastoral relevance for the knowledge and service of God in the life of the churches today. Pastoral counseling and its larger context of pastoral care will be pushed from one unexamined set of fadistic assumptions to another without this serious endeavor as a primary concern. Theory and practice cannot be neatly separated except for competitive purposes among insecure classroom teachers who are still trying to find a place in already overcrowded divisions and subdivisions of the college, university, seminary, and medical school curricula.

The more we plumb the depths of the practice of the Christian ministry, the more the basic nature of man before God emerges as a primary concern. The more we plumb this primary concern, the more we begin to ask questions about the crudeness and ineptness of our pastoral practice. Consequently, such a study of the religious dimensions of personality may, it is fondly hoped, be a happy meeting place for an enriched and stimulating conversation between all the disciplines of theological study as well as between the theologians and the scientists of personality.

Such a hope, however, necessitates a clear word about the method of inquiry I am using here. This will need restatement at at least one more point later, but an early statement of it is imperative at this point. The method of inquiry I am using here is briefly this: On matters of fact, facts which elucidate personal and interpersonal processes of either a developmental or a redemptive sort, I believe that empirical observation is indispensable. This empirical observation must be participant, existential, and scientific at one and the same time. Therefore, any statements concerning the religious dimensions of personality that pretend to elucidate processes and yet are not ready to do the grimy work of faithful observation and examination are misguided. On the other hand, however, the function of faith in relation to psychology is to give clues, to set forth value-presuppositions, and to insist that questions be asked because of their importance and not merely because of the methods by which they may be studied. Consequently, asking these questions is in and of itself necessary to the exploration of the religious dimensions of personality, and, in my opinion, integral to the total study of personality.

NOTES FOR CHAPTER I

1. Gardner Murphy, *Personality: A Biosocial Approach to Origins and Structure* (New York: Harper & Brothers, 1947), p. 919. By permission.
2. G. E. Zunini, "La Psicologia e L'Uomo," *Riv. Filosofia Neosc.*, Luglio, 1940.
3. Emil Brunner, *The Christian Doctrine of Creation and Redemption: Dogmatics,* Vol. II, trans. Olive Wyon (Philadelphia: Westminster Press, 1952), pp. 46-47.
4. Karl Barth, *Church Dogmatics,* Vol. III, 2, trans. A. C. Cochrane (Philadelphia: Westminster Press, 1953), p. 26.
5. Hendrik Kraemer, *Religion and the Christian Faith* (London: Lutterworth Press, 1956), p. 48.

6. Diderot, *Supplement au Voyage de Bougainville* (1771), *Oeuvres,* ed. Assezat, Vol. II, pp. 199 ff. Quoted in Ernst Cassirer, *The Philosophy of the Enlightenment* (Princeton, N. J.: Princeton University Press, 1951), p. 135.
7. Kraemer, *op. cit.,* p. 169.
8. Gordon W. Allport, "European and American Theories of Personality," *Perspectives in Personality Theory,* eds. H. P. David and Helmut Von Bracken (New York: Basic Books, Inc., 1957), p. 9.
9. Hendrik Kraemer, *The Communication of the Christian Faith* (Philadelphia: Westminster Press, 1956), p. 60.
10. Kraemer, *ibid.,* p. 71.
11. Murphy, *op. cit.,* p. 919.

CHAPTER II

A SYNOPTIC DEFINITION
OF RELIGION AND PERSONALITY

THE WORDS "RELIGION" AND "PERSONALITY" will be used so often in the following pages that they will be meaningless unless carefully defined. As one pulls down his dictionary and other authoritative sources and tries to pin down the meaning of these two words, he is impressed by the fact that in some instances they are used almost interchangeably, in others similar definitions are given, and in still others a kindred sort of vagueness appears as the authors admit the inadequacy of any definitions.*

MISCONCEPTIONS OF PERSONALITY AND RELIGION

Some common misconceptions of personality and religion arise from overclassifying them with one particular aspect of either. For instance, personality is often overidentified with "mind"; religion is similarly overclassified with "reason" or "emotion." Such pigeonholing of religion and personality as a part of life leads to faulty thinking, vagueness of definition, and damaging practice. Neither personality and "mind" nor religion and "emo-

* Notes and credits for this chapter begin on page 50.

31

tion" are coextensive terms. This distinction in itself is not clear without some plain examples.

Leuba, for instance, defined religion by dividing definitions current at the time of his writing into the "intellectualistic," the "voluntaristic," and the "affectivistic." He himself defined religion as a "type of rational behavior."[1]

In line with this overclassification, religious conversions are often rejected upon the value-judgment that they are "emotional" experiences. A more precise example of confusion wrought by overclassifying religion and personality with reason is found in discussions of mental illness. Pickett quotes St. Thomas Aquinas as saying:

> I answer that of actions performed by man, those only are properly called human which are proper to man as man. Now man is different from irrational animals in that he is the master of his actions. Wherefore those actions alone are properly called human of which man is the master. Now man is master of his actions through his reason and his will: whence also free will is defined as the faculty of will and reason. Therefore those actions are rightly called human which proceed from a deliberate will. And if any other actions are found in man, they may be called actions of a man but not properly human actions, since they are not proper to man as man.[2]

Such a hypothesis about personality assumes that when reason or "mind" departs, then the mentally sick person is something *less* than a person, something other than human. This is not what Pickett and St. Thomas necessarily *mean* to say, but it is exactly what the populace *hear* them say. Such a point of view does not have to be repeated more than once to prompt the treatment of mentally ill people as animals such as Philip Pinel encountered at Bicêtre. (Pinel, it will be recalled, was an early psychiatrist in France who astounded his patients by releasing them from cages and chains in which they had been bound by former superintendents of the hospital.) Mental patients—people "without reason"—were caged and used for Sunday afternoon amusements of persons who visited the place as if it were a zoo. The Gadarene villagers accorded this kind of treatment to the demoniac. They consigned him to the graveyard without the benefit of a funeral. If his "reason" was gone, he was no more "useful" than the dead.

Such overclassification of both personality and religion with reason or "mind" is also reflected in the popular superstition that if a person is said to be mentally ill, it necessarily means that he is not bright intellectually. The college counselor, in talking with the family of a mentally sick student, will hear them say, "Our son *couldn't* be mentally ill. He has made straight A's in all his work up to this year!"

The concept of "mind" as being the total person has been challenged by men like Kurt Lewin. He considered this as part of an outmoded method of thinking. He saw the intellectual or cognitive aspect of personality as only *one* dimension of the dynamic personality. Attitudes such as have been described are essentially value-judgments of persons rather than dependable and constructive descriptions of the nature of personality, according to Lewin.[3] Consequently, to overidentify personality with a personal desire to glorify the "intellectual" or "rational" dimensions of human life as a whole does little more than obscure rather than clarify the meaning of personality and religion.

Of course, overclassification of the nature of personality with mind and reason is the obverse side of the rejection of the body as a legitimate part of the personality and of the concerns of religion. This is alien to the biblical conception of the wholeness of man. To be drawn into such misconceptions results in the kind of confusion of which Goethe speaks when he says:

> . . . none e'er comprehended
> How soul and body wedded are blended,
> Hold fast, as if defying separation
> Yet never cease their mutual irritation.[4]

But more than this, the director of religious education, the college counselor, and the pastor see the results of such confused thinking in counseling with students who perceive their basic bodily needs as evil or as without either moral or religious dimensions, or both.

The "mutual irritation" due to distorted teaching adds insult to injury for the developing attitudes of persons, particularly in their preparation for and participation in marriage. The rigid dichotomies of flesh and spirit underlying many of the conflicts that prevent people from having happy marriages are alien to the Hebrew mind, the prophetic witness, and to great seers of history such as Browning. Therefore, the division and over-classification of personality or religion must be carefully rejected. In the spirit of Browning,

> Let us not always say,
> "Spite of this flesh today,
> I strove, made head, gained ground upon the whole!"

> As the bird wings and sings;
> Let us cry: "All good things
> Are ours, nor soul helps flesh more now, than flesh helps soul."

THE ETYMOLOGY OF "PERSONALITY" AND "RELIGION"

What do the dictionaries and lexicons say about the meaning which men have given to the two basic concepts of religion and personality?

The word "personality" is derived from the Latin word *persona*, a noun which is derived from a verb form *personare* which means "to sound through." The word has two usages in the Latin. The first meaning is "a mask," used by players in a drama to cover the whole head and to be changed to fit the character to be represented. The second meaning is "a personage, a character, a part," and is used to refer to the part, the role, or the character played by a person in the drama. This can be expanded a bit to refer to life itself as a drama, as did Shakespeare when he said that all the world is a stage and each of us is an actor. Thus a secondary meaning is derived in which *persona* means the "part" or character which anyone "plays" in the world. This can be further developed in use to refer to any human being, and especially to his *personage*, or that certain standing that a person has by reason of his age, sex, or marital status, among his fellows. This latter was particularly important in the Roman world in which the word *persona* was used to distinguish a freeborn citizen from a slave.

The Hebrews had no word for personality. Nor did they have a word for body. The body was the man, and there was no differentiation between the physical and psychical, the natural and supernatural. In Hebrew thought, the *nephesh* is the inner aspect of the body, and the body is the outward form of the *nephesh*. "What happens to the body happens to the *nephesh*, so that even the mutilation of the dead body can be a terrible thing."[5] To read the Greek idea of "the soul" into the Hebrew word is a mistake, because the word "describes the unity we call man," and may at times be used to mean "life" itself. *Nephesh* refers to "self," and "stands for personal pronouns— I, Thou, or He."[6]

Leb is another Hebrew word which, like *nephesh*, traps the elusive Hebrew understanding of that which the Western mind has come to call "personality." This word, usually translated "the heart," is used frequently "to denote the personality as a whole on its inner side, the inner life or character."[7] *Nephesh* is the total person as a whole, and the heart is its inner value and being. These are the two words native to the Hebrew understanding of the meaning of personality. Rust attributes the latter references to *ruach* or spirit as over against other constituent parts of man's personhood as being due to the extraneous influences of the Exile on Hebrew writers' thinking about the nature of personality.[8]

In Jesus' teachings the word *kardia* is used in the same sense that the Old Testament uses the Hebrew word *leb* for heart. The heart is the center of man's being, the source of the issues of life, and the core of man's spiritual motivation. In Jesus' teachings *psuche* and *pneuma* are used in companionate but not synonymous meanings. *Psuche* referred to the very life of man, which was more precious than anything else, that which it did not profit a man to gain everything and lose. *Pneuma* is a word which puts this in relation, not just to itself and its own preciousness, but to God, and was used to refer to the eternal, God-encountering dimension of man's total life-relationships.

The Hebrews of the Old Testament did not have a word for the body, but thought in terms of the whole body being exercised at any given and living moment through any given part of the body. However, in the New Testament, and particularly in the teachings of Paul, two words, *sarx* and *soma*, translated *flesh* and *body*, capture the New Testament meaning of personality most completely. As Robinson says, these two words underscore the relational character of the religious dimensions of personality. In essence they

> designate different aspects of the human relationship to God. *While sarx stands for man, in the solidarity of creation, in his distance from God, soma stands for man, in the solidarity of creation, as made for God.*[9]

Also, Rudolf Bultmann says that this word for "body" is the "most comprehensive term for the total personality of man. He confesses with others that it is the "most complex," and understanding it is most difficult. But in his own definite way he says:

> Man, his person as a whole, can be denoted by soma. . . . *Man is called soma in respect to his being able to make himself the object of his own action or to experience himself as the subject to whom something happens.* He can be called soma, that is, *as having a relationship to himself*—as being able in a certain sense to distinguish himself from himself. Or, more exactly, he is so called as that

self from whom he, as subject, distinguishes himself, the self whom he can perceive as subjected to an occurrence that springs from a will other than his own. It is as such a self that man is called *soma*.[10]

Consequently, the rich inner diversity of man's selfhood as a self in dialogic relationship with itself and in encounter with God emerges. The New Testament conception of personality presents this in a way which is missing in the monolithic concepts of the Old Testament and the segmented views of the Greek and Roman world.

Another Greek word *prosopon*, used in the New Testament gives a rich and lucid meaning to personality. This word is usually translated "face," or "countenance" in the literal sense, but it is used with several different connotations which reflect the essentially religious overtones of the meaning of personality. Its usage is quite akin to the Roman or Latin usage of *persona* with some significant additions. Four passages from the New Testament reflect the various shades of meaning with which the word is invested. In Matthew 6:16 Jesus refers to the Pharisees who disfigure their faces in fasting to be seen of men. He urges his disciples to be different. The face as a deceptive mask, hiding the real self, a pseudoself of appearances reflects the rift that may come in personality between the apparent and the real self.

Anne Morrow Lindbergh gets at this dimension of duplicity between the apparent and the real self in personality when she writes:

> I find I am shedding hypocrisy in human relationships. What a rest that will be! The most exhausting thing in life, I have discovered, is being insincere. That is why so much of social life is exhausting; one is wearing a mask. I have shed my mask.[11]

Socrates expresses this lucidly also in his prayer:

> O Lord, give me beauty in the inner soul
> And may the outward man and the inward man be at one!

In a second passage which uses *prosopon* Paul, in Galatians 2:11, describes his face-to-face encounter with the apostle Peter over his having refused to eat with the Gentiles. Here personality is seen as the direct encounter of selves-in-relation to each other. The third passage refers to personality in terms of the personage, role, or status of a person, just as does *persona* in the Latin. This is exemplified in II Corinthians 5:12 in which Paul talks about men priding themselves on the positions that they hold, the status they have achieved, and so on. Sincerity and inner integrity are missing.

Finally, a fourth connotation is given to the word in Luke 9:51 in which the purposive nature of personality is symbolized in the fact that Jesus "set his face steadfastly to go to Jerusalem." Here the idea of purpose, goal, and intention is clearly marked out as an identifying dimension of personality. In these four passages, which could be paralleled by other relevant passages, personality is defined in terms of the real self as over against the pseudoself; it is defined in terms of the dynamic interactions of an interpersonal nature in the *betweenness* situations of men, as Buber calls it; it is defined in terms of the purposive striving which characterizes a person's life; it is identified in terms of the role that men take in the drama of society.

Similar lexical definitions of religion are enlightening in the face of the discussions of the meaning of personality. The word "religion" itself is a transliteration of the Latin word *religio* meaning to bind, to bind fast, or to fasten up. It is defined as reverence for God or the gods, or the fear of God. The word also carries with it a connotation of scrupulousness, anxiety to fulfill a covenant or an obligation. Furthermore, it refers to the objects of worship, veneration, and sacred feeling. The word is obviously related to another word, *religo*, which carries the meaning of chaining or fastening or holding back. This catches up two philosophical definitions which accent the ethical seriousness and the moral sensitivity to peril that usually goes with religion.

Immanuel Kant defined religion as "the recognition of all our duties as divine commands." Also, Bergson related the religious character of man to his need to hold back his own intelligence from destroying him. Religion is the chaining of man's intelligence much as Prometheus was chained to the rock after having stolen the fire from heaven. Also, man's search for redemption began, according to the Hebrew faith, when he came to know good and evil. But the common interpretation put on the binding quality of religion is that men are religious in a community of faith in which a tie of common worship "binds their hearts together" in the love of their God. The betweenness situation of the Greek is thus accented in the binding character of religion as seen through the Latin.

The word "religion" is not in very good repute in the New Testament. The word which is translated "religion" is used three times. In Acts 26:5, Luke uses it to refer to Judaism; in Colossians 2:18 it refers to the worshiping of angels; in James 2:17, the word is used in the good sense to refer to the practical work of caring for orphans and widows. But usually the word "religion" is rather foreign to the concerns of the New Testament. The contemporary defensiveness about religion on the part of people who are involved in professional religious work was of little concern to the writers of the New Testament. Usually, as did the eighth-century (B.C.) prophets, they found themselves against what was ordinarily thought of as being religion in their day. This is not to taboo the use of the word "religion" today. Its meaning has been enriched with all the great gains of the Christian faith as a living religion. At the same time, this negative use of the term, native to the original prophetic attitude, still serves to remind the modern Christian of the difference between folk-religion, or primitive nature religion, and the worship of the true and living God in Christ. However, the words for personality are rich with positive meaning in the New Testament, as has already been seen.

PHILOSOPHICAL AND PSYCHOLOGICAL DEFINITIONS
OF RELIGION AND PERSONALITY

The recurring themes in the definitions of personality and religion as they are set forth by philosophers and psychologists are too nearly alike for even the casual observer to miss the similarity. About five of these themes are apparent.

Supreme Value

First, both personality and religion are seen as the highest value of mankind. As Goethe poetically states it:

> Folk and serf and conqueror
> These concede in every age:
> The sons of earth find greatest joy
> In personality alone.[12]

Personality is perceived as being of supreme value, then. And as Allport defines religion,

> A man's religion is the audacious bid he makes to bind himself to creation and to the Creator. It is his ultimate attempt to enlarge and to complete his own personality by finding the supreme context in which he rightly belongs.[13]

The supreme value of personality is in itself an expression of religious concern. This was the hallmark of the ethical teachings of Jesus. Jesus said: "The Sabbath is made for man and not man for the Sabbath." He reflected this in his treatment of people, in the way he manifested tenderness to those whose persons were facing destruction, and in the way he martialed his aggressions toward those who exploited human life and avoided their own selves in the process. They thought that they did God a service, that is, that they were religious.

This dimension of the supreme value of personality and, for that matter, of life itself, comes to the surface of man's thoughts when the idea of suicide occurs to him. More primitive and unsophisticated individuals would express this insight in terms of a taboo. Uneducated persons might incorporate it into the familiar theological colloquialism that "all people who commit suicide are thereby sent to hell." Others may go so far as to say that this teaching is "in the Bible," although it is not.

But even the most sophisticated cannot laugh away this feeling of ultimate responsibility for deciding to maintain or to end life. In fact, they may say that the main reason for the wrongfulness of suicide lies in the fact that there is a God. He has created man and not man himself. To thus end this creation, is to break the human bond and, hence, any bond with its Source. It is to attempt to be God, to think that one can dispose of his own destiny. Thus, the sense of ultimate value in human personality and human life pervades all these reactions.

Uniqueness of Individuality

A second theme in philosophical and psychological definitions of religion and personality is that of the uniqueness of individuality of the person. Schleiermacher epitomizes this:

> For every man has in him all that another man has, but it is all differently determined; and the greatest similarity is only a diminishing or [relatively] vanishing difference.[14]

Cattell, on the other hand, defines personality as "that which enables us to predict what [man] will do in a given situation."[15] In other words, it is that pattern of dependable individuality which characterizes him. This helps his fellows to know him as an individual different from other people.

Just as personality is defined in terms of individuality, of the uniqueness of the person, so also is religion defined by Whitehead in terms of man's solitariness. He says that "religion is what the individual does with his own solitude." [16] He accents this by calling religion man's solitariness. This, Whitehead says, is symbolized by Prometheus on his rock, Mahomet brooding in the desert, Buddha under his tree, and the lonely Christ on his cross. Whereas this facet of Whitehead's thinking reflects his main thrust about mutuality in human life, and the isolated sentence does him injustice, nevertheless this partial hearing of him has been picked up by arch-individualists and used as denoting the essence of religion. The remarkable diversity of American religious life may be the outworking of such individualism in the religious life, as such, and in the American culture as well. Heavy emphases upon a highly individual conversion, as well as the insistence of the nonconformists upon the communion with God through nature, the arts, and personal meditation give some empirical credence to this point of view. Berdyaev appreciates loneliness in religious living in a remarkably poignant way when he says:

> Only when man is alone . . . does he become aware of his personality, of his originality, of his singularity and uniqueness, of his distinctness from every one and everything else. A man may feel himself definitely more alone in the midst of his co-religionists than in the midst of men of totally different beliefs and persuasions.[17]

The English romantic poet, Lord George Gordon Byron, caught the quintessence of the religion of solitude and its dimensions in personality in his *Childe Harold's Pilgrimage:*

> There is pleasure in the pathless woods,
> There is rapture on the lonely shore,
> There is society where none intrudes,
> By the deep Sea, and music in its roar;
> I love not Man the less, but Nature more,
> From these our interviews, in which I steal
> From all I may be, or have been before,
> To mingle with the Universe, and feel
> What I can never express, yet cannot at all conceal.[18]

The fact still remains that the need to withdraw from the clattery external interferences into one's own inner communion with the Infinite articulates the religion of many people today and characterizes them as persons.

The Communal Definitions

But conversely, the theme of individuality and solitude in the definitions of personality and religion stands over against the third theme of the communal definition of both religion and personality. Berdyaev does not stop with individuality in his definition of religion, for instance. He sees it in tension with the need of man for relationship with his fellows and says that absolute solitude would be synonymous with hell and nonbeing.[19]

> Religion implies a relationship; it may be defined as an attempt to overcome solitude, to release the Ego from its seclusion, to achieve community and intimacy. . . . But only God is capable of overcoming solitude.[20]

In the spirit of the New Testament aversion for identifying things of the spiritual life with what is commonly known as "religion," Berdyaev continues the preceding quotation by saying:

> Religion only implies a relationship, and, as such, can only be secondary and transitory. Transcendence and plenitude, as well as the purpose of existence, are only manifest in God. There is a tendency to overlook the fact that God is the primary consideration, that religion can prove an obstacle to man's communication with God.[21]

Certainly Harry Stack Sullivan would be among those psychotherapists who identify personality with man's need for relationship and say that personality *is* relationship and apart from the interaction that goes on between man and man personality does not exist. As Sullivan puts it, "people behave in interpersonal fields." [22] Roughly speaking, a whole grouping of contemporary psychologists of personality define a person in terms of the interactions of persons with each other.[23]

*But in the main this accents a theme of interpretation of per-
sonality that needs separate identity: the individual's need for
community.* The basic conviction of certain psychologists is that
personality becomes what it is by reason of the dynamic confrontation between persons. The contemporary philosopher who has
drawn the attention of many different fields of inquiry today is
Martin Buber. He, too, identifies personality with community.
In his book, *Between Man and Man,* he says that

> . . . modern collectivism is too often mistaken for community, but
> collectivity is not a binding but a bundling together: individuals
> packed together, armed and equipped in common, with only as
> much life from man to man as will inflame the marching step. But
> community . . . is the being no longer side by side *with* one another
> of a multitude of persons and this multitude, though it also moves
> towards one goal yet experiences . . . a dynamic facing of, . . . a
> flowing from *I* to *Thou.* . . . Bundled together, men march without
> *Thou* and without *I.*[24]

The whole discussion of personality and religion as individual, as
over against community, points to a basic polarity that exists between the individual and his community. Personality and religion
are more often defined in terms of this reciprocity. Angyal
chooses a term, the "biosphere" to cover these two forces in life
itself. Within the biosphere is the organismic autonomy and the
environmental heteronomy which are at one and the same time
parts of each other. "Every process which is a resultant" of these
two forces in relation to each other is part of the life process.
These are really not antagonistic forces. They are "only degrees
of ego proximity and ego distance. The degrees of ego proximity
and ego distance are the symbolic expression of the gradient of
autonomy and heteronomy." [25]

This is not unlike Schleiermacher's interpretation of life and
personality as the "alternation between an 'abiding-in-self'
(*Insichbleiben*) and a 'passing-beyond-self' (*Aussichheraustre-
ten*) on the part of the subject." [26] In another place,[27] Schleier-

macher says that the single and the particular are not possible except by means of a unity with God and community. The sum total of religion is the feeling of dependence upon the Absolutely Dependable.

T. S. Eliot poetically states the ever-existing tension of polarity between individuality and community in religion and personality when he says:

> What life have you if you have not life together?
> There is no life that is not in community,
> And no community not lived in praise of God.
> Even the anchorite who meditates alone,
> For whom the days and nights repeat the praise of God,
> Prays for the Church, the Body of Christ incarnate.[28]

Ethical Definitions

The definitions of religion and personality both move in the direction of ethical absolutes at many points. Immanuel Kant, as one would expect, accentuates the ethical dimensions of personality and religion. As has already been noted, he defines religion as the interpretation of all duties as divine commands. In talking of personality, he says that everything in creation except personality "can be used by man as a means to an end; but man himself, the rational creature, is an end in himself. He is the subject of the moral law and is sacred by virtue of his individual freedom." [29] Furthermore, Berdyaev again says that personality "has an autonomous validity which prevents it from being converted into a means." [30] As Goethe has said, "with all its hundred thousand pranks, the World is one enormous Fool!" [31] But the autonomous nature of personality is such as to make it always a subject rather than an object. It will not be fooled into being treated long as a thing!

This is the moving spirit of the writings of Martin Buber who focuses the religious quest and the quest for the meaning of personality together into a synoptic view. The I-Thou relationship is characterized by loving, encountering, and participating. The person is not an *It* but is either an *I* or a *Thou* in encounter. The moving dynamic of this encounter is love. As Berdyaev says, "love transforms the Ego into a personality." [32] This is why Brunner makes the ethical distinction that the individual truly becomes a person by responsible love for others in community. "Individuality," he says, "is fulfillment of our creation as persons destined for community." [33]

Religion as Purposiveness

Such a creative tension between the individual and the communal character of personality and religion, however, begins to give point, direction, and purpose to personality. This suggests the definitive statements about personality and religion. A consistent theme of the *purposiveness of personality* tends to separate philosophically oriented psychologists from the purely descriptive psychologists. Prescott Lecky gives the clearest statement of this point of view as a psychologist of personality in his posthumously published book when he says:

> Personality is a concept of the organism, created by us as a means of assisting our understanding of psychological phenomena. Personality goal is the striving of the individual to maintain a unified organization.[34]

Gordon Allport, in the Terry Lectures of 1954, challenges his fellow psychologists to enlarge their horizons without sacrificing the gains they have made. He emphasizes the purposes of mankind that not only preserve life but make it meaningfully worth living. These purposes have a futurity to them and do not dwell merely on the past history of the individual. Personality is characterized in Allport's interpretative definition by an ongoing purposive growth which he calls "becoming." Religion to him represents the "final meanings achieved by unique personalities in diverse lands and times." [35]

COMMON EMPHASES IN ATTEMPTED DEFINITIONS
OF PERSONALITY AND RELIGION

A synoptic definition of personality and religion, then, reveals that research men and interpreters in the two areas, writing independently of influence from each other, are defining religion and personality in the same basic themes. Often they use different nomenclatures. They voice, however, many of the richest insights of the poets in every generation, as has also been evident. The common witness of widely selected attempts at definition reflects that both religion and personality can be defined in any one of an inseparable series of working hypotheses.

Religion and personality both defy adequate definition because they share the emphasis on the vital unity and indivisible totality of man in relation to himself, his attendant created order, and the Creator. (1) Religion and personality can be defined ethically in terms of that which is of supreme value in the universe. (2) Religion and personality can be defined in terms of man's uniqueness, either as a race or as an individual, but always as that which makes him separate from other species and an individual apart from other members of the human race. (3) Religion and personality can be defined as *interpersonal* or communal in essence, as man in relation—always. (4) Religion and personality both can be and have been defined in terms of the dynamic tension existing between man's solitariness and his communal nature, thereby underscoring the basic ambiguity of his quest for life's meaning. (5) Religion and personality both may be defined in terms of the difference between personality and material things. This is a difference in meaningful quality and not in essential substance. It is the difference between *things* that are used as means, and *persons* whose natures defy any attempt to use them as anything less than an end in themselves. Again, this introduces the ethical element of justice and value into the basic definition of a *person*. (6) Finally, this points toward the intrinsic purposiveness of personality as a basis for its definition. Consistency of purpose and clarity of direction become both a religious dimension of personality and a psychological dimension of religion at one and the same time.

CHRISTIAN THEOLOGY AND THE DEFINITION
OF PERSONALITY

Even casual observation of the reflections of Christian theologians reveals how uncritically and often unconsciously they have drawn their definitions of personality from the prevailing thought patterns of their day. For instance, the influence of Neo-platonism and Manichaeism upon the thought of Augustine as he described the workings of human personality lie unassessed alongside his profound interpretations of the image of God in man. A more recent theologian of lesser repute, R. C. Moberly, in his book, *Atonement and Personality,* adopts a tripartite definition of personality in terms "first of free will; secondly of reason and wisdom; and thirdly of the divine faculty of love." [36] He reflects knowledge neither of the careful word studies of the Hebrew-Christian primary sources on the nature of man nor of the vast research on personality being conducted by scientific psychologists at the time of his writing and within a stone's throw of his home city. Yet, he—like E. Y. Mullins—was under the sway of a poorly transmitted Aristotelian conception of personality.

The result of such neglect of the courses of one's knowledge of the meaning of personality has two contrary effects. The first is a secularization of the theologian's view of personality when he inhales, without noticing the strangeness of the air, the commonly accepted perspectives of personality being breathed even by the man on the street of his day. Without a specific, conscious, and ordered study of personality in both its theological and scientific dimensions, the theologian and the preacher cannot avoid interpreting the basic nature of the Christian faith in what may be essentially non-Christian terms. The unalert theologian by his neglect of this study not only permits but also participates unwittingly in the secularization of religion. Much of the research on the psychology of personality consists of a humanistic handling of the basic issues of the Christian faith. The ease with which definitions of religion by theologians and the definitions of personality by psychologists can be seen synoptically is mute testimony to the heavy overlapping of concern by persons who move from quite different philosophical and theological presuppositions.

Therefore, a positive word needs to be said in conclusion as to the exact relation of the psychology of personality to the Christian doctrine of man. As Gregory Zilboorg has acutely observed, the psychologists have presented empirical descriptions of man as a sinner.[37] Mary Thelan has described the antireligious philosophies of Karl Marx and Sigmund Freud as "secular theories of the fall of man."

> Marx, in his picture of capitalist exploitation, and Freud, in his discovery of the unconscious suffering of the neurotic, had highly original appreciation of the degree to which man is enslaved by evil. Each had a theory, moreover, of the nature of the forces which had brought man into this bondage, and of how freedom from them might be secured.[38]

If this be true, then the theologian has empirical materials in the depth views of personality and the diagnoses of these men for interpreting man's need for redemption. Likewise, he has taken the first step at confronting the political materialist and the naturalistic psychoanalyst with the claims of the Christian faith in that he really knows their mind-set.

Yet, these secular doctrines of man offer their own "ways of salvation" which are essentially doctrines of man's enlightened self-sufficiency. In doing so, they fall short of an adequate definition of personality, in that the essential Hebrew-Christian view would see this as the deification of human personality, which is the core of original sin in and of itself. This is a rejection of the creaturely, finite, and circumscribed nature of man under God, an affirmation of man in his distance from God rather than his I-Thou encounter with God. In the Christ we see the perfection of human nature through redemptive love and sacrifice rather than a restless and anxious rejection of humanity as it strives to "become God." Until man encounters God in Christ, his own efforts to understand himself and to define the nature of his own personality go unaided and fraught with ambiguities and contradictions.

NOTES FOR CHAPTER II

1. James H. Leuba, *The Psychological Study of Religion: Its Origin, Its Function, Its Future* (New York: The Macmillan Company, 1912), pp. 3-22, 339-361.
2. S. Thomas Aquinas, *Summa Theologica*, I-II, q.1, a.1, in *Opera Omnia* (33 vols, in 17 tomes, Parisiis: Apud Ludovicum Vives, 1871), Vol. II, tome 1: *"Respondeo dicendum, quod actionum quae ab homine aguntur, illae solae proprie dicuntur humanae quae sunt proprie hominis, in quantum est."* Colin R. Pickett, *Mental Affliction and Church Law* (Ottawa, Ontario: The University of Ottawa Press, 1952).
3. Kurt Lewin, *A Dynamic Theory of Personality* (New York: McGraw-Hill Book Company, Inc., 1955), pp. 15, 16.
4. Johann Wolfgang von Goethe, *Faust*, Part II, Act II, Scene II (New York: Random House, Inc., 1950), p. 77.
5. Eric C. Rust, *Nature and Man in Biblical Thought* (London: Lutterworth Press, 1953), p. 104.
6. *Ibid.*, pp. 105 and 102.
7. *Ibid.*, p. 107.
8. *Ibid.*, p. 109.
9. John A. T. Robinson, *The Body: A Study in Pauline Theology* (Chicago: Henry Regnery Company, 1952), p. 31.
10. Rudolf Bultmann, *Theology of the New Testament*, Vol. 1 (New York: Charles Scribner's Sons, 1954), pp. 192, 195-196. Used by permission.
11. Anne Morrow Lindbergh, *Gift from the Sea* (New York: Pantheon Books, Inc., 1955), p. 32.
12. *West-Oestlicher Divan, Buch Suleika;* quoted by Gordon W. Allport, *Personality: A Psychological Interpretation* (New York: Henry Holt & Company, Inc., 1937), p. 32.
13. Gordon W. Allport, *The Individual and His Religion* (New York: The Macmillan Company, 1950), p. 142.

14. Friedrich Schleiermacher, *The Christian Faith* (Edinburgh: T. & T. Clark, 1928), p. 47.
15. Raymond B. Cattell, *An Introduction to Personality Study* (London: Hutchinson House, 1950), p. 21.
16. Albert North Whitehead, *Religion in the Making* (New York: The Macmillan Company, 1926), p. 16.
17. Nicolas Berdyaev, *Solitude and Society* (London: The Centenary Press, 1938), pp. 68-69, 92.
18. From Canto the Fourth, "The Ocean," CLXXVII.
19. Berdyaev, *op. cit., ibid.*
20. *Ibid.,* p. 91.
21. *Ibid.*
22. Harry Stack Sullivan, "The Study of Psychiatry," *Psychiatry* 10, 1947, pp. 355-371.
23. Bernard Notcutt, *The Psychology of Personality* (London: Methuen and Co., Ltd., 1953), p. 25.
24. From *Between Man and Man* by Martin Buber (London: Routledge & Kegan Paul, Ltd., 1947), pp. 31, 32, 33. Used by permission of The Macmillan Company, New York.
25. Andras Angyal, *Foundations for a Science of Personality* (New York: The Commonwealth Fund, 1941), p. 115.
26. Friedrich Schleiermacher, *The Christian Faith* (Edinburgh: T. & T. Clark, 1928), p. 8.
27. Friedrich Schleiermacher, *Speeches on Religion: Its Cultured Despisers* (London: Kegan Paul, Trench, Trubner & Co., Ltd., 1893), pp. 49-50.
28. T. S. Eliot, "Choruses from The Rock," *Collected Poems 1909–1935* (New York: Harcourt, Brace & Company, Inc., 1950), p. 188. By permission.
29. Immanuel Kant, "Kritik der Praktishen Vernunft," *Gesemmelte Schriften,* Bk. V (Reimer-Verlag, 1908), p. 87.
30. *Op. cit.,* pp. 122-123.
31. *Faust,* Part II, Act I, Scene III.
32. Berdyaev, *op. cit.,* p. 89.
33. Emil Brunner, *Man in Revolt: A Christian Anthropology,* trans. Olive Wyon (Philadelphia: Westminster Press, 1947), p. 325.
34. Prescott Lecky, *Self-Consistency: A Theory of Personality* (New York: Island Press, 1945), p. 44.
35. Gordon W. Allport, *Becoming: Basic Considerations for a Psychology of Personality* (New Haven, Conn.: Yale University Press, 1955), p. 98.
36. R. C. Moberly, *Atonement and Personality* (London: John Murray, 1904), p. 219.
37. Gregory Zilboorg, *Mind, Medicine, and Man* (New York: Harcourt, Brace & Company, Inc., 1943), p. 326.
38. Mary Thelan, *Man as a Sinner* (New York: Kings Crown Press, 1946), p. 32. By permission of Columbia University Press.

CHAPTER III

THE RELIGIOUS DIMENSIONS
OF MAN'S HEREDITY

MAN, FROM HIS CONCEPTION TO HIS DEATH, experiences himself both as a *being self* and as a *becoming self,* as an actual and as a potential person. The religious dimensions of personality, therefore, must be explored from both these points of vantage. When man contemplates his essential nature as well as his potential as a person, one of the first questions he asks concerns his biological heritage, his birth, his heredity. Ever since Ezekiel reminded Jerusalem of her birth, men have perceived their destiny as having been, somehow or other, cast as in a die at their conception. He said to Jerusalem:

> Your origin and your birth are of the land of the Canaanites; your father was an Amorite, and your mother a Hittite. And as for your birth, on the day you were born, your navel string was not cut, nor were you washed with water to cleanse you, nor rubbed with salt, nor swathed with bands. No eye pitied you, to do any of these things to you out of compassion for you; but you were cast out on the open field, for you were abhorred, on the day that you were born.* [1]

* Notes and credits for this chapter begin on page 70.

"Most men . . . ," Tacitus said, "cannot part with the belief that each person's future is fixed from his very birth." [2]

This is easy for a person like Saul, who was "head and shoulders" above his brothers, to believe. This is difficult for a person like Shakespeare's Gloucester to forget. Horribly disfigured from birth, he had to say:

> I, that am rudely stamp'd, and want love's majesty
> To strut before a wanton ambling nymph;
> I, that am curtail'd of this fair proportion,
> Cheated of feature by dissembling nature,
> Deform'd, unfinish'd, sent before my time
> Into this breathing world, scarce half made up,
> And that so lamely and unfashionable
> That dogs bark at me as I halt by them . . .[3]

Christians are likely to repeat the question asked by the disciples of Jesus concerning the man who had been blind, "Who sinned, this man or his father?" Anatomy may not be destiny, as Sigmund Freud said; however, the biological heritage of man does interact reciprocally with man's assumption that he can react voluntarily to life, that he can determine the destiny that takes specific shape in the personality that he ultimately becomes.

Therefore, the factual evidence concerning the biological heritage of man needs careful attention. Equally important are the considered opinions and interpretations of the research scientists who have given us these facts. But even these facts and interpretations should be taken with a healthy skepticism and deep hope for more light, for in no area do men's deep feelings about their birth color their research and interpretations more than in discussions of heredity.

WHAT IS HEREDITY?

Clear thinking calls for dependable definition of terms. Some of the most bitter and verbose controversies have been waged over the biological heritage of man. Bradley M. Patten, professor of anatomy in the University of Michigan Medical School, says "*Homo sapiens* is not always sapient with regard to his own breeding." [4] Therefore, in order that this discussion may proceed on a clearly understood basis of shared meaning between the writer and the reader, several terms need an agreed-upon definition.

Heredity. This is a "broad term referring usually to the sum total of biological influences which at the time of conception determine an individual's capacity for growth and development." [5] Careful note should be made that "the science of genetics deals with those phenomena which are determined at the time of conception." Heredity does not refer to those changes that occur in the intra-uterine existence after conception. Heredity refers to those characteristics conferred upon an individual by his parents through the genes and chromosomes. For instance, mental retardation has many causes, one of which is hereditary. It may or may not be hereditary. Careful diagnosis is necessary, even in this instance.

Congenital. This word refers only to those changes that occur during the embryological development of a child. In other words, the intra-uterine life of the growing individual, strictly speaking, would be synonymous with his congenital life. But many writers use the term to refer to any condition or trait which exists at birth. At the risk of being exceptionally strict in the use of the word, let us "save" the word "congenital" for only those influences and changes which occur after conception and before birth. The birth experience itself deserves separate consideration. The science of embryology, strictly speaking, concerns itself with these changes, as does the practice of obstetrics.

Birth trauma. Birth itself creates changes in the organism. These have come in for their own separate consideration in the psychological and medical literature. Birth itself has been interpreted as a trauma by some. More specifically birth injuries may occur in the passing of the child from the womb through the pelvic aperture into independent existence. Therefore, the term "birth trauma" will be used to refer to the experience of birth itself and the changes that occur in the organism at that time.

Innate. This is a more general term than either "heredity" or "congenital." Innate refers to those characteristics "existing within and belonging to the essential nature of human nature." "Inborn" is the Anglo-Saxon term meaning the same thing. In the main these terms are used to cover the characteristics of the species, of man as man when he is distinguished both from things and from other organisms, that is, *homo sapiens* characteristics. Philosophically, Plato referred to innate ideas within man as man. Kant referred to certain categories, such as God, morality, immorality, as being innate. John Locke rejected the conception of innate ideas. Biologically, certain drives are innate to the organism, such as hunger, thirst, sex, sleep. In other words, innate characteristics are "such as are common to man."

Constitutional. This word is used as almost synonymous with the term "innate." However, a special connotation is attached to it by the psychopathologists, Hinsie and Shatzky, in terms of the "relatively constant physiological composition and biological make-up of the human organism by which its resistances are governed." In the realm of workaday hospital diagnosis, the term is used often as a "lumping category" or catchall word for those undesirable aspects of personality that make living difficult for the individual and his associates but which are not susceptible to known psychological and educational techniques of changing the person. In this latter sense it really is used to mean "incorrigible." As such it may or may not be a specific term in understanding the biological and social heritage of man.

THE HEREDITARY BASES OF PERSONALITY

With clear definitions in mind one can think consecutively and meaningfully about many of the unexamined assumptions which the average person carries about with him concerning his biological heritage. The first pair of questions needing attention is: What dispositions in personality are hereditary? What are the religious implications of these facts?

The answers to these questions run from a deadly certainty voiced by a research man like Stockard to a cautious sense of reserve expressed by Patten. Stockard says that "the most important part of individual existence for man is passed and over before birth . . . the union of . . . two gametes . . . to form the new person—is the supreme consequence in individual existence." [6] On the other hand, Patten says that wishful thinking in this field helps to becloud the proper understanding of heredity. Although the laws of heredity are intricate and our knowledge is limited, "biological laws are inexorable and, by and large, like begets like!"

Mendel's Law

The mechanism of heredity has been named *Mendel's Law.* This law was first observed

in the inheritance of many characters in animals and plants discovered by Gregor J. Mendel (Austrian Augustinian abbot, 1822–1884) in breeding experiments with peas. He showed that height, color, and other characteristics depend upon determining factors (genes) which behave as units.

The following example shows the operation of the law: Tallness being due to a factor T and shortness to a factor t, a tall plant, arising by the union in fertilization of two germ cells both bearing the factor T is TT; a dwarf is tt. Crossing these, crossbreds, Tt, result (called generation F_1). In their formation a process (Mendelian segregation) occurs such that germ cells, whether male or female, are produced of two kinds, T and t, in equal numbers. T and t, being thus alternatives, are called *allelomorphs.*

The offspring, generation F_2, which arise from the chance union of these germ cells in pairs, according to the law of probability, are on an average in the following proportions:

1 TT; 2 Tf; 1 tt

and thus plants (homozygotes) pure in tallness (TT) and dwarf-
ness (tt) as well as crossbreds (heterozygotes) (Tt) are formed.
Frequently, the individual Tt is itself indistinguishable from the
pure form TT. The factor T is then called *dominant* and t called
recessive.

Generation F_1, containing only the Tt form, consists entirely of
dominants (tall plants) and generation F_2 consists of three dominants (2 Tt, 1 TT) to one dwarf (tt), which is called *recessive.*

Such qualitative and numerical regularity has been proved to
exist in regard to very diverse qualities or characters which com-
pose living things, both wild and domesticated, as colors of flowers,
of hair or eyes, patterns, structure, chemical composition, and
power of resisting certain diseases.[7]

The groups of genes found in the chromosomes are the trans-
mitters, then, of hereditary characteristics. One needs to ask
specific questions as to what characteristics are thus inherited.
The geneticists are cautious as to statements about what is and
what is not inherited. Research in heredity is a highly complicated
study that calls for controlling many variables in determining the
hereditary factor. The methods of determining hereditary factors
have usually been the use of the pedigree or "family tree" method,
the contingency method of statistical prediction, and the study
of dizygotic (fraternal) twins and monozygotic (identical)
twins. Even these techniques have been questioned as to validity.
Hans W. Gruhl [8] has pointed out that Mendelian laws are laws of
probability for large samplings of individuals. He says that research in human heredity has, in the psychological and psychiatric sphere, yielded definite results in such instances as Huntington's disease, but not many more. He challenges researches in
the inheritance of social or criminal behavior as lacking a solid
methodological basis. Likewise, he questions the generalization
about large segments of the nontwin population on the basis of
twin research inasmuch as they are a unique psychosocial phenomenon in their own right.

However, more cautious research people seem to be represented by Gardner Murphy who says that

> genes and chromosomes are neither a miniature of the later adult
> life form nor a prophecy of what it is to be. They are simply keys
> to potentials for differential responses which will ultimately appear
> under environmental pressure.[9]

This is T. L. Kelley's point of view in that the whole problem
should be looked upon in the light of "inner urge and outer opportunity," and that Mendelian transmission, although taken into
account, should be avoided as a prejudice that keeps observers
from making independent studies of mental inheritance.[10]

When the more guarded approach is taken, the problem of
heredity can be evaluated in terms of three categories of transmitted characteristics: (1) those traits which have a low probability of hereditary determination; (2) those individual traits
with a moderate probability of hereditary determination; (3)
those individual traits in which hereditary transmission is highly
indicated.

*Individual differences with low hereditary probability. The
basal metabolism rate,* indicating the use of energy in relation to
food intake and governed by the activity of the thyroid, has
some hereditary determination. It is related to such problems as
dieting and obesity. *The threshold of sensory stimulation,* related
to the individual's sensitivity to pain, is structurally involved with
heredity, many contend. This is significant in the ministry to
physically ill people, particularly terminally ill cancer patients
for whom physical pain is acute. The anxiety reactions of patients
to such pain varies considerably from individual to individual,
and such research persons as Frank J. Otenasek at Johns Hopkins
University and Donald Moore of the University of Louisville have
contended that the principal use of the operation of the prefrontal lobotomy is in lowering the patient's anxiety response to
pain from malignant disease.[11]

Another lowly weighted, but nevertheless important, hereditary factor in personality is that of the balance of the *outward and inward reactions of individuals*. Outward reactions are controlled by the central nervous system, and inward reactions by the autonomic nervous system. These, as Murphy says in summarizing the results of the work of Jones and Macfarlane, are related both to genetic and early environing factors. Some infants react to stimuli in terms of internal, gastrointestinal, cardiovascular responses, whereas others respond in terms of external activity of the striped muscles. Culler, in an earlier research, describes these endocentric and exocentric behavior patterns.[12]

Murphy says that the typology of overtness and internalness in response is "as good a hypothesis for a constitutional typology as we have." [13]

Individual differences with moderately weighted hereditary probability. Research men speak with a good deal more positiveness when they discuss the relationship between body build and temperament. W. H. Sheldon has done the most conspicuous work in this field. In his book, *The Varieties of Temperament*,[14] he modified the terminology of Kretschmer who earlier related different kinds of body build, such as the aesthemic, athletic, and pyknic forms, to temperamental types of persons such as the psychiatric classifications present. Sheldon chose the term *ectomorphic* to refer to the thin, lean, rather puny, angular, and long body build. The temperament he associated with it was "cerebretonia," consisting of shyness, sensitivity, intenseness, and inhibitedness. The *mesomorphic* body build in Sheldon's system described the more heavily limbed, rugged, and muscular person whose temperament Sheldon named "somatotonia," which consisted of assertiveness, adventuresomeness, uninhibitedness, and muscular activitiness. The *endomorphic* body build was associated by Sheldon with a "visceratonic" temperament of easygoingness, comfort-lovingness, and so forth. The schizophrenic personality and the manic depressive syndrome were associated by Sheldon with the ectomorphic and endomorphic body builds respectively. Some effort has been made outside the literature to correlate the mystical and activistic religious outlooks with body build. Leroy and Medakovitch,[15] for instance, hint at the heredi-tary character of mystical religious temperament in their report of twins who developed a religious mysticism together and were admitted to the hospital within a few days of each other. The de-lirium concerned devils, and they thought they had been to heaven and had received a revelation from God. After a short time in the hospital, they died at almost the same hour. How-ever, one may wryly raise the question: "Is this body build idea not really an elaboration of the Lombrosian idea of phrenology?"

Moderately weighted hereditary probability is also attributed to *certain emotional and social disorders of personality.* Franz J. Kallman, in a study of 691 schizophrenic twin index families, found an ascending percentage of incidence of schizophrenia as he moved from 1.8 per cent of step-siblings to 2.1 per cent for marriage partners, 7 per cent for half-siblings, 9.2 per cent for parents, 14.3 per cent for the full-siblings; 14.7 per cent for dizy-gotic twins, and 85.8 per cent for monozygotic twins. However, Kallman also says that this does not mean that schizophrenia can-not be prevented as well as cured.[16]

Similar studies reflect a 70 per cent occurrence in which, if one identical twin would be in prison, the other twin would also be in prison, whereas only 35 per cent of fraternal twins would both be in prison. However, the whole research method stands or falls upon the feasibility of comparing the total population with the cases of twin studies inasmuch as twins present a separate psy-cology as well as eugenics. However, R. G. Hoskins agrees with Jennings and says that "what is passed on from parent to off-spring is *potentiality* of a given development. What actually ap-pears in the completed offspring is dependent not only on genic composition but also upon the circumstances attendant upon the unfolding process. The hereditary potentials may or may not be realized." [17]

Individual differences with very high weighting of hereditary probability. Coloring of hair, eyes, complexion, teeth, and so on are most certainly determined in groups of hereditary characteristics. *Intelligence,* ruling out intra-uterine, birth trauma, and later disorders affecting the brain, is directly traceable to heredity, although heredity is only one of many factors in mental retardation. *Manic-depressive* psychoses are essentially temperamental disorders and related to heredity. In one study, where both parents were manic-depressive, 67 per cent of the children of such unions were so affected. However, this does not mean that the cycloid person cannot learn a meaningful and useful way of life. Nor does it mean that *all* persons who have mentally ill parents necessarily must become ill themselves.

Myoclonic epilepsy, which is only one of several different types of epilepsy, has a strong hereditary determination. *Huntington's chorea,* a degenerative disease of the central nervous system, appearing in adult life and usually ending in dementia, is a specifically hereditary disease. When such disorders as have been mentioned here appear, it is highly important that the individuals so affected and their families get a thorough diagnosis and clear pattern of medical advice rather than to depend upon hearsay and superstitition.

THE RELIGIOUS IMPLICATIONS OF HEREDITY

Gathered about the core of factual information that we have about heredity is an ever-widening circle of religious assumptions about the mystery of man's heritage. The line where this shades into magical thinking and superstition is hard to locate. A clear overview of the religious implications of heredity is astonishing, as will be seen.

Is Man Fated by Heredity?

For instance, fatalism as a way of life draws much of its strength from the sense of helplessness men feel about their births. Laymen take even the proved results and what is yet theory in the field of eugenics as reason for believing that whatever is inherited is totally unchangeable and useless. Gemelli, the Italian psychologist, rightly observes that research in psychiatry and psychoanalysis has "delivered us from the conceptions of biological determinism and . . . that liberty is the functional law of the mind." [18] The balancing of research in eugenics with other research softens fateful and deterministic religious assumptions.

From the point of view of revelational theology, the same problem of fate and free will have been of lasting interest to the theologians. Early efforts to relate the spiritual dimensions of personality to creation at conception and birth were made by the philosophers and theologians of the ancient world. Aristotle, Jerome, and Pelagius evolved *the creation theory of the soul* which held that the soul of each separate human being was evolved at conception, at birth, or at some time in between these two events as the immediate, direct, individual act of God. This theory was in contradistinction to *the pre-existence theory of the origin of the soul* held by Plato, Philo, and Origen to the effect that the soul always existed in the realm of the transcendental and took an empirical form in the body, that the body was a sort of fleshly drape for the soul. Traditional and orthodox theologians have held to *the traducian view of the origin of the soul* in order to account for the purposes of God for man as well as the observable facts about heredity, individual differences, and other phenomena. Traducianism is the contention that the soul was created in Adam and propagated through natural generation. All souls since Adam are only mediately and not directly created by God. This was implicit in the thought of Augustine when he said:

> For we all were in that one man, when we were that one man.
> . . . For not yet was the particular form created and distributed to
> us, in which we as individuals were to live, but already the seminal
> nature was there from which we were to be propagated.[19]

Tacitly running through all these attempted explanations are the
apprehensions of the theologians about the responsible relationship of God to man's biological heritage. Implicit in them is the
theologians' concern about the freedom and yet the responsibility of man. Even Calvin is reluctant to accept the fated sense
of necessity that is best expressed in the words of Chaucer's
Troilus:

> "I am," he said, "but done for, so to say;
> For all that comes, comes by necessity,
> Thus to be done for is my destiny.
> I must believe and cannot other choose,
> That Providence, in its divine foresight,
>
> . . . .
> . . . plans things as he thinks both best and right,
> . . . as was arranged for by predestination." [20]

To Troilus, "free choice is an idle dream."

Calvin frankly says that man's prideful rebellion against the
sovereignty of God "obliterated" the divine image in him. "This
is that hereditary corruption which the fathers called *original
sin.*" Man's guilt is "the origin of that curse which extends to
every part of the world, [and] it is reasonable to conclude its
propagation to all his offspring." [21] Yet at the very outset of this
chapter he says that the fact of his defection can be known by
man and that man is responsible for responding to this self-knowledge. As he puts it,

> . . . the knowledge of ourselves consists, first, in considering what
> was bestowed on us at our creation, and the favours we continually
> receive from the Divine benignity, that we may know how great
> the excellence of our nature would have been, if it had retained its
> integrity; yet at the same time, recollecting that we have nothing
> properly our own, may feel our precarious tenure of all that God

has conferred on us, so as always to place our dependence upon him. . . . we are inflamed with fresh ardor to seek after God, to recover in him these excellences of which we find ourselves utterly destitute.[22]

This is in line with the contention of Emil Brunner that even a man's decision that he is fated represents a response on his own part to his situation in life. As Brunner says in another but relevant connection, "Even this answer *is* an answer, and it comes under the inherent law of responsibility." Brunner would say that this is a response on the part of man to his situation which in itself depicts a kind of sense of responsibility. This in turn reflects a limited kind of freedom which is presupposed in the image of God within man.[23] In discussing the facts of heredity which have been presented in the above discussion, Brunner also states that

all these facts must be taken into account, if we aim at the truth about man. . . . At the bottom [though] they do not tell us any more [about man] than we have always known. Thus if in spite of this knowledge people do not cease to believe in a certain freedom of self-determination, and if the Christian faith makes responsibility the heart of existence, all this means that these facts do not touch the ultimate, central, secret heart of personal existence.[24]

Nevertheless, in practical theological encounter with working people in the parish, students in the corridors, and men ready to be drafted, the sensitive Christian layman and teacher, pastor and friend confronts the sense of fated necessity that many people feel with a quiet sense of inner desperation. Much of it they lay at the door of bad birth. For example, the person who has homosexual fears or confirmed homosexual behavior will use heredity to explain his situation. He may even feel somewhat persecuted by others for not being in agreement and sympathy with him. Likewise, just as these pages have been written, a counselee asked the author if her husband's alcoholism would be inherited by her children. Another example is the parents of mentally retarded children who interpret the condition of their child as the direct punishment of God for specific sins that they as parents have committed. Underneath all these responses is the reaction of responsibility to the facts of human heredity. Many of them are misguided or unguided reactions that result in superstition rather than mature faith. Nevertheless, they *are* reactions, awaiting the light of a factual interpretation of both human heredity and the Christian faith. In many instances, the reactions are foils for a basic unwillingness to change or to accept the need for changing behavior. As such, human heredity becomes the master scapegoat for the human propensity to irresponsibility. But God calls everyone, so Karl Barth declares,

> into freedom within the limits of his vocation, that is—of the station in life at which each one happens to find himself, the historical situation assigned him, his personal capability, his special field of activity.[25]

Is One Race Superior by Heredity?

Scientific as well as biblical information has been pressed into service by propagandists on both sides of intense race conflicts. Persons like H. R. Sass would argue for the protection of "our 350-year-old system of keeping our races pure." [26] Others, like Arnold and Caroline Rose, go so far as to state that "all races are biologically equal." [27]

But Brewton Berry is probably much more in touch with reality, as far as the hereditary basis for racial distinctions is concerned, when he says that such statements on either side of a tense issue can hardly be supported for this reason:

> Science, indeed, has not been able to prove any race superior to the others; but it does not follow that races are therefore equal. Nor has science been able to prove that races are equal in their innate abilities, but this failure does not justify one in concluding that they are therefore unequal.[28]

He goes on to say that a suspended judgment on the problem of racial mental differences should await more information, either as to equality or difference. The important fact is, as Simpson and Yinger say, that people *feel* racial differences and attribute inferiorities and superiorities to races. These are sociological and psychological realities, although they are not grounded in discernible evidence from genetics and physical anthropology, inasmuch as we have "a lack of full genetical data on human beings." [29] Heredity is probably quite indifferent to the whole problem. The same could be said for the argument for and against the idea of a "pure" race, for as Dobzhansky points out:

> Pure races conforming to a single genetic type could exist in sexually reproducing organisms only if heredity were transmitted by blood instead of by genes . . . but in reality groups of genetically uniform individuals—clones and pure lines—exist only in asexual and self-fertilizing populations . . . when applied to such sexually reproducing populations the notion of "pure" race is absurd. [30]

The most recent discussion of this whole problem, however, is a May, 1957 publication of the Group for the Advancement of Psychiatry. This research group of the American Psychiatric Association say that whereas IQ levels of white and Negro school children *as groups* may differ, *some* Negro children do better than the average white child. They aver that group-average IQ levels of Negro students tend to be lower "due to life circumstances," and that "the consensus of expert opinion . . . is that there is no scientific evidence of inborn difference in intelligence between Negroes and whites." [31]

Nevertheless, religious dimensions have been added to the special pleadings of both sides of the racism conflicts in such a way as to re-enforce misinterpretations of scientific fact. Biblical passages are quoted to support propaganda adduced from incomplete scientific evidence. Confusion is multiplied, and the people are confounded. God, having created us with individualities both personal and racial, is probably indifferent to the ways in which men have become respecters of themselves to the point that they cannot respect each other's uniqueness. Edmund

Davison Soper is right when he says that the security of the numerically inferior white man depends upon his changing of his fearful attitude toward the numerically superior races of different color which he usually justifies on some appeal to inherent or hereditary inferiorities.[32]

HEREDITY ASSUMPTIONS AND PASTORAL THEORY

When theology moves into the marketplace and takes its stand with people in their quiet inner desperations as they try to do their daily work and earn their daily bread, the problem of heredity appears to the pastoral theologian in many forms. For instance, several different recurring types of pastoral care situations could be named. First, the pastor encounters the problem of heredity in the fears that people have that the troubles of their parents and siblings will be visited upon them. This is always a covert or pronounced fear in the reactions of the family of a mentally ill person. They are likely to say, "Well! We have never had anything like this in our family!" Also, the parents of an epileptic child or a feeble-minded child may have severe difficulties in accepting the reality of the child's condition by assuming that only "trashy people" have such things in their family. Children of alcoholics live under the dread possibility that this is "in the blood." The relatives of a person who has committed suicide may also be plagued by the fear that they will do so themselves.

The delicate gearing of the need for survival with the demanding responsibilities of life is obvious in all these pastoral problems. The intricate interweaving of the need for self-preservation with one's ethical values, therefore, is apparent. This weaving process has caused some, such as Bull, to assume that the concept of self-preservation is the source of all values, that ideas of good grow out of our experiences of benefit and ideas of evil out of our experiences of harm. Security and danger are other names for good and evil.[33]

However, a deeper basis of ethics is apparent in Paul Tillich's conviction that a man's real ethical values spring from his courage to affirm life in the presence of the threats of destruction.[34] This is a much more fruitful pastoral approach, more in keeping with the Pauline conception of the sharing of the sufferings of life as a preparation for ministry to others who "are in any affliction" (II Corinthians 1:3 ff.). Such a view of the sufferings described above is less likely to produce either a Bedouinlike fatalism of the constantly threatened Arab or the prudential ethics of much American "success" religion.

Such an approach to the religious dimensions of man's hereditary endowment also leaves no room for the use of heredity as the scapegoat for personal unwillingness to accept responsibility for repentance and insight, decision and change. The passive irresponsibility of the confirmed and overt homosexual is an example of this. To blame his condition on heredity relieves him of the necessity for therapy, change, insight, or redirection of his life.

But probably the most penetrating criticism of attempts to explain human life entirely in terms of heredity or of subsequent influences lies in the flagrantly false views of science, personality, and causation they reflect. Specific causes for specific effects have been sought on the assumption that the universe is a simple and not a complex reality. Every cause is actually an effect and every effect simultaneously a cause. All these are caught up in a dynamic, complex, purposive sphere of life itself. The relationship between the given and the acquired in personality is not a cleft, detached relationship; it is a flowing continuum. In the very genius of what is known as heredity, can be seen the uniqueness of man appearing. In this connection Edmund W. Sinnott, dean of the Graduate School at Yale University, has said:

> Each self is not only a knot of purposes and predilections but has its own particular and private character. Each man and child is not a unit or a statistic only, but a person. In any plans that we

may have for man, this unique individuality of every member of his race must never be disregarded. Dollars are all alike, and miles and pounds, but not men. There is no Bureau of Standards to make them uniform, and let us hope there never will be.[35]

A clear understanding of the inexhaustible creativity of God is apparent in man's response to his inheritance. Alfred Adler states it in this way:

It goes without saying that the inheritance, primarily of . . . human potentialities is not subject to any doubt whatsoever. But what matters ultimately is what the child, the individual does with the equipment he inherits. . . . How and for what purpose or objective he molds and shapes these various formative factors becomes manifest through the millions of variations in individual styles of life.[36]

In the definition of these purposes and goals, in the choosing of the meaning of one's vocation in life, in Barth's sense of the word "vocation," in response to the call of the Eternal, the religious dimensions of man's hereditary endowment appear. In the intensity of the conflict when a man or woman decides how he or she is going to react to the fact of his heredity the religious dimensions of personality begin to emerge.

NOTES FOR CHAPTER III

1. Ezekiel 16: 3-5, RSV.
2. Tacitus, *The Annals*, Book VI, Sec. 21.
3. *Richard III*, Act I, Sc. 1.
4. Bradley M. Patten, *Human Embryology* (Philadelphia: The Blakiston Press, 1946), p. 12.
5. *The New Dictionary of Psychology*, ed. Philip Harriman (New York: Philosophical Library, 1947), p. 161.
6. Charles R. Stockard, *The Physical Basis of Personality* (New York: McGraw-Hill Book Company, Inc., 1948), p. 26.
7. *Webster's New International Dictionary of the English Language* (Springfield, Mass.: G. & C. Merriam Company, Publishers, 1948), p. 1535.
8. Hans W. Gruhl, "Inheritance of Psychic Traits," *Deutsch Med. Wschr.*, 1947, pp. 72, 62-63.

9. *Ibid.*, p. 53.
10. T. L. Kelley, "The Inheritance of Mental Traits," *Psychologies of 1930* (Worcester, Mass.: Clark University Press, 1930), pp. 423-433.
11. *Bulletin of the Isaac Ray Library*, 1953, I, pp. 83-95.
12. E. Culler, "A Phobic Case," *British Journal of Medical Psychology*, 1930, X, pp. 46-69.
13. Gardner Murphy, *Personality: A Biosocial Approach to Origins and Structure* (New York: Harper & Brothers, 1947), p. 82.
14. William H. Sheldon, *The Varieties of Temperament* (New York: Harper & Brothers, 1942).
15. "Mystical Delirium in Two Twins," *Annals of Medical Psychology*, 1929, 87 (II), pp. 265-269.
16. Franz J. Kallman, "The Genetic Theory of Schizophrenia," *Personality in Nature, Society, and Culture*, eds. Clyde Kluckhohn and Henry A. Murray (New York: Alfred A. Knopf, Inc., 1949), pp. 60-79.
17. R. G. Hoskins, *The Biology of Schizophrenia* (New York: W. W. Norton & Company, Inc., 1946), p. 36.
18. A. Gemelli, "The Nature and Genesis of Character," *Quarterly of Psychiatry*, 1930, 17, pp. 41-61.
19. *Civitas Dei*, 13:14.
20. *Britannica Great Books*, Vol. 22, p. 106, Geoffrey Chaucer, "Troilus and Cressida," stanzas 137-138.
21. John Calvin, *Institutes of the Christian Religion*, trans. John Allen (Philadelphia: Presbyterian Board of Publication and Sabbath Work, 1902), Vol. I, Book II, Chapter I, pp. 225-226.
22. *Ibid.*, pp. 221-222.
23. Emil Brunner, *The Christian Doctrine of Creation and Redemption* (Philadelphia: Westminster Press, 1952), II, pp. 55-57.
24. From *The Christian Doctrine of Creation and Redemption* by Emil Brunner, The Westminster Press, 1952. Used by permission.
25. Karl Barth, *Church Dogmatics:* Int. Report, V. II: to V. III:4, trans. A. C. Cochrane (Philadelphia: Westminster Press, 1953), pp. 247-248.
26. H. R. Sass, "Mixed Schools and Mixed Blood," *Atlantic Monthly*, Vol. 198, No. 5, November, 1956, pp. 45-49.
27. Arnold and Caroline Rose, *America Divided* (New York: Alfred A. Knopf, Inc., 1948), p. 275.
28. Brewton Berry, *Race Relations: The Interaction of Ethnic and Racial Groups* (Boston: Houghton Mifflin Company, 1951), pp. 95-96.
29. George E. Simpson and J. Milton Yinger, *Racial and Cultural Minorities: An Analysis of Prejudice and Discrimination* (New York: Harper & Brothers, 1953), pp. 63-64.
30. Theodosius Dobzhansky, *Evolution, Genetics and Man* (New York: John Wiley & Sons, Inc., 1955), pp. 135-136.
31. *Psychiatric Aspects of School Desegregation* (Group for the Advancement of Psychiatry, 1790 Broadway, New York 19, N. Y.), pp. 65-66.
32. Edmund Davison Soper, *Racism: A World Issue* (New York: Abingdon Press, 1947).
33. N. Bull, "The Biological Basis of Value," *Science Monthly*, 1941, 53, pp. 170-174.

34. Paul Tillich, *The Courage to Be* (New Haven, Conn.: Yale University Press, 1952).
35. Edmund W. Sinnott, *The Biology of the Human Spirit* (New York: Viking Press, Inc., 1955), p. 158. Used by permission.
36. *The Individual Psychology of Alfred Adler*, eds. Heinz and Rowena Ansbacher (New York: Basic Books, Inc., 1956), pp. 206-207. By permission of the editors.

CHAPTER IV

RELIGIOUS DIMENSIONS
OF MAN'S BIRTH

MANY OF THE "RUDE STAMPS" OF THE HUMAN organism arise independently of hereditary transmission through the genes and chromosomes. They occur either in the embryological development of the individual or in the actual process of birth itself or both. When one reads a book like Bradley M. Patten's textbook on *Human Embryology,* he gasps with awe at the fearful and wonderful miracle that the preponderant majority of the human race enter life well-formed without suffering the mishaps of gestation and birth.*

However, if these failures of development and accidents of birth happened to only one person, this would be of deep significance to the spiritually sensitive person. The fact is, however, that many, many people "enter into life maimed."

One of the main mistakes existing in the minds of people about the handicaps which they bring into life is that of confusing the malformations which occur after conception with the inheritance of characteristics through the genes and chromosomes. These two factors in personality development are related. They are most

* Notes and credits for this chapter are found on page 84.

certainly not identical. This in itself is a great comfort to many persons whose children are malformed for one reason or another.

CONGENITAL MALFORMATIONS OF THE BODY

Arey classifies the anomalies or malformations of the developing embryo and fetus into six groups. A brief study of these will give some concrete facts for thinking about congenital malformations in personality development. Anomalies or malformations of the human organism, according to Arey, fall into several categories relating to the general nature of the defective development:

1. Developmental failure. In these instances the primordium fails to appear. The primordium is the first beginnings of a future organ or part before it has taken on its characteristic features. For instance, the ectodermal thickening in front of the optic cup is the primordium of the lens, as is the arm bud of the arm. When this happens, what is known as *agenesis* occurs. An example of agenesis is the child that is born without an arm or a kidney. One child in the author's city was born without the prefrontal lobe of the brain.

2. Developmental arrest. Here progressive development falls short of completion. A common example is the cleft palate or the undescended testes. In other instances temporary structures or states which serve only a passing function in development may continue or persist. For example, the umbilical cord is a temporary structure, but a persistent hernia may occur. The anal membrane may remain, also. Or, in other instances, normal growth simply fails, as is exemplified in the case of the dwarf or of persons with an infantile uterus.

3. Developmental excess. Anomalies of this type consist of the exaggeration of growth, as is exemplified in gigantism. They may consist, rather, in the multiplication of normal numbers of which a body is usually in possession, such as extra fingers.

4. Developmental misplacement. In these individuals organs occupy abnormal locations. Examples of this would be the transposed viscera or the palatine teeth.

5. *Fusion or splitting.* Examples of this would be the horseshoe kidney or cleft ureter.

6. *Atavism.* These are ancestral recurrences. As Arey says in another place, some embryonic organs neither disappear nor take on permanent functions. They rather persist throughout life as vestiges. Nearly 200 of these have been listed for man. Many of them will no doubt be eliminated from the developmental course of man. But *atavistic characters,* or ancestral reversions are somewhat different from vestiges. "These are features that normally have been dropped from development but may, on occasion, reappear. They are due to the inheritance of genes which are able to reassert themselves whenever the proper embryonic conditions are re-established." [1] Examples of atavisms are the azygos lobe of the lung, as in quadrupeds and the elevator muscle of the clavicle, as in climbing primates.

PRENATAL DEVELOPMENT, BIRTH TRAUMA, AND MENTAL DEFICIENCY

Although it may be safely assumed that a variously estimated majority of cases of mental deficiency are hereditary, "The diagnosis of hereditary mental deficiency is usually made by eliminating other specific causes," [2] many of which occur in the congenital development or the birth experience of the individual.

These nonhereditary occurrences include fertilization of imperfect ova, imperfect implantation of the fertilized ovum, diseases which arise in the mother between conception and birth, and anomalies of development in the congenital period. Many things can happen, such as Rh incompatibility, maternal rubella during the early pregnancy, maternal embryonic irradiation, prematurity, to produce mental deficiencies. Prematurity or birth accidents can occur in parturition, causing brain damage and other injuries. Clumsy medical procedure can produce brain damage during exceptionally difficult labor in the birth process. This can eventuate in retardation of mental abilities. Birth injuries, for instance, are far more frequently the cause of mental deficiency than was previously recognized.[3]

Cretinism is the best known and most frequent physiological and nutritional disorder related to mental deficiency. This disorder "is due to an almost complete lack of the thyroid gland, which atrophies shortly before or after birth, without known cause in most cases."[4] Thyroid medication administered early is very effective in changing this condition.

RELIGIOUS AND PSYCHOLOGICAL DIMENSIONS
OF PRENATAL AND BIRTH EXPERIENCES

The religious and psychological dimensions of prenatal and birth experiences extend all the way from some rather grim ethical problems in medical practice to highly developed psychological and philosophical theories which have been applied to these experiences, and are raised to another level in the highly poetic and symbolic interpretations of the religious life. At first the implications of all the foregoing scientific information for a religious conception of personality seem remote. But if one stays with the subject and searches the literature, he begins to see vast implications.

Ethics and the Handicapped

The ethical implications of the unfortunate results of medical practice in the assistance of mothers in the delivery of their babies are often hidden away in the institutions for the feeble-minded, such as they are. The medical profession itself could well finance research on the improvement of the condition of traumatic birth injury patients. The institutions for the care of these patients are sparse in number and poorly staffed in many cases. Social ethics calls for redoubled effort in the way in which states are caring for the feeble-minded. Often psychiatric experts remark about the damage done to personalities by clumsy religious teachers. Similar remarks, without any desire to be vindictive, need to be made about the blunders of the medical profession. A visit to the state institution for the feeble-minded will be a revealing experience at this point.

The churches and the Christian ministry also have an unfelt burden of ethical responsibility for those handicapped from birth. The ministry of Jesus to the man blind from birth reflects both the theological confusion of his contemporaries and the courageous concern of Jesus that the man be helped. The disciples asked the question that is regularly presented to the under-shepherds of Christ today: "Rabbi, who sinned, this man or his parents, that he was born blind?" (John 9:2.) Implicit in this question is a twofold reaction of the human heart to inevitable sufferings such as birth injuries or congenital deformities.

First, there is the "response of responsibility," the need to affix judgment and to deal with human guilt. Second, there is the persistent primitive need to think of God as an enemy who inevitably visits the sins of the fathers on the sons, whether he does or not! But Jesus saw in this the same kind of speculation that has always made it easier to talk about a problem than to accept responsibility for doing something about it. He chose to glorify God as the friend of the injured. Therefore Jesus answered: "It was not that this man sinned, or his parents, but that the works of God might be made manifest in him. We must work the works of him who sent me, while it is day" (John 9:3-4).

On another occasion Jesus expressed his compassionate insight into the situation of eunuchs who had been rendered incapable of marriage by reason of congenital deformities (Matthew 19:12). He did not comment extensively at this point, but the context is that of his discussion of marriage. He reflected the inseparable connection between birth and marriage as two destiny-shaping events; many of the variables in the decision to marry are set at the moment of birth. Of course one of the major points of ethical tension with reference to the grossly handicapped person is whether or not he should be permitted to marry and, if so, whether he should be permitted to have children. The Catholic prohibitions against sterilization, for instance, have been challenged by Joseph Fletcher in his book, *Morals and Medicine*.[5]

An even grimmer thought occurs to the parents who have given birth to a monstrosity of a child. Are they ethically bound to let it live? Early in my pastoral ministry I participated in the pastoral care of a family at the birth of a badly malformed child. The normal desire to cherish life, to love a child, collided with the sheer wisdom that the child would be better off dead. I remember the painful, jerking emotion the father felt when the nurses in the hospital used extreme, frantic measures to keep the child alive. I remember the clashing emotions of grief and relief that accompanied the news to the parents that the child died after three weeks of life. Yet to leap to the conclusion that the death of the weak and the survival of the perfect is the highest good has been the hallmark of the worship of the State throughout the centuries. This theory was the spawning ground of the Nazi practice of extermination of the "weak" prior to World War II.

The apostle Paul refers in I Thessalonians 5:14 to the "feebleminded" as it is translated in the King James version. However, closer scrutiny of the original text reveals that this is really a poor translation of a word that means "fainthearted." Calvin used it to refer to a "broken and afflicted spirit," and interpreted the passage to be a general exhortation to console and care for the weak with kindness and humanity.[6] This is a significant mistranslation, in that it reflects the way in which the hundreds of different kinds of birth injuries and congenital malformations are all lumped together to mean weakness of mentality. For instance, this attitude is often leveled at all the 550,000 cerebral palsied children living in the United States by many of their fellow citizens who do not know that cerebral palsy is most certainly not identical with mental retardation, although it may be associated with it.

Once this attitude is corrected, then the deepest meaning of the suffering of the handicapped appears and the companionate character of God *in* suffering becomes apparent. God works after the fact of such suffering in redemptive endowment of the handicap with meaning and purpose. The meaning of the Christian fellowship becomes clearer in the mutual bearing of burdens. Our acceptance and not our explanations of suffering open the way for new light on its meaning in God. The apostle Paul gave the main meaning of suffering when he set it within the context of the fellowship of the Christian community. Suffering, he said, is an instrument whereby we become a comfort to those who are in trouble. By means of suffering we are enabled to be ministers of reconciliation, comfort, and hope. (II Corinthians 1:3-7)

ANXIETY, THE BIRTH EXPERIENCE, AND
THE SPIRITUAL RENEWAL OF LIFE

The psychologists have sought to fathom the depths of meaning implicit in the intra-uterine experience, the birth trauma, and organic inferiorities for the continuing life of the individual. Notable among these have been Otto Rank and Alfred Adler.

Otto Rank, a student and colleague of Freud, interpreted the psychotherapeutic experience of healing in terms of the resolution of anxiety set in motion during the experience of birth. The individual before birth abides within the dependent, cloistered protection of the womb. Birth thrusts him forth into an independent existence at peril of life itself. The experience of anxiety set in motion may take the form of a neurotic reproduction of the birth trauma itself. It may be handled through symbolic adaptation. It may even be expressed in the sublimations of religious experience. Concerning this, Rank says:

> Every form of religion tends ultimately to the creation of a succouring and protecting primal Being to whose bosom one can flee away from all troubles and dangers and to whom one finally returns in a future life which is a faithful, although sublimated, image of the once lost Paradise.[7]

Rank interpreted the relationship to the analyst in psychotherapy as a recapitulation of the prenatal existence of the individual. "The freeing of the libido from its object, the analyst, seems to correspond to an *exact reproduction* of the first separation from the first libido object, namely of the newborn child from the mother." [8]

Sigmund Freud, in commenting upon this theory of Rank, said that the biological factor of helplessness created in the process of birth "brings into being the first situation of danger and creates the need to be loved which the human being is destined never to renounce." [9] However, Freud felt that Rank's theory hung "in mid air," and that no trustworthy investigation gave indisputable evidence that difficult and protracted birth was related to the development of neurosis.

At a later date, Phyllis Greenacre reviewed the literature on the whole problem of birth traumatic influences on personality development. She concluded that real evidence exists for assuming a preanxiety reaction occurring in foetal life. This preanxiety is evident in reflex actions, and it may be increased by "untoward prenatal, natal, or postnatal conditions." However, she feels that much of this is genetically determined. Variations in the birth process may increase and heighten the anxiety potential and thereby lay the foundation for severe reactions later in life.[10]

Rank correlated his theoretical presuppositions about birth trauma with his practical treatment of patients in psychotherapy.

The birth fear before the trauma of birth is transmuted into a death fear after birth which he calls an "undifferentiated feeling of insecurity on the part of the individual, which might then better be called fear of life." [11] Rank likened the therapeutic experience to a birth process in which the individual was born out of death fears into the affirmation of life. Neurosis is an individual attempt at healing against the "arch enemy of mankind, the death fear." [12] The neurotic is the man whom extreme fear keeps from paying the price of death as a basis for life, and "who accordingly seeks in his own way to buy himself free from his guilt." [13] His self-punishment is really an attempt at self-atonement. Spiritual experience consists in dying as a way to life in the inner sense of the word. Rank likened this "dying and rising" to birth into life out of death. He used "end-setting" techiques with his patients when their time of fulfillment would come.

Of course, this psychological frame of reference can easily be appropriated by Hindu ideas of reincarnation. Its promulgation in America as a psychological form of therapy has further opened the American mind to the plausibility of Hinduism. Usually psychologically sophisticated students and faculties sit in their seats without much squirming when these researches of Rank, Freud, and Greenacre are presented. They even become entranced at the fascinating ways in which a non-Christian religion like Hinduism might be synthesized with such scientific hypotheses. However, long familiarity with Christianity may have caused them to overlook the teachings of the Fourth Gospel in that the new life in Christ is described as a new birth. Nicodemus asks the question: "How can a man be born when he is old? Can he enter a second time into his mother's womb and be born?" Jesus answered ". . . unless one is born of water and the Spirit, he cannot enter the kingdom of God" (John 3:4-5). Yet this falls with such familiarity that we are likely to say, "All this I have heard from my youth up," and go away sorrowing because it is no new thing.

One of the criticisms leveled at Rank is that he has been over-awed by the more mechanical aspects of the birth process. But others feel that he not only took the literal birth process seriously, but also followed it metaphorically as well. This distinction was the turning point of the discussion between Jesus and Nicodemus. Nicodemus balked at the purely literal discussion of the new birth. Otto Rank reaffirms the importance of a spiritual rebirth of life. His thesis throughout is upon breaking the earth-bound idolatries of a god in human form by the risk of creativity symbolized in birth itself. However, the Christian raises the question of continuity and stability of the new birth. He asks whether this idea of Rank may not equally as easily be appropriated by theories of continued and repeated reincarnation as by the Christian doctrine of the new birth.

The Spiritual Dimensions of Organic Inferiorities

Alfred Adler is best known for his evaluation of the psychology of inherent handicaps in individuals. He first noted this in the way in which one kidney will compensate for the loss or failure of the other kidney. "If in the organ-environment interaction, the balance threatens to turn against the organism, it responds through attempts at compensation." As Adler himself describes it,

> The fate of the inferior organs is extremely varied. Development and the external stimuli of life press toward overcoming the expressions of such inferiority. Thus we may find approximately the following outcomes with innumerable intermediate stages: inability to survive, anomaly of form, anomaly of function, lack of resistance and disposition to disease, compensation within the organ, compensation through a second organ, compensation through a psychological superstructure, and organic or psychological overcompensation. We find pure, compensated, and overcompensated inferiorities.[14]

Although this concept is not identical with Walter B. Cannon's theory of homeostasis, it is closely related to it. This is the law of a maintained balance in the psychophysiologic organism.[15]

The "psychological superstructure" of compensation of which Adler speaks has specific religious dimensions. For instance, Adler calls attention to the way in which Aaron was asked to help Moses to compensate for his speech handicap. Such profound religious meaning is attached to the fact that Jacob acquired a withered hip that the infirmity is interpreted by the author as a *result* of his spiritual struggle. To the contrary, the thorn in the flesh was to Paul a governor on his pride, "lest he be exalted overmuch" (II Corinthians 12:7).

Adler points out how genius, degeneracy, or neurosis, depending upon the reaction of the individual with his particular "styling" of life, can be one of at least three types of compensatory reactions to the handicaps of the organism. The extremely tall, short, fat, or thin person, develops a style of life in reaction and compensation to his deviation from the average. His individual response takes a patterning that is distinctly his own as he deals with his limitations. When the organically imposed handicaps become accepted, then the individual is set free to use them creatively rather than to be used by them destructively. Adler says:

> Self-boundedness (*Ichgebundheit*) is the central point of attack of *Individual Psychology*. The self-bound individual always forgets that his self would be safeguarded better and automatically the more he prepares himself for the welfare of mankind.[16]

The religious dimensions of the inferiorities bequeathed to an individual at birth, then, are difficult to measure. Coming to terms with limitations is the universal human struggle at the base of which lies the religious difficulty that all men, not just organically handicapped men, face: that they are men and not gods. The eternal qualitative difference between men and God, once sensed, is the beginning of either salvation or despair for man. This awareness comes much earlier for the congenitally malformed person than it does for others. They, then, like their comparatively more fortunate fellow human beings, may find the way through their limitations to dependence upon God and deep social feeling for their neighbors. Or they may retreat and shrink back into self-rejection, insensitivity to the needs of others about them, a dependence upon fantasies of what life "might have been" under other circumstances. They have this alternative in common with all human sufferers.

NOTES FOR CHAPTER IV

1. Leslie B. Arey, *Developmental Anatomy: A Textbook and Laboratory Manual of Embryology* (Philadelphia: W. B. Saunders Company, 1947), pp. 19, xx, 173.
2. Mandel Sherman, Ph.D., M.D., "The Mental Defective," *An Introduction to Clinical Psychology*, eds. L. A. Pennington and Irwin Berg (New York: Ronald Press Company, 1948), p. 91.
3. Sherman, *ibid.*, p. 93.
4. *Ibid.*, p. 95.
5. Princeton, N. J.: Princeton University Press, 1954.
6. *Calvin's Commentaries* (Grand Rapids, Mich.: William B. Eerdmans Publishing Company, 1948), pp. 293-295.
7. Otto Rank, *The Trauma of Birth* (New York: Robert Brunner Publishers, 1952), p. 117.
8. *Ibid.*, p. 4.
9. Sigmund Freud, *The Problem of Anxiety* (New York: W. W. Norton & Company, Inc., 1936), p. 100.
10. Phyllis Greenacre, "The Predisposition to Anxiety," *Psychoanalytic Quarterly*, 1941, X, pp. 66-94.
11. Otto Rank, *Will Therapy* (New York: Alfred A. Knopf, Inc., 1945), p. 123.
12. *Ibid.*, p. 127.
13. *Ibid.*, p. 126.
14. *The Individual Psychology of Alfred Adler*, eds. Heinz and Rowena Ansbacher (New York: Basic Books, Inc., 1956), p. 24. By permission.
15. Walter B. Cannon, *The Wisdom of the Body* (New York: W. W. Norton & Company, Inc., 1932).
16. Adler, *op. cit.*, p. 112.

———————— ✦ ————————

CHAPTER V

RELIGIOUS DIMENSIONS
OF MAN'S INNATE DESIRES

HOMER SAID THAT "ALL MEN CRAVE THE GODS." * [1] Probably a more accurate statement of it would be that all of man's cravings have religious overtones. Primitive religions have consisted in many instances of the deification of man's desires for food and drink, for relief from sexual tension, for procreation, for rest and health. Even sectarian interpretations of Christianity and other living religions can be seen as the centralized emphasis of a given group upon one or more of man's desires. For instance, the elaborate health and security emphasis in many sects and cults is a case in point. Therefore, the main thrust of this chapter is to evaluate the religious dimensions of the universal human desires or needs of man.

WHAT ARE THE UNIVERSAL DESIRES OF MAN?

A moot theme of much psychological conversation has been the enumeration of man's basic desires, to try to answer the question: "What are the universal human desires?" W. I. Thomas

* Notes and credits for this chapter are found on page 106.

elaborated his theory of four wishes of man. He said that the underlying motivating forces of human conduct are the wish for security, the wish for response, the wish for recognition, and the wish for adventure. Herbert Carroll, in a widely acclaimed book, *Mental Hygiene,* spoke of four human needs: the need for physical security, the need for emotional security, the need for mastery, and the need for action. A. H. Maslow analyzed human motives on the various levels of human need, in a sort of spiral-like hierarchy of needs. On the first level, he said, the basic physiological requirements for continued existence must be met before needs on higher levels can emerge or be recognized. On the second level, Maslow put safety from external dangers. Once hunger has been satisfied, then life is governed by motives of safety. At the third level of motivation, the need to be loved appears. As its requirement is met, then the need for self-respect or integrity becomes important. The crowning need of human life is the need to achieve and master, said Maslow.

These writers brush on a large canvas with a free hand in their attempts to portray human desires that are "innate," universal, and characteristic of human beings as human beings. But the more highly detailed and carefully etched portraits of human needs may be found in the writings of William James, William MacDougall, Sigmund Freud, and Alfred Adler. Under the aegis of various instinct theories, they sought to identify that which regularly recurs in human desires at all times and all places. William James, in his *Principles of Psychology,* commented on both animal and human psychology. He talked about the instinctive character of reflexes such as blushing, sneezing, coughing, laughing, dodging, and keeping time to music. Then he discussed "special human instincts," listing reflexive behavior such as sucking, biting, clasping, crying, carrying to the mouth an object, turning the head aside as a rejecting action, holding the head erect, sitting up, standing, walking, and vocalization. He moved beyond these more or less automatic kinds of behavior in the human being, which become manifest in time. He listed a whole continuity of more complex needs: imitation, rivalry, pugnacity, anger, resentment, sympathy, the hunting instinct, fear, acquisitiveness, constructiveness, play, curiosity, sociability, secretiveness, cleanliness, modesty and shame, love and jealousy. He says that "these are the most prominent of the tendencies which are worthy of being called instinctive in the human species." [2]

William James' listing of human needs was more pointedly and clearly stated by William MacDougall. He listed thirteen primary instincts or needs: the parental or protective instinct, the instinct of combat, the instinct of curiosity, the food-seeking instinct, the instinct of repulsion, the instinct of escape, the gregarious instinct, the instincts of self-assertion and submission, the mating instinct, the acquisitive instinct, the constructive instinct, and the instinct of appeal. Then he named scratching, laughter, play, and imitating as "some minor instincts." [3] He, like James, was assured that wherever one finds human beings he will find these needs manifesting themselves.

Sigmund Freud, under the general discussion of his libido theory, preferred to group all these various impulses of human life under two groupings of instincts, the *self-preservative* impulses which he named *Eros*, the sexual instincts for life; and the *self-destructive* impulses, which he named *Thanatos*, the aggressive impulses for death. These were in polar tension with each other in the thrusts and recoils of life. His student and rival, Alfred Adler, grouped all the needs of human life under one great need, the striving for mastery and the achievement of individuality.

Probably no comprehensive psychologist of personality has emphasized the importance of the *need to communicate* more than has Harry Stack Sullivan. In his book, *The Interpersonal Theory of Psychiatry*, [4] he set forth a conception of the development of the total personality in terms of the universal human need to communicate oneself to one's fellows and receive communication from them.

When we boil all these schemata of the universal human needs and desires down to a dependable set of "tangibles," we can safely identify six basic needs of human life in the order of their usual appearance in the development of a person: (1) food and drink (2) sleep (3) communication (4) walking (5) cleanliness (6) sexual satisfaction. These are the rawest simplicities of life. Wherever we find people, we find them building the hymns, the symphonies, the jazz, the folk-tunes, or the tom-tom rhythms of their lives out of these basic notes in the scale of human existence.

WHAT ARE THE RELIGIOUS DIMENSIONS OF MAN'S DESIRES?

The basic desires of man become complex very quickly. They undergo radical transformation breathtakingly soon after birth. Human needs for food, sleep, and so on, as in other creatures, are quite automatic and pressing. But they undergo refining processes that convert them to higher and higher scales of complexity and meaning, both individual and social. And, as Herbert Spencer said, "they begin to lose their automatic character," and "that which we call Instinct will merge into something higher." [5]

Precisely at the point of the merging of the basic needs of man into "something higher" do the religious dimensions of man's basic desires appear vividly. Each of these needs is essentially a biological tension in and on the whole organism. It is a basic note struck in the consciousness of the individual. But these notes have resounding overtones that add substance, depth, and richness to the essential need. The individual not only has the need; he reacts to the need as a total person. In the sphere of reaction the individual's basic biological needs present him with larger issues: his total destiny as a human being and the ultimate meaning he attaches to his life as a whole.

For instance, each one of these basic biological needs takes on a psychological meaning to the individual which, if and when it is developed, may become a full-fledged religious concern. This religious concern accrues to itself tremendous symbolism and ritual. Furthermore, these needs cannot be met in isolation. The psychological meanings and religious concern, and the symbols and rituals are of a distinctly communal character in the fellowship of other human beings. In addition to this, these needs encounter the necessity of deferment and limitation, that is, deferment in time and limitation in extent of satisfaction. This accentuates the ethics of human needs. Finally, these needs must be co-ordinated with each other so that, as Plato cautions, one is not made to do the work of the other nor all the rest made to be the slave of one. At these points, at least, the religious dimensions of human needs become manifest.

All these "for instances," however, are pretty vague until specific applications of them are made to each of the six great human needs just named. This will, one could fondly hope, make the whole picture clear and concise.

Religion and the Need for Food

Let us take the need for food as the first example. A baby is born into the world, rudely severed from his mother, without the lifeline of the umbilical cord to sustain him any longer. He feels insecurity first as hunger. To be fed is to be made secure. Therefore, in proportion to his being fed does he feel secure. The need for security, which Thomas, Carroll, and Maslow all three put first in the hierarchy of human needs is a derivative of the need to be fed. But very early, the psychological need for security overlays the need for food. Then the child becomes secure in terms of the *way* in which he is fed. He does not have to be many hours old before it becomes a matter of great importance to him as to whether he is jerked up and dropped down as he is fed. Here security is reminiscent of having been held closely within the womb before birth. Being dropped, not being held when being fed, being left alone—all these stimulate basal fears, intolerable insecurity, in the child.

Imperceptibly the need for security, therefore, is transmuted into the need for love, to receive warmth and tenderness. This is the first movement of the symphony of the human spirit. It is associated with eating, being fed, taking food into oneself, incorporating one's environment in oneself. The need for security has now become the need for love, and the child tells whether it is loved through the way its need for food and security is met. Very soon the need for love ties into the spiritual necessity for a trustworthy world.

The very helplessness of the human individual makes the elementary experience of food-getting a distinctly social experience. No man lives to himself, even in the simplicities of getting enough food for survival. Here, at the threshold of life, dependency is etched into human nature never to be erased. As the experience of helplessness, limitation, and dependence become a part of human life, religious concern begins to hasten around the crib of a child. For here, the parents feel for the first time a little of what it is like to be God; a tiny, helpless, human life is in their hands.

Little wonder is it, then, that whole primitive religions have been naturalistically developed which center in the need for food. The agricultural deities, built around the gods of the crop and the harvest, reflect man's dependence upon the co-operation of the elements to get food. Likewise, in systems of philosophy such as Marxism, economic security is made the main center of life. Marxist criticisms of religion, also, slant heavily toward correlating Protestantism with the rise of capitalism as an economic system. The demonic character of such systems lies in the fact that they have taken a facet of the Christian gospel and thrown it out of focus with the rest of the ministry of the church to human needs. For the basic relevance of the economic need is never minimized in the mind of Christ; but the idolatry of this or any other need is radically challenged. Jesus enjoined his disciples to pray for daily bread, but it was this same Jesus who hungered for forty days and nights in the wilderness. Jesus spoke kindly of John the Baptist who "neither ate nor drank." Yet, he himself both "ate and drank," and added his blessing to the wedding feast at Cana. The same Jesus who multiplied the loaves for the multitude, warned his disciples about the way in which mammon can compete with God for first place in their loyalty. He taught them of a trustworthy heavenly Father who met their needs for food as he met the hungers of the children of Israel with manna from the dew of the morning. His own sacrificial offering of himself was referred to as the Bread of Life. In his death he imparted a symbolic meal of bread and wine. At every Emmaus Road experience since the first one he has somehow or other been made known to his followers in "the breaking of bread."

In human life the fellowship of faith is caught up in the concern of the "haves" for the "have-nots," the willingness of the Jew to eat with the Gentile, the solidarity of the family epitomized in the saying of grace at meals. Here the instinct of self-preservation is transmuted into something higher, the preservation not only of oneself but of one's fellows, even at the expense of oneself. When this Rubicon is crossed, the simple deification of a man's own security is set aside in terms of his having "taken up a cross." The guilt that Americans feel about overeating cannot be assuaged, for instance, by appealing to their sense of vanity for looking "slimmer" than their years. It can best be handled by a sense of stewardship that considers the plight of whole nations of starving people.

At such a level as this, the raw necessities of human hunger become intensely important to the elevated insight of our Lord Jesus Christ. It was Jesus who said to the Pharisees when they criticized his disciples for partaking of ears of corn on the Sabbath:

> Did ye never read what David did, when he had need, and was hungry, he, and they that were with him? How he entered into the house of God when Abiathar was high priest, and ate the showbread, which it is not lawful to eat save for the priests, and gave also to them that were with him? [6]

Apparently, when men are hungry, the smaller niceties of the law are set aside. Not only time, but hunger, makes ancient good uncouth!

Religion and the Need for Sleep and Rest

The satisfied hunger for food, or for any other thing for that matter, prepares the individual for a relaxed sleep. The relaxation of tension is in itself rest. The newborn child spends much of its day asleep. (Working fathers wish that it would spend more of its night!) Some research persons such as Otto Rank would interpret the psychological meaning of sleep as a return to the security the child enjoyed before birth. In the vein of Shakespeare, others would interpret sleep as gathering up "the ravell'd sleeve of care." They would interpret sleep as a restorative force that heals up man's despair at the ceaseless demands of life and strengthens his courage to face another day.

The anxieties that collect around sleep today underscore the undisciplined lack of attention to the meaning of sleep in the religious world-view of the average person. For instance, one of the most common complaints of parents about young children is that their child "does not follow the book" in his sleep schedule. Their fears take the form of "not spoiling" the child while he goes to sleep, or of having to hold him for fear of not giving him love. But another example is obvious in the preoccupation of adults with their own inability to sleep. Hundreds of thousands of dollars' worth of sleeping pills are sold in America every year. A local church installed a telephone that gave back phono-

graphically recorded words of comfort to restless people. The
response was so great that three telephones had to be added to
take all the incoming calls. This pinpointing of anxiety around
the experience of sleep is religiously significant. We need to
ask in what way it is significant.

The Asklepion temples of the fourth century B.C. and following formed quiet refuges where exhausted people might be re-
stored through rest. Temple sleep, or incubation, was used as a
means of therapy. It consisted of having the patient sleep in a
sacred sleeping part of the temple. During his sleep "the god
Asklepios appeared to him in a dream and told him that he
would awake healed or gave him instructions as to what he
should do." [7] Obviously here religious ritual took sleep and
dreams very seriously as a part of an early form of suggestive
psychotherapy within the context of a pagan religious setting.

In setting the boundaries of man's limitations, the God of
Abraham, Isaac, and Jacob is portrayed in the biblical account
as one who "fainteth not and neither is weary." But at the same
time man's finitude is accented in his need for rest. The Sabbath
is the social institution of rest. The distinctly religious dimensions
of sleep itself, however, begin to emerge at two points: First,
men give specifically religious interpretations to what goes on
during their sleep; and, second, tend to interpret religion in
terms of their need for rest, relaxation, and renewal.

As will be seen later, E. B. Tylor explained the origin of religion in terms of animism, or the belief in spirits. Man first observed the separation of his spirit from his body in sleep as he
dreamed. Likewise, he tended to interpret death as a kind of
sleep during which, nevertheless, he would be quite active to
the point of needing his hunting implements, food, and wives,
even! The biblical writers took man's sleep seriously. They
brought this realm of experience under the ethical and spiritual
domain of their encounter with God. Albert Meiburg has demonstrated this effectively in his study of dreams as a means of

divine revelation in the biblical account.[8] He points out that dreams are a form of mental activity during sleep in which some of the most creative literary, musical, and theological insights, such as Coleridge's *Kubla Khan,* Tartini's *Devil's Sonata,* and Peter's insight into the missionary message of Christ have come to pass.

In the overstimulating environment of contemporary business and professional life, the increases in heart failure and emotional disorders are strained testimonies to the fact that the basic need of men and women for a meaningful sleep has not been plumbed religiously. The emergence of "aspirin religions" is as much a criticism of the "production jags" of "quota-happy" and architecturally preoccupied churches as it is of the shallowness of the "peace-of-mind" preachers. The God who said that in returning and rest shall be our strength is certainly a "still, small voice" in contemporary activistic religious living. Such main-strength-and-awkwardness religion is a far cry from the sleeping Messiah in a tossing boat on a restless sea. The secret of the charwoman about whom Leslie Weatherhead spoke is missing. He tells of a charwoman who could sleep between her mop and bucket during a bombing raid on London. When asked how she could do it, she said, "The good Lord says that he stays awake and watches over his own. There is no use of both of us being awake!"

Religion and the Need for Communication

The child is not many weeks and months old before he comes out of his own noncommunicative world; he senses that he is in a talking world filled with sign language and all sorts of nonverbal communication. James and MacDougall posit a separate instinct for laughing, turning the head, and so on. This can be dealt with by saying that these, like speech, are means of communication, accenting the need for just that. They represent motions toward and away from relationship with others. Sleep itself, for that matter, is a total withdrawal from relationship except in so far as it is bepeopled in dreams. The learning of language, then, is one of the truly human skills of meeting the need for relatedness. By its very nature communication is a social experience, even when it is carried on within the self, for there must be a community of selves for it to be heard.

Therefore, man discovers the "internal dialogue of the self," as Reinhold Niebuhr describes it. "We may safely say that the human animal is the only creature which talks to itself." [9] But before he does so, man usually has already had some self-encounter with a community of other selves for this experience to be meaningful. More than that, he is concerned for their approval and sensitive to their disapproval. Their values, therefore, become acutely important in his building of his conception of himself. What he says with words and communicates with gestures to other people becomes the stuff of which his own values are made. To say that this is the point at which religion and ethics become dimensions of the growing personality is almost to be guilty of wasting printers' ink, it is so patently obvious.

The building of a religious language and the exclusion of irreligious language becomes of first concern in the life of the child who is learning to talk. "Okay" and "Non-Okay" ways of saying things are passed or censored in the common coin of household language. The revealing, concealing, bartering, and losing power of words becomes the stuff of which the religion of the growing mind is made. So predominant do words become that they are often mistaken for religious experience itself. The Society of Friends bear a silent witness against this. In their fellowship they remind us all that the deepest things of both God and man are ineffable and known best in silence. The ineffable depths of religion can be obscured by words. We could never have really gotten this clear thought, however, had it not been for the miracle of human language.

Religion and the Need to Stand Erect and to Walk

Much research has been done as to the psychological dimensions of such biologically oriented needs as feeding, sleeping, talking, and keeping clean. But little evaluation has appeared in the literature, it seems to me, concerning the self-reference meanings which a growing child attaches to standing upright on his "own two feet" and learning to walk. Every nursery teacher knows that something radically different is going on in the life of the child that can travel "under his own steam" as compared with the one who has to be moved by others. Every mother who has asked her toddler to get out of the refrigerator for the seven-thousandth time knows that child to be vastly changed from the child who did not know how to walk. In fact, this dramatic change is usually taking place most drastically at the same time that the child is being toilet-trained.

Much that has been attributed to the aggressive-sadistic behavior of children during toilet-training essentially grows out of the fact that children have learned that they can stand on their own two feet and outrun their parents at these same times. Dexterity with hands and feet has been described by Gesell, Ilg, and Ames, but in psychoanalytic thought preoccupation with oral, anal, and phallic dogma has caused the analysts to glide over psychological significance of the use of the arms and legs.

One does not really see the importance of this dexterity until he observes the handicapped child who has been deprived of these skills. The crucial personality issues drawn in terms of the growing child's personhood, identity, and interpersonal competency magnify the vast spiritual implications of standing erect and walking as a distinctly human need and function. This, like human language, separates the human infant from quadrupeds. This separates him from other creatures and ties him to his own kind, the human species.

The assertion of independence is full-blown in the achievement of the skill of walking. The child is now *really* on his own, not just symbolically. These are *his* feet, not someone's else. His intellectual functions are activated afresh. He really has to take heed lest he fall! He also experiences fatigue in a way that he has not up to this time. He runs and he gets weary. He also learns to hide and to keep a secret during this adventure as a walker and a runner. He can run away from home. He wanders away from his parents. He gets lost from them. All of this, like his ability to talk, begins to take on religious and moral significance in terms of obedience and disobedience, rebellion and compliance.

As personality grows older, such significance of the ability to stand and to walk emerges in the symbolism of religious experience. The Lord said to Ezekiel, "Stand upon thy feet, and I will speak to thee" (Ezekiel 2:1). Jesus, in his teaching, related "standing" to singularity, integrity, and sincerity of purpose. He said that Satan's kingdom could not stand because both Satan and his kingdom were divided (Mark 3:24-25).

Paul counseled the Ephesians "to put on the whole armor of God, that ye may be able to stand . . . and having done all, to stand" (Ephesians 6:11, 13). This symbolism is rich; the Old and New Testaments both are laden with it. Equally elaborate is the use of the symbols of walking. The Christian life itself is a "walk of life," and Christians were first known as those of "the Way." Christians are enjoined to "walk in the newness of life, and not after the flesh" (Romans 6:4, 8). We walk "by faith and not by sight" (Colossians 5:7). The walk of the Christian is his vocation under God. He is to walk worthy of the vocation wherein he is called (Ephesians 4:1) and "as the Lord hath called him, . . . so let him walk" (Colossians 7:17). Man's sense of uprightness and integrity, on the one hand, and his sense of direction and purpose, on the other hand, are symbolized in standing and walking. But it would have little meaning apart from the rather humble skill being learned by a two-year-old, namely, to walk and to choose a direction to walk. In fact, coupled with the analogy of the new birth, these symbols carry the same developmental sequence in the spiritual life!

The Religious Dimensions of the Need for Cleanliness

As has already been pointed out, the need for cleanliness develops at about the same time as does the need for standing and walking. The control of the bowels and bladder, as well as learning to feed oneself, are skills or developmental tasks which cluster around this common need. Freud and Abrahams, aided and abetted by English and Pearson,[10] have permanently contributed to the literature of personality in interpreting the psychology of these acts. The development of orderliness and precision as personality traits emerges in connection with these habits.

Cleanliness is partly motivated by the older need for survival and partly by the recent discovery that disease is bred through filth. Cleanliness is partly motivated by personal comfort in that disgust, nausea, and even pain are associated with unattended human excreta. Cleanliness is partly motivated by fair play in that each individual can go on only so long expecting others to clean up after him. Therefore, the need for cleanliness may start into the substratum of human life as one main root supporting the superstructure of personality but it spangles off into many subroots. The essentially social character of the need cannot be missed, however.

The child does not always share this social feeling. In fact, he may revel in being an individualist to the point of splattering his urine and smearing his feces! As far as he is concerned the whole race can die of typhoid, the whole family can be nauseated to vomiting, and the idea of fair play has never occurred to him. On the other hand, the child may be extremely tidy, easily nauseated, and solicitous for attention in learning this skill just right. He may even be extremely obstinate and withhold his excreta until it hurts. These various extremes, dealt with by psychoanalysts in the treatment of emotionally disturbed children and adults, have led them to classify personalities in terms of "retentive," "hoarding," and "expulsive" types of people.

The psychological drift of these emotional reactions to the need for cleanliness may be spelled out in terms of the conformity and nonconformity of the individual to social demand, the orderliness or disorderliness of the personal habits of the individual. These characteristics become apparent in the religious consciousness of the person and his group at many points.

For instance, on a cultural basis, the Jewish laws concerning ceremonial cleanness as a way to God reflect the need to preserve the race that God has given them, to keep from offending both the nostrils of God and man, and to demand fair play from their fellow men without becoming personally involved with them. These are usually the functions of "the rules" in a community. However, Jesus challenged compulsive preoccupation with the rules by eating without washing his hands. In the days of the theocratic state, however, all these minor matters of the law had to be carried on by the priests. We sometimes overlook this in our easy condemnations of the legalism of the Jews. Today these laws—food inspection, sanitation, and the like—are carried on in this country by a state which is separated from the church. However, some real problems of religious concern hover around the easy conscience with which churchmen own property that is so unsanitary as to breed disease.

Furthermore, on a personal basis at least two pertinent observations may be made concerning the need for cleanliness and orderliness in life. First, the Hebrew ideas of ceremonial cleanliness, as reflected in the teachings of both the Old and the New Testament, have often been seen by Western interpreters through the eyes of Plotinus and Mani, the founders of Neoplatonism and Manichaeism respectively. Both these non-Christian teachers had extreme views as to the uncleanness and evil of the human body, as such. This idea is alien to the Hebrew mind that has not been tampered with by Western and Persian forms of dualism.

As a consequence of this clouding of our perceptions concerning the meaning of the Old and New Testament teachings about cleanness, we miss the basic meaning of these Scriptures. We almost regularly read them to refer to sexual impurity. In reality the passages refer to the ceremonial system of Judaism in which, as is true in Romans 6 for instance, the body and its instruments are cleansed and dedicated to Christ as were the instruments of the Temple. This includes any kind of undisciplined or false use of life, and not just sexual selfishness. In fact, a deceptive sense of imagined sexual spotlessness can be as obviously a withholding of the instruments of life from dedicated use for reasons of pride as was Ananias' deceptive use of his funds!

A second observation about the personal religious dimensions of the need for order and cleanliness is in the area of the vocational meaning that this gives to some people's lives. Extreme care about detail, orderliness, and precision seems to be the main motif of some individual lives. Less tightly defined persons tend to justify their own nonchalance about order and detail. They may even try to change their more impeccably orderly neighbors. They may even "write them off" with a psychological "cuss-word" like compulsive, or obsessional. A more creative approach would be to enable them to find vocations in which "precision-personalities" are desperately needed.

For instance, it is entirely possible that a person in the teaching profession may live a life of quiet desperation and impatience with sloppy-minded and carefree students. In reality this same teacher would be much more effective as a research man in highly detailed areas of pinpointed research. Likewise, some good statisticians and architects have been nudged into the pastoral ministry, if the way in which statistics and church architecture drain their attention from the pastoral care of their people is any index!

The Religious Dimensions of Sexual Needs

The sexual needs of the human person appear on at least four stages in the pilgrimage of life, and maybe more than that. *The first stage is in childhood, when the child is, through identification with his parents, defining his gender.* This is not what an adult means when he uses the word "sexual," but it has tremendous importance for later sexual maturity. Rather, it is the experience in which, quite unreflectively, the child accepts or rejects the particular masculine or feminine role which corresponds to the kind of body he or she has. He or she decides that he or she is happy to be a boy or a girl, as the case may be. At this time, the child finds in the parent of the same sex the kind of person he or she wants to become and feels that the parent of the opposite sex will love him or her that way. If this is not a clear-cut decision for "boyness" or "girlness," then confusion attends later attempts to satisfy the sexual need.

The second stage in sexual-need expression is when the preadolescent child establishes confidential companionship with a member of his or her own sex. Here he or she learns how to trust a member of his or her own sex. Through the experience of having been successful in winning the respect of a comrade, he or she is freed of the curse of jealousy later. On a more conscious level, he or she has a friend with whom to compare notes secretly about the ways of the opposite sex. This "chum" imparts courage in the movement toward the opposite sex.

The third stage of sexual encounter is the experience which includes dating, courtship, engagement, and marriage. Here the sexual role is implemented, and full abandon to the surge of sexual desire is felt. The great social and spiritual rituals of marriage dramatically spell out the individuals' acceptance of responsibility for each other in sexual union and prospective parenthood. In this stage, thrill seeking, curiosity, awe, mystery, experimentation, and the learning of sexual and parental skills preoccupy the attention of the persons involved. The early experiences of sex may be guilt-laden, but more often are clumsy, inept, and embarrassing. Even the deeper experiences of parenthood in its earlier days are obscured by the sheer business of learning the mechanics of the pre- and postnatal care of children.

The fourth stage of sexual encounter has received little attention in research, as compared with the first three. This is what I have chosen to call *the stage of stabilizing the sexual life and enhancing its creativity on a durable basis.* This usually comes in the mature years of marriage. Here the basic skills have been learned, but the meanings have not been enriched. All the surface mysteries have been revealed. Then the couple either face each other as persons or retreat into boredom in which the acts of sex themselves become meaningless rituals. In this stage of spiritual necessity, the ultimate meaning and destiny of the combined lives of the man and woman either coalesce or diverge. Sexuality and vocation either merge or compete. These are the crucial years of the sexual life. Both the most dramatic spiritual advances and the most sordid spiritual defeats are experienced here.

The common denominators of spiritual dimensions in all these stages of the encounter of men and women with their sexual needs may be said to be fourfold:

First, if we lay to heart the religious accounts of the creation of man and woman, we must affirm the fact that sexual needs must be taken seriously by the religion that lives; for in man and woman's encounter with each other their personalities are complete. *Second,* the release that comes to men and women in sexual relationships and parenthood is a human experience of revelatory power, letting them know what self-abandon may be in the deeper encounter with God. This was true of Hosea. It has been true of others. *Third,* sexual experience draws clearly the issues of absolute responsibility for human action and the sense of guilt upon failure to accept this responsibility. Even when we see people who have committed gross violations of sexual ethics, but do not reveal much conscious guilt, we may be dealing with their numbed feelings of responsibility. We cannot always go by their emotional responses in the stress of a crisis. *Finally,* in a degree not true of the other human needs, the whole race has a sense of corporate responsibility for itself at the point of sexual needs and ways of meeting these needs. Hence, more elaborate controls, more extensive and varied ways of satisfaction, and more religious rituals are clustered about this human need than is true of the other needs.

THE ETHICS OF MAN'S INNATE DESIRES

Underlying all the human desires are the ethical problems involved in the expression and control of these needs. Ase G. Skard has summarized nine laws (rephrased below in italics) governing organic needs and desires.[11] They show clearly the indispensable connection between ethics and the psychology of religion. It is worth while to dwell on them for a short time:

1. A need not satisfied tends to store its energy. The denial of a need increases its strength. The human desires are not simple but complex. For instance, the need for sweets by girls working in a candy factory is complicated by prohibiting them from eating. They eat less candy when they are permitted to eat all they want!

2. The stronger a need is, the less particular we are about the way we satisfy it. This was dramatically illustrated in concentration camps during World War II where hunger was so acute that men would eat anything, and some were tempted by cannibalism. This is a vital factor in brain-washing techniques.

3. Indifference and excessive indulgence produce disgust. This is one of the arguments used by Catholic moralists to justify the use of the "safe period" as a technique of birth control in marrige relationships. They argue that the longer period of abstinence makes the returning to union a recapitulation of the honeymoon with the added factor of past experience!

4. *Social influences may stimulate or inhibit our needs.* An example is the socially shy person who hungers profoundly for acceptance, communication, and yet who is inhibited in the presence of people who are trying to break through the shyness to commune with him.

5. *If a strong need remains unsatisfied, other needs often tend to be neglected.* One of the most obvious examples of this is the way in which the double work schedules of professional students and their wives deprive them of sleep. Fatigue in turn undercuts their communication with each other, and their sexual needs are neglected as well.

6. *Needs which are not satisfied may sometimes be replaced by other needs.* The husband away from home and yet faithful to his wife may find that his need for sexual union with her is offset by eating more heavily. The businessman who is completely absorbed in making money often lets this become food, drink, sleep, wife, and child to him. This is what Plato calls allowing a part of the soul to rise up against the whole. This, incidentally, was one of Plato's definitions of sin.

7. *Many of our needs and desires tend to conflict with each other.* Our need to stand erect and walk our own way, to achieve, and to succeed may outstrip all our other needs. We may imperil our health and bypass opportunities for a happy home in the pursuit of ambition. Or, the need for self-preservation may conflict seriously with our sense of commitment to a certain way of life. This is where we begin to talk about the cross in human experience.

8. *Needs tend to combine rather than to conflict.* A very simple example is the way in which the need for communication is combined in social rituals with the need for food. As R. W. Pickford says, "It is impossible to catalogue all the impulses satisfied at meal times." [12]

9. *None of the basic human needs can be fulfilled in social isolation.* In these needs, man shares a common humanity with his fellows, and they cannot be met apart from an enduring community.

These laws point up some concluding remarks about the religious dimensions of human desires. Stated in theological frames of reference, we have seen that the main threat in meeting any human desire is that the desire itself shall be deified. This is apparent in the agricultural religions of primitive peoples, the "relaxation" and "health" religions of today and yesterday, and the fertility cults of primitive religions and the worship of sex today. The First Commandment speaks directly to this temptation.

Again, these desires are in conflict with each other apart from the integrating power of the God who is great enough to be interested in all of them without excluding any of them. The supremacy of the search for the Kingdom of God is the only sure way of satisfaction. Even so, Christianity has often been institutionalized as a nature religion rather than a gospel of risk which makes the desires of man secondary to the will of God. The institutionalization of the crises of life around a sacramental system—baptism at birth, confirmation at puberty, holy matrimony at marriage, Holy Communion as the renewal of the nature, unction at death—represents in many instances the building of God's action around man's need. The seasonal adaptation of the Christian year lays hold of the cycle of an agricultural year, and utilizes the nonrevelational modes of primitive religion. Done with insight these rituals can be aids to worship. Without revelation and regeneration, they can become subtle forms of nature religion.

This explanation underscores the essential conclusion to the whole matter: the plain fact remains that complete satisfaction of human desires is not a possible but an illusory goal. One of Edna Ferber's characters says, "Money solves any problem except for them that's got it!" The deeper desire of man for self-realization through self-sacrifice has only begun to be tapped by the psychological interpreters of human existence. Here the "desire for the durable" in life, the search for that which lasts in interpersonal relationships is uncovered. The thirst for the Living God is the "burst-through" of the ultimate which gives a main purpose to life, to which all other satisfactions are but finite additions. This is the main difference between "religion" and "faith."

NOTES FOR CHAPTER V

1. Od. iii, 48.
2. William James, *Outlines of Psychology*, Vol. II, Ch. 24, pp. 383-441 (New York: Henry Holt & Company, Inc., 1950).
3. William MacDougall, *Outline of Psychology* (New York: Charles Scribner's Sons, 1927), pp. 130-176.
4. New York: W. W. Norton & Company, Inc., 1952.
5. Herbert Spencer, *The Principles of Psychology* (New York: D. Appleton and Co., 1892), Vol. I, p. 443.
6. Mark 2:25-26.
7. Spencer L. Rogers, "Psychotherapy in the Greek and Roman World," *Ciba Symposia*, Vol. IX, 1 and 2, April-May, 1947, p. 625.
8. Albert L. Meiburg, "An Understanding of the Dream as a Means of Divine Revelation" (unpublished doctoral dissertation, Southern Baptist Theological Seminary, 1954).
9. Reinhold Niebuhr, *The Self and the Dramas of History* (New York: Charles Scribner's Sons, 1955), p. 6.
10. O. Spurgeon English and Gerald H. J. Pearson, *Emotional Problems of Living*, rev. ed. (New York: W. W. Norton & Company, Inc., 1955), pp. 43-75.
11. Ase G. Skard, *Character and Personality*, Vol. VIII, No. 1, pp. 28-41.
12. R. W. Pickford, "Ethics and Instincts," *Ethics*, Vol. L, No. 4, July, 1940, p. 395.

CHAPTER VI

—————— ◆ ——————

THEORIES ON THE ORIGIN
OF THE RELIGIOUS DIMENSIONS
OF PERSONALITY

The PRECEDING DISCUSSION of the innate needs of mankind raises several questions: Is religion an inborn dimension of personality, an instinct, in other words? If so, how does one identify this instinct and distinguish it from others? If religion is not a separate instinct, then how do we explain the origin of the religious dimension of personality? Whence comes the religious concern of mankind, anyway?

Throughout the history of philosophy and psychology, concerted efforts have been made to answer these questions. Many of the major psychologists, for instance, have been impelled to write about the nature of religion.* [1] Anthropologists concerned with comparative religion have been deeply involved in this kind of inquiry, as is evident in the work of Schmidt, Tylor, Frazer, and others. This was one of the first projects to which psychologists of religion addressed themselves, as is particularly evident in the work of Leuba. We usually classify such research as "the

* Notes and credits for this chapter begin on page 136.

phenomenology of religion." The presupposition of such study is that religion has more or less specific origins, that these origins can be observed and explained empirically, and that religion can be explained in terms of these origins.

This effort to "explain" religion as springing from one or more specific sources is, in fact, a nineteenth-century mode of scientific thinking. One characteristic of nineteenth-century science was the conviction that all effects tend to have a *single* cause. If one could discover the cause, he could thereby control and, if need be, destroy the effect. Thus he had reduced any given effect to its origin and had thereby explained it. The result of much of this was the attempt to "explain away" the validity of religion, *per se*. Twentieth-century science has shifted the emphasis away from naïve causation theories to a distinctly relational and holistic conception of the meaning of phenomena. This has resulted in a growing conviction that points of origin are only one aspect of the total relational field of which a given phenomenon, such as religious customs, may be an expression. This has led to a much more reflective and careful evaluation of religious experience as observed and interpreted by contemporary psychologists of personality.

Furthermore, nineteenth-century scientists tended to interpret religion in the light of their hope for "total" objectivity, when in reality their own biases are apparent in the conclusions they drew. They moved on the assumption that man's description of himself as a religious person can be free of his own ambiguous relationship to himself which distorts that which he describes. However, contemporary scientists, particularly in the field of the social sciences, are speaking more readily of *participant* observation. The relationships of the observer to the observed are a part of that which is observed.

But whether we approach the phenomenological study of "religion" from the nineteenth- or the twentieth-century scientific point of view, the *Zeitgeist* of Reformation and biblical theology

was radically removed from preoccupation with or even friend-
liness toward "religion," as such. "The word 'religion' as it is
used today can hardly be said to be a biblical word at all." In
the Bible it refers to the outward practices of religion as "cultus"
or "systems of worship," all of which are incidental and may be
antithetical to the encounter of man with God in Christ. In some
contexts in the New Testament the word "religious" is used almost synonymously with "superstitious," and in others refers to
pagan idolatry. For example, in Acts 17:22, Paul, standing in the
middle of the Areopagus, said: "Men of Athens, I perceive that in
every way you are very religious." In doing so, he stood in the
prophetic tradition of Elijah, Amos, and others who found their
main contention to be with the "high things" that exalted themselves against the knowledge of the Living God.[2] The "doctrine
of 'religion,'" Karl Barth says, "is . . . a feature of the 18th and
19th century thought." It is a "pietistic, rationalistic modernism"
which "popped up" as a third alternative between Catholic super-
naturalism and Reformation theology.[3]

This interpretation of biblical and systematic theology must be
counted in as a wholesome corrective of the easy tendency to
equate the Christian faith with any and every kind of religious
expression. However, here again we see the "left-handed" use of
the word "religion" which, nevertheless, does not do the work
that the vernacular use of the word accomplishes. The fact remains that to great numbers of informed, devout, and effective
Christians today the word "religion" does not carry the scurrilous
reputation that it had in the days of Paul.

Nevertheless, the following discussion of theories of the origin
of religion will reflect the shifting emphases in the philosophy
of science toward an interpretation of religious experience in
terms of interpersonal relationships. Likewise, the unique contribution of revelational theology to the correction and purifica-
tion of the theories themselves will be interjected all along the
way. Calm note needs to be made of the fact that both the Refor-

mation theologians and the Catholic theologians have somewhat allowed the study of personality to go by default to the "pietistic, rationalistic modernists," as Karl Barth calls them. They have operated on the assumption of a completely *revealed* knowledge of human nature and have often mistaken their own logic for revelation. Consequently, they have withdrawn from the conversation with scientists who have operated on the assumption of a completely *hidden* revelation and have often mistaken their own ignorance of God for a factual description of the universe. An effort will be apparent in the discussion of theories of the origin of religion to keep these two types of knowledge—revealed and hidden—in touch with each other.

CONCEPTIONS OF THE ORIGINS OF RELIGION

Considerable overlapping of emphasis makes any discussion of conceptions of the origin of religious concern in man a sort of blending spectrum of interpretations. Sharp lines of demarcation are both impossible and misleading. The different emphases must be seen together to be appreciated, understood, and evaluated properly.

Religion as an Instinct?

The most obvious point to begin with in the discussion of theories of the origin of religion is with those persons who, like Morris Jastrow, at the turn of the century frankly regarded religion as an instinct of man:

> The certainty that the religious instinct is, so far as the evidence goes, innate in man, suffices as a starting point for a satisfactory classification . . . the definite assumption of a religious instinct in man forms part of almost every definition of religion proposed since the appearance of Schleiermacher's discourses. . . .[4]

Jastrow not only takes this position himself, but he also imputes it to everyone else! This point of view is not explicitly taken by

Rudolf Otto,[5] but the upshot of his contribution points toward a separate "category" or "faculty" for religion. He comes very nearly to positing a "nonrational category" as a fourth estate of personality in relation to the tripartite faculty psychology which Kant bequeathed to us.

Göte Bergsten, a more recent writer, steeped in the pastoral literature which has grown out of psychotherapeutic approaches to man's emotional needs, says that "it is not necessary to deny that religious needs may be innate because one discards the idea of a religious instinct." When he speaks of "a religious tendency," he means an innate religious sensitivity. This tendency may be "aroused by something spiritually objective," or it may "remain latent; a mere potentiality sleeping in the inmost being of men." [6]

One would raise the question as to whether or not the "instinct" explanation of religious origin is not a restatement of the older Calvinistic doctrine of predestination and election. If religion is an instinct, it certainly does not manifest itself significantly in some people, only the elect and the "concerned." John Calvin stated it in this fashion:

> The covenant of life not being equally preached to all, and among those to whom it is preached not always finding the same reception, this diversity discovers the wonderful depth of the Divine judgment. Nor is it to be doubted that this variety also follows, subject to the decision of God's eternal election . . . salvation is freely offered to some, and others are prevented from attaining it. . . .[7]

Apparently discussions of basic theological issues such as this are not shut off completely by the advent of the scientific era. Rather the context for the discussion is shifted from the categories of revealed theology to those of an empirical science such as biology, psychology, or physics. The basic issues remain; the areas of investigation are narrowed as they were in Schleiermacher's system, and the terminology undergoes much change.

Religion as a Derived Reality

A second group of thinkers perceive religion as arising, not from any one instinct, but *as being derived* from the organization, integration, direction, and refinement of the impulses. Edwin D. Starbuck, one of the pioneers in the psychology of religion, puts this point of view as follows:

> It should constantly be borne in mind that religion has not been nourished from a single root, but that, on the contrary, it has many sources. Among the facts in the preceding chapters there are evidences that other deep-rooted instincts besides that of sex have been operative in religious development. Out of the instinct of self-preservation and the desire for fulness of life in the physiological plane, there seems to have arisen, by progressive refinement and irradiation, the religious impulse toward spiritual self-enlargement. . . . The process of religious development has consisted in arousing discharges from [instincts and lower nervous centres] through the higher psychic centres and in working them into a higher synthesis.[8]

In other words, religion, from this point of view, is a derivative of human development. The "higher synthesis" to which Starbuck refers reflects a definite evaluational approach to levels of integration, leaving room for much ethical consideration. More pessimistic interpreters might say that from this point of view religion is *nothing but* an epiphenomenon of human development. More optimistic interpreters could reject such reductivism and say that religious dimensions of personality begin to appear when the individual reflects upon the *direction* and *meaning* of his development, his pilgrimage of growth. Where is it all going, and where is *he* in the web of social relationships in which his growing takes place?

Starbuck's point of view can be found also in Coe, Ames, and others, and has made an enduring contribution to religious education. No interpreter of the religious life, since these men, can safely do his work without taking seriously the processes of growth and development. Gardner Murphy says that the human personality begins to cogitate upon the nature of the totality of the self in relation to others. In this process the interpreter of the religious dimensions of personality asks the same question Murphy asks:

> Should the student of personality . . . postulate a non-empirical entity distinct both from the organism and from its perceptual responses to the forms and symbols which are called self? [9]

Murphy would say "no" to this question but at the same time he later confesses that the difficulty of personality theory "seems to be not with our research or our definitions as to personality, but with plain fogginess as to the nature of man." [10] Whether we like his answers or not, we must say that he is asking some basic questions that are essentially religious in nature. As he has meditated upon and described the process of differentiation, growth, and experience through which the self becomes the self, he stands on the same fog bank with many others and asks, "What is man?" Starbuck answers by saying that man is a growing, developing, seeking personality. He becomes religious as he works all his impulses into a higher synthesis. His religion is derived from the maturing necessities and the chosen directions of his growth.

Religion as an Illusion

Operating upon some of the same developmental assumptions as did Starbuck and others, Sigmund Freud and others arrived at different conclusions. He said that religion represents a childish stage of human development—both individual and social—which man needs to outgrow. Religion is an illusion, the composite of the childlike hopes of man, they would say. Freud puts it in this way:

> When the child grows up and finds that he is destined to remain a child forever, and that he can never do without protection against unknown and mighty powers, he invests these with the traits of the father-figure; he creates for himself the gods, of whom he is afraid, whom he seeks to propitiate, and to whom he nevertheless entrusts

the task of protecting him. Thus the longing-for-the-father explanation is identical with the other, the need for protection against the consequences of human weakness; the child's defensive reaction to his helplessness gives the characteristic features to the adult's reaction to his own sense of helplessness, i.e., the formation of religion.[11]

When Freud fixed his attention upon the psychical origin of religious ideas, then he concluded that "they are illusions," by which he meant the "fulfilments of the oldest, strongest, and most insistent wishes of mankind," and that the strength of religion lies in "the strength of these wishes." [12]

Freud had other very important aspects to his theory of religion. These ideas concerning his theory of illusion are only part of his conceptions. But these are the ones on which he made his reputation concerning religion. These are the ones most people heard. The others will be discussed in subsequent sections of this chapter.

Karl Marx is another who considered religion to be an illusion, a recoil against the disappointments of life. He described religion as being an illusory counterpart of the real world. He said:

> The religious world is but the reflex of the real world. . . . The religious reflex of the real world can, in any case, only then finally vanish when the practical relations of everyday life offer to man none but perfectly intelligible and reasonable relations with regard to his fellowman and to nature.[13]

He castigates Protestantism for its identification with trading nations and for converting men into producers of commodities for sale. Such religion, to Marx, becomes a means for keeping people happy on the hopes of an unreal world in the presence of the shattered hopes and bitter disillusionments of a real world. Therefore it is an opiate of the people, a soothing reassurance in the presence of the harshness of reality, a reaction-formation against things as they are. As the waggish parody of a great poet puts it, so Marx would describe the religious man:

> He sits in a green grotto
> With a bucket of lurid paint
> And paints the thing as it isn't
> For the Great God of things
> As they ain't!

The prophetic faith of Isaiah, however, would be equally impatient with the way Israel, after Yahweh taught her to walk, insisted on going off after superstitions, magic, and idols. This is where Freud and Marx were prophetic but also in the dark as to the God of Isaiah.

Religion as Reverence-for-Life

The poignant sadness of the thoughts of the melancholy prophets, Freud and Marx, is washed of its cynicism but left poignant in the thought of Albert Schweitzer. He identifies religion itself with the reverence for life and the will-to-live. He says that *veneratio vitae,* reverence-for-life, is the "most direct and at the same time the profoundest achievement of my will-to-live," and that "ethics, too, are nothing but reverence for life." [14] Our religious world-view, according to Schweitzer, would then arise from being grasped by the will-to-live, which is the ground of all being. As he puts it, "world-view is a product of life-view, not vice versa." [15] Religion originates in the active will-to-live and one's theology is an after-reflection of this.

Very akin to this kind of thinking is the point of view of William Ernest Hocking, who feels that religion starts when man begins to value life as life. He does not give in to the assumption that religion springs from curiosity nor to any lesser thing than the deep-going desire, as deep as the will-to-live itself.

> Religion is to be understood as a product and manifesto of human desire; and that of no secondary or acquired desire such as curiosity, but of deep-going desire, deep as the will-to-live itself. . . . If we should venture to name this deep-set desire which we call religious it might be represented as the ultimate demand for self-

preservation: it is man's leap, as individual and as species, for eternal life in some form, in presence of an awakened fear of fate.[16]

Such a spirit is obvious in the experience of Fyodor Dostoevsky, who was condemned to death by the firing squad. He had no way out of the death sentence. He was led out to be shot. Just as he was to be killed—the soldiers with their guns loaded, shouldered, and cocked to fire—the emperor issued a reprieve. Dostoevsky, commenting later in his book, *The Idiot,* says:

> What an eternity! What if I did not die. All eternity would be mine. Oh, then I would change every minute into a century; I would not lose a single one; I would keep track of all my instincts, and would not spend any of them lightly.[17]

This is something of the deep sense of urgency that gripped the fellowship of the early church when they knew that at any moment they, like their Master, could be hauled before the tribunal and killed. Also, their firm belief in the imminent return of the Lord made life itself very precious and very religious. The will-to-live was heightened. To it they must be true. As Schweitzer puts it:

> The highest knowledge, then, is the knowing that I must be true to the will-to-live. . . . The essential nature of the will-to-live is determination to live itself to the full. It carries within it the impulse to realise itself in the highest possible perfection. In the flowering tree, in the strange forms of the medusa, in the blade of grass, in the crystal; everywhere it strives to reach the perfection with which it is endowed. In everything that exists there is at work an imaginative force, which is determined by ideals. In us, beings who can move about freely and are capable of pre-considered, purposive working, the impulse to perfection is given in such a way that we aim at raising to their highest material and spiritual value both ourselves and every existing thing which is open to our influence.
>
> How this striving originated within us, and how it is developed, we do not know, but it is given with our existence. We must act upon it, if we would not be unfaithful to the mysterious will-to-live which is within us.[18]

However, the Christian faith would probe deeply the believer's conception of life itself. The pantheist can reverence life for its own sake. The bereaved person who has lost his nearest of kin can reverence life so dearly that he will despair of his own life at the loss of his loved one. The apostle Paul was aware that life itself could be a separating power in the relationship to God, and was persuaded that "neither life nor death" could separate him from the love of God in Christ. The injunction that the saving of life can be accomplished only through the loss of life has been interpreted ascetically. But on the other hand this same command of Christ cuts through the ethical confusion that can arise out of the idolatry of a time-bound, finite, restricted understanding of the meaning of what life is.

Religion as an Encounter with the Infinite

The very effort to define life reminds man of the infinite nature of that which he is seeking to define. Some, like Gilbert Murray, trace the religious dimensions of man's personality to his encounter with the infinite. Murray says that

> . . . religion essentially deals with the uncharted region of human experience. A large part of human life has been thoroughly surveyed and explored; we understand the causes at work; and we are not bewildered by the problems. That is the domain of positive knowledge. But all round us on every side there is an uncharted region, just fragments of the fringe of it explored, and those imperfectly; it is with this that religion deals.[19]

Also Max Muller, rejecting the idea that religion arises from a separate faculty or theistic instinct, insists that religion emerges from a sense of the infinite:

> One of the essential elements of all religious knowledge is the admission of beings which can neither be apprehended by sense nor comprehended by reason. Sense and reason, therefore, in the ordinary acceptation of these terms, would not be sufficient to account for the facts before us. If then, we openly admit a third

function of our consciousness for the apprehension of what is infinite, that function need not be more mysterious than those of sense and reason.[20]

In the same context Muller says that although each religion has its own peculiar growth, "the seed from which they spring is everywhere the same. That seed is the perception of the infinite." [21] He says that although the fragments of our finite knowledge may cover this sense of the infinite, it is always there. He urges that we dig deep enough and promises that we will find this seed, buried, supplying the life to the fibres and seeders of all true faith.

Pascal, the seventeenth-century mathematician and physicist, who Martin Buber says "became homeless in infinity," [22] stimulated religious feeling in his readers by appealing to their awareness of the infinite:

> Returning to himself, let man consider what he is in comparison with all existence; let him regard himself as lost in this remote corner of nature; and from the little cell in which he finds himself lodged, I mean the universe, let him estimate at their true value, the earth, kingdoms, cities, and himself. What is man in the Infinite?" [23]

Religion as Man's Encounter with Finitude

Man's contemplation of the infinite thrusts him into a painful awareness of his own finitude. As Hocking again says, "Religion is a reaction to our finite situation. . . . This reaction seems to be, at its heart, as instinctive as a start or a shudder." [24] This is that state of helplessness of which Freud spoke and with which he himself struggled. As Schleiermacher contemplated the nature of religion, he was impressed with the feeling of dependence which to him was universally apparent among men. He said that "in the midst of finitude to be one with the Infinite and in every moment to be eternal is the immortality of religion." But this comes from having encountered one's ultimate dependency. He says that "the feeling of absolute dependence [is] a coexistence of God in the self. Consciousness, the totality of being from which all determination of self-consciousness proceed, is comprehended under the feeling of dependence." In another place he says that "to feel oneself absolutely dependent and to be conscious of being in relation to God are one and the same thing." [25]

Rudolf Otto expressed the theme of finitude as a source of the religious dimension of personality in his idea of the creatureliness of man. He saw religion historically and psychologically as arising from the feeling of awe, fear, dread, attraction, and fascination in the presence of the numinous, *mysterium tremendum*. Such numinous experience enriches reason and gives heart to morality. It eludes or transcends comprehension in rational or ethical terms and is essentially ineffable.

Paul Tillich, in his definition of man's religious dimension in terms of his ultimate concerns, thrusts this concern over against the backdrop of man's finitude. Man tries to "grasp the infinite with the categories of finitude, the really real with the categories of experience, and . . . it necessarily fails." [26] Tillich feels that the concept of finitude is central to the understanding of God, "for it is the finitude of being which drives us to the question of God." [27] Religious experience roots in this handling of finitude. As Tillich points out, man realizes his finitude through the experience of *time* (having to die) and *space* (fear of losing one's place in life or not having a place in life) and *causality* (being dependent on something or someone else), and *substance* (the fear of losing one's self, one's identity).[28] And, as he defines it, finitude is "the possibility of losing one's ontological structure" and, with it, one's self." [29]

In fact, the experience of sin, as an encounter with man's own finitude, may be considered as "holding out on the possibilities of losing one's self." The elevation of the self against God, rejecting one's own humanity willfully represents man's pride. Revelational theology has usually considered the fact of original sin as more than just finitude, or man's desire to be infinite. Man's first disobedience to God arose when he willfully rebelled against God by erecting himself as God. This is what Freud, in describing neurotics, called a "childish feeling of omnipotence."

The Interpersonal Sources of Religion

Man soon learns that he is not only finite as an individual; he also lives among a people of finitude, a people of sinfulness. The social scientists have been quick to form theories of the origin of religion. Also kinship-covenant approaches to religion have been articulated by certain theologians. For instance, Pederson aptly states this in his penetrating study of the religious life of Israel:

> When we look at the soul, we always see a community rising behind it. What it is, it is by virtue of others. It has sprung up from a family which has filled it with its contents and from which it can never grow away. The family forms the narrowest community in which it lives. But wherever it works, it must live in community because it is its nature to communicate itself to others, to share its blessings with them.[30]

Also, W. Robertson Smith, in interpreting the religion of the Old Testament particularly, was impressed by the way in which Semitic religion was rooted in the solidarity of the community. So marked and obvious was this solidarity in the Old Testament that H. Wheeler Robinson has called it "corporate personality," affirming that the sense of the community preceded the awareness of individuals. Smith says forcefully:

> From the earliest times religion, as distinguished from magic and sorcery, addresses itself to kindred and friendly beings, who may indeed be angry with their people at times, but are always placable except to the enemies of their worshippers or to renegade members of the community. It is not in vague fear of unknown powers but with a loving reverence for known Gods who are knit to the worshippers by strong bonds of kinship, that religion, in the only sense of the word, begins.[31]

Here the idea of a covenant-making God, so inseparable from a Hebrew-Christian view of religion enters with full force, for the covenant was always made with an individual with *a people* in mind. Sin was interpreted as a breaking of that covenant, as a disruption of a relationship to God and his people.

Emile Durkheim, at the same time he did much special pleading for sociology as a separate science, set forth an essentially communal or kinship theory of the origin of religion. He pointed out that "nearly all the great social institutions have been born in religion," and that "if religion has given birth to all that is essential in society, it is because the ideal of society is the soul of religion." [32] In so many words, he says that the "*sui generis* out of which religious experience is made is society." [33]

Sigmund Freud gave a much more profound conception of religious origins than his illusionistic conception. Drawing heavily upon the writings of W. Robertson Smith, he set forth a distinctly social psychology of religious myth in his book, *Totem and Taboo*. He followed Charles Darwin and assumed that men originally lived in comparatively small groups or hordes. (The word horde in Freud's vocabulary means an organized group of limited size, and not the large mass which it connotes in English.) The jealousy among the younger brothers of the oldest and strongest clan or horde leader inhibited sexual promiscuity of the men with women. The brothers rose up and killed the leader, and the *father clan* was replaced by the *brother clan*. Religion, therefore, arose out of the need to handle the sense of guilt, shame, and remorse which the brothers felt for having killed the leader. The leader's image was transformed from that of a threatening enemy to that of a forgiving friend. Morality, although based on the necessities of society, nevertheless has a deeper rootage in the need for atonement for the sense of guilt the clan bears for having destroyed their leader.

The religious meal, or the totem feast in primitive religion, as Freud described it, is that occasion in which "the clansmen acquire sanctity by consuming the totem: they reinforce their identification with it and with one another." [34] Thus their hostility has taken the form of repentance; their rejection has become adoration. They receive the communal meal as a symbol of forgiveness. They take into themselves the likeness of their dead leader who now lives again through them. In speaking in another place of the Christian community, Freud said that "the tie which unites each individual with Christ is also the cause of the tie which unites them with one another." But this tie of love which was formerly competition, has now directed its hostility outward toward unbelievers.

> Fundamentally indeed every religion is . . . a religion of love for all those whom it embraces; while cruelty and intolerance toward those who do not belong to it are natural to every religion.[35]

Another Jew, Martin Buber, more contemporaneously interprets the religion in interpersonal terms. He observes children's "instinct to make everything into a Thou, to give relation to the universe," even to the point of carrying on conversation with a simmering kettle. This universal need for encounter with a Thou is the fertile source of religious concern. Religion is found in community, but not just any kind of community, says Buber. "The community is built up out of living mutual relation, but the builder is the living effective Centre." [36] Buber comes very near to making the need for a Thou into a separate entity, but to draw this conclusion is to miss his inherent mysticism. In a word, the need to be "in touch," for tenderness, to be in creative relationship with *an* other and the Other, is the source of the spiritual dimensions of personality.

Religion and Man's Individuality and Uniqueness

Those who emphasize the interpersonal origins of religion represent both sides of man's struggle for individuality and uniqueness as the ambivalent aspect of the religious dimensions of personality. This is what Buber calls the "separated I," [37] or the "unique one." [38]

Yet man could not be an individual except in relation to a community. Out of the deep tragedy of his own life, Søren Kierkegaard demarcated the struggle to become a self as the pilgrimage of the religious person. He correlated man's despair with the ambiguities involved in becoming a self. Even if one succeeded in becoming a self, he would fall into despair for having done so! [39] And becoming a self before God is a lonely experience in which one exists "before God," and feels the awfulness of the eternal qualitative difference between him and God.

This existential struggle of man to discover who he is and to identify himself in relation to the basic anxieties of his humanity is also highlighted by Paul Tillich when he calls this process of becoming a self before God "the courage to be." [40]

Also, Gordon Allport defines the developed religious sentiment in terms of a "comprehensive attitude whose function is to relate the individual meaningfully to the whole of being." [41] Although Allport rejects any simple, one-cause explanation of religious origins, and says that mature religion is a "rich pudding, smooth and simple in its blend, but intricate in its ingredients," he emphasizes repeatedly the "ultimate individuality of the religious sentiment." [42] He perceives the major task of psychology in relation to religion to be increasing man's self-knowledge. Increased self-knowledge will enable man to "bind himself wholesomely and wisely to the process of creation." [43]

The science of psychology has emphasized the varieties of religious experience, the importance of the individual in religion, and the diversity of religious truths with an undergirding commitment to the uniqueness of each man's personal religion. Allport's psychology of personality calls for an explanation of the uniqueness of each life, that which separates it from every other life.[44] In the same context he says that each life has a necessary, separate, unique patterning different from that of every other life.

This insistence upon the uniqueness of man as an individual necessarily points man's religious quest in the direction of the discovery and realization of his individuality. God has made himself known in his creation of the individual by setting him apart from the rest of creation in some particular ways. Thus he has stamped his own image on the person as surely as he gave him fingerprints, a tone of voice, and many other visible and audible evidences of uniqueness. Man's religion is realized in his discovery and creative demonstration of his individuality. However, Buber would consider such insistence upon the uniqueness of man to be an artificial understanding of man's true nature. He says that "individuality neither shares in nor obtains any reality" and that "individuality in differentiating itself from others is rendered remote from true being." [45]

Leadership and the Origin of Religion

When an individual begins to separate himself from the community and to assert his uniqueness, the fact still remains that he cannot do so in isolation from the community. He must either reject the community of which he is a part or draw it after him as its leader. In this sense Buber is right when he says that "no man is pure individuality." [46] On the other hand, a community inveterately develops some kind of leadership. As Aristotle and Homer both pointed out, even the gods on Olympus had to have a king.[47] Therefore, the religious dimension of personality is closely associated with man's need for leadership. And Aristotle's *Politics* bears a direct relationship to his interpretation of the spiritual life of man as emerging from his search for a First Cause, an Unmoved Mover, as an ultimate source of authority and responsibility.

When we turn to the Hebrew-Christian tradition, only a casual glance is needed to see the intense preoccupation of religious people with the demand for a king in the Old Testament story. As the spiritual kingdom was built, leaders such as Abraham, Isaac, Jacob, Moses, Samuel, David, and Solomon supplied the meaningful motifs of the spiritual strivings of the people. The communal disintegration of the Exile was accompanied by the leadership of the prophets and the emergence of the Messianic Hope, the hope for a delivering leader upon whose shoulders would rest the "government of the people."

The divine right of kings, as it has emerged from time to time historically, is forcefully relevant to the leadership theory of the origin of religion. The corruption of this so-called divine right of kings has appeared regularly in dictatorships when, from Alexander the Great to Hitler, despotic rulers have sooner or later either deified themselves or been deified by their subjects. In the psychotic manifestations of religious concern the extreme delusions of grandeur in which the patient is persuaded that he is God, Christ, or the father of God further reflect the curious elision of the need for individuality and the need to be a king.

The conflictual division among religious groups cannot be totally explained in terms of the struggle for leadership and the need of the group for a leader. But obviously this is a large component, for instance, in the fragmentation of Protestantism today. The emerging goal of both the mature person and the healthy religion at this point is the balanced handling of the problems of authority and responsibility. We can point to similar secularized struggles for authority and leadership in conflicts in the field of psychology. The leadership of this or that psychologist became a determinative factor in interpretation of personality and therapy!

This could be one of the reasons for intense fascination that Darwin's theory of the primal horde and his leader had for Sigmund Freud. He himself was the leader of a community which expressed well-nigh religious devotion for him. He felt keenly the rivalry of his near contemporaries. He feared, apparently, their destructive criticisms. The divisions within "Freudianism" have been surpassed only by those within Protestantism.

Religion and the Unity of Man's Being

Obviously the struggle to achieve individuality is linked with the leadership need of man. This is rooted in the need of a community to symbolize itself. Such pressures within man are not always in harmony with each other. The unity of his selfhood is constantly under threat from this and other conflicts that assail his being. Therefore, some efforts to explain the origins of the religious dimensions of personality suggest that man's need to maintain the unity of his being is a fertile source of religious concern.

Aristotle said that there are three souls—the nutritive, sensitive, and rational souls of man—but he threw his whole weight against the idea that these were separate souls. Rather, he chose to use the term "soul" to apply to the cohesive reality in man's essential nature. He said that if there were a force which held the soul together, it would be more fitting to call that the soul than the parts which were supposed to be souls.[48] Furthermore, this unitive need of man is reflected in the Genesis account of the creation of men and women, that man and woman are, in some sense or other, partial beings without each other. The twain become one flesh. This *henosis* is, as Derrick Sherwin Bailey has pointed out, the ontological basis of the sexual relationship.[49] Also, this unitive striving of mankind, according to A. R. Johnson, is the most distinctive characteristic of Hebrew interpretations of personality.

> This recognition of the mental activity of the Israelites as predominantly synthetic, the awareness of totality, is important. It is, perhaps, hardly too much to say that it is the "Open Sesame" which unlocks the Hebrew language and reveals the riches of the Israelite mind.[50]

The Hebrew conception of the resurrection of the body, made most articulate in primitive Christianity, further represents the depths of the religious dimensions of man's need to maintain the unity of his being, even in the resurrection.

Prescott Lecky developed a theory of personality and motivation which provides a personality-model counterpart for this kind of interpretation of the source of religious concern. He calls his point of view "self-consistency." He says that as long as man is alive

> . . . he must be thought of as a unit in himself, a system which operates as a whole. . . . One source of motivation only, the necessity to maintain the unity of the system, must serve as the universal dynamic principle . . . We assume a constant striving for unity.[51]

Gordon Allport, in an imaginative dialogue between a student and his professor of psychology, explores the meaning of religion as a quest for unity in the disorder of life. The essential intent of the religious consciousness is to fulfill life's highest potentialities. Allport concludes that the Christian philosophy that motivates the self to strive for comprehensive and unified goals is conducive to mental health.[52]

Of course, E. B. Tylor's theory of animism, which explains the origin of religion in man's belief in spirits, is a sort of "reverse twist" of the need of man for the unity of his being. Man, according to Tylor, developed his religious life from his experiential encounter with spiritual separations within his being. He first sensed these separations within himself in sleep, dreams, visions, ecstasies, and the deliria of illness. Then he saw the departure of "the spirit" from his fellows when they died. Ancestor worship, nature worship, totemism, polytheism, and the like built rapidly upon this encounter of spirits and man's attempts to stay in touch with the "better part" of himself.[53]

Contemporary experience in counseling reflects the almost panicky fear people have of "going to pieces," and the way they exhort themselves and each other "to pull themselves together." The fear of mental illness today has become the modern counterpart of the fear of hell in the Edwardian period of American revivalism. In fact, it may be called a secularization of the doctrine of hell in which the main fear is what Tillich has called "the threat of destruction," and "the threat of nonbeing." The nameless anxiety, which Tillich calls "basic" anxiety, causes man to ask what the basic meaning of his life is. He becomes ultimately concerned in terms of his encounter of the abyss of meaningless, shattered and scattered selflessness.

Comprehensive approaches to medicine, commonly known as psychosomatic medicine, point up the segmentation of selfhood that occurs when the spiritual dilemma of a patient is converted into physical symptoms and/or when emotional tensions actually produce lesions in the tissue structure. The "healing team" approach to the needs of the whole patient, combining the resources of medicine, religion, education, social work, and so on, reflects the sensitivity of the helping professions to man's need to achieve and maintain the unity of his being. Hence the religious dimensions of personality become all the more obvious in man's need for the coherence of his being, particularly in the light of the Hebrew understanding of the oneness of man's person.

Man's Contradictoriness and the Religious Dimensions of Personality

However, man is essentially a contradictory being, especially as we see him in his unredeemed war with himself. Spiritual concern which arises out of the essential contradictions in man, is a deeper insight into religious origins. For example, Henri Bergson would contend that no single element of religious concern manifests itself in an "unadulterated state," but comes amalgamated with others. He sees the religious order emerging creatively from tension between man's intelligence on the one hand

and the natural desire to preserve the life and balance of man on the other hand.[54] As a result of this tension, Bergson says that

> *looked at from this first point of view, religion is a defensive reaction of nature against the dissolvent power of intelligence.* [italics author's] [55]

The thought behind this seems to be that in man's intelligence is the power to destroy himself. Religion becomes a form of control of this power. On the other hand, man's intelligence gives him the capacity to perceive his own finitude, his inevitable death. Therefore, Bergson says,

> *Looked at from this second standpoint, religion is a defensive reaction of nature against the representation, by intelligence, of the inevitability of death.* [italics author's] [56]

The creation story identifies man's fall and subsequent need for salvation with his rebellious and uncontrollable desire to be "like God, knowing good and evil." The upshot of the tension between natural self-preservation and intelligence, according to Bergson, is what he calls "static religion," which

> when it stands alone, attaches man to life, and consequently the individual to society, by telling him tales on a par with those with which we lull children to sleep.[57]

But the thesis of the nature-intelligence antithesis gives rise to another polarity, the tension between intelligence in its finite setting and the larger, mystical striving of man. "We know," says Bergson, "that all around intelligence there lingers still a fringe of intuition, vague and evanescent." [58] This conflict between man's finitude and his mystical power to touch the "transcendent cause of all things," gives rise to a second kind of religion, the only kind worthy of the name, *dynamic* religion. This kind of religion is rare, but "in the innermost being of most men [there is] the whisper of an echo" of it.[59]

A more profound understanding of the contradictoriness of

personality as a source of religious concern is that of Anton T. Boisen. According to Boisen in his book, *Religion in Crisis and Custom*,[60] the great periods of spiritual creativity occurred when individuals and groups were under severe stress and in great crises. He takes the Great Depression as an example, and through the use of social surveys correlates the emergence of many smaller religious groups of pentecostalists with the crisis of economic privation. As these spontaneous religious awakenings occur and begin to consolidate their gains, they develop customs, rituals, and institutions for defining and transmitting their heritage. Here the pull between institutional and intensely personal or charismatic religious expressions becomes apparent.

Boisen also correlated severe mental illnesses with "reactions to a sense of personal failure" in personal crisis situations in the lives of mental patients whom he studied. He evaluated the prognosis of the patient in terms of the nature and direction of "concern" in the patient. The tension between traditional and personal religious loyalties, between the need for individual freedom and the approval of "those whose approval the patient considered most worthwhile . . ."[61] was the spawning ground for both great religious ideas and distorted mental pathologies. The critical situation could go either way: toward the benign solutions of an effective religious expression of the deepest within the patient or toward the more malignant concealment and defense of the real person.

Andras Angyal, in his "theoretical model" of personality, points out the polarity that exists between the homonomous trends and the autonomous trends within the biosphere, or the total person. Whereas he says that "religion contains many elements," and these "have very different origins and character," nevertheless he accents the homonomous features of religion and identifies them as man's need to "share in a meaningful cosmic order."[62] He sets these homonomous trends over against the absolute necessity, however, for autonomous achievement in the creative artist, the saint, the hero. He even suggests a religious, artistic, and social typology on the basis of the predominance of one or the other of these trends in the given individual. The whole of man is expressed in the paradoxical tension of these trends.

The Christian doctrine of man has always, when stated in keeping with its biblical and historical sources, been more concerned with the origin of man himself than with the origin of religion. Man is a creature, made in the image of his Creator. This origin, as man, puts him into inescapable dialogue with his Creator. Subsequent to his creation, man affirmed his own freedom through negation of and rebellion against his Creator. Man was thrust into a "life of conflict" with himself, covetousness in relation to his fellows, and unreality in his estrangement from God. Hence, as Emil Brunner says, "The Christian doctrine of man . . . takes this conflict seriously, and does not try to explain it away or neutralize it in any direction." [63] The contradictoriness of man's need for individuality and community, for affirmation of release from his finitude, and his fearful attempts to control and yet have use of his intelligence—all this reflects the essential ambiguity of man's existence. The anxiety thus created is the precondition of distorted and sinful behavior which in turn burdens man with a load of guilt. His need for forgiveness, reconciliation, and restoration becomes the precondition of his return to God by faith through Christ, which is the essence of Christian experience.

AN OVERVIEW OF RELIGIOUS ORIGINS

This discussion began with the conception of religion as arising from a special instinct and has progressed to the point of considering the creation and fall of man. The movement toward the integration and wholeness of personality away from atomistic conceptions of this or that part of a person as the source of religious concern has been another discernible movement. The earlier theorists reduced both personality and religion to a simple, one-factor "phenomenon." But the more recent thinkers in the field, such as Allport, Angyal, and others see both religion and personality as complex, comprehensive expressions of life itself, moving toward wholeness and consistency of organization. Allport declares:

> For if the religious sentiment were of uniform composition, marked by a single phenomenal core, then our task of psychological analysis would be straightforward; but . . . this simplicist . . . approach is not acceptable . . . and our attack must be pluralistic and varied.[64]

Religion, Allport says, "is a white light in personality which, though luminous and simple, is in reality multicolored in composition." [65] Therefore, what we have is a spectroscopic analysis in the description above of the various attempts to identify the source of religion in personality. Each one of the interpretations blends into all the others when we push it far enough.

It needs to be repeated: Allport's approach represents a definite shift in the modes of scientific thinking in midtwentieth century as compared with nineteenth century scientific theory. The simple causation approach to science in which A causes B, especially in the case of human actions, is really a psychologizing of natural processes for teaching purposes only. This is what Felix Mainx calls an "inadmissible" turning of "ideas into natural objects." We can do this only so long as "we isolate partial causes from the event and do not take fully into account, or do not fully know, the constellations of conditions given in the system itself." [66]

In the same vein of thought, H. A. Overstreet says that the most important change "in respect to causality that science has introduced into our contemporary thinking is to turn the age-old 'linear' conception into a 'field' conception. As in a field of force, everything is both cause and effect." [67] He goes even further to say that "what is *the* cause . . . is one of those monocausal

—and really nonsensical questions that no disciplined mind now asks." [68]

Therefore, when we apply this kind of energetic, field, interaction conception of causation to the origins of religious concern in human personality, the reduction of religion to this or that one-cause explanation is as naïve in the field of science as it appears to the disciplined theologian. The reductivist, as well as his logic, is outmoded! When, therefore, we hear someone say that "religion is nothing but . . ." regardless of what he reduces it to, we can conclude that he is either a professor who has quit studying, or a sophomoric thinker whose teachers have kept him in the dark!

The earlier phenomenologists of religion did a great deal of special pleading for this or that branch of science, usually their own specialty. Leuba made a strong case for making theology "a branch of psychology." Durkheim identified religion with society, and naturally the study of religion would become a branch of sociology. More recently Erich Fromm has made a deep impression upon theologians, but the impression he tends to leave is that religion should be a branch of psychoanalysis. This is certainly the impression left by ministers who insist upon psychoanalysis for *every* minister. In such approaches the one-cause theory of religion is shifted into a panacea theory of religion, or a one-cure theory of a given science. Thus specializations in the field of science, especially in the area of the helping professions, tend in either theory to have their beginning in a marked rebellion against religion followed by later efforts to encompass religion in their developing specialty. Such segmented thinking also grows out of scientific thinking which has been outmoded by a more comprehensive understanding of the unity of the fields of science. Competitive special pleading for this or that science has led to a semantic morass which hinders the intracommunication of the scientists themselves. Little wonder is it that the scientific interpretations of religion have been characterized by this same segmentation.

However, more recent scientific activity reflects a comprehensive interpretation of life. It rejects partial explanations of human personality by special pleaders for this or that budding profession. A holistic, communicative, and co-operative approach to human personality is emerging. Professions are seeking to find themselves, not only in relation to themselves, but also in relation to each other. Multidisciplinary approaches are being developed in hospitals and educational institutions. More and more the religious dimensions of the personal needs of individuals and groups are being provided for by trained chaplains in hospitals, for instance. All this activity and thought emerges from comprehensive rather than segmental approaches to human personality.

Therefore, the reader who started this chapter seeking for a one-cause explanation of why people are religious is deflected toward a more profound understanding of religious concern. He sees that religious concern emerging in human personality at every point the theorists say it does but it does not *just* emerge at any one of them. He sees religious concern as the permeating meaning and the "set" direction of the total personality as that person lays his whole life upon a given course of life considered ultimate and unconditional for him. This becomes God *for him.* The Christian would say, "Take heed that it is not an idol!" The theological task in relation to the psychological evaluation of religion as a phenomenon is to introduce the science of the nature of God in order to separate the false gods from the true God. The distortions of human life, studied so carefully by the psychologist, in turn become empirical descriptions of man in contradiction, revolt, and estrangement; in other words, man in sin.

The discerning student of Henry Nelson Wieman's account of values would be prone to read his value-judgment conception of religion into what has just been said. However, this is not what is intended by any stretch of the imagination. Here again the "ambidextrous" meanings of the concept of religion itself can be underscored. The neo-orthodox understanding of the Christian faith has contributed much toward correcting the homocentric kind of theology that measures truth in terms of its value to man, unreconstructed and unredeemed. They have emphasized man's distressing need for redemption. Likewise, they have emphasized a conception of the science of theology which balances up the empiricism of such approaches with a deductive kind of science based upon both biblical and historical revelation. However, great care needs to be exerted, in shifting from one of these approaches to the other, that they are historically understandable only when seen as critical correctives of each other and not in isolation from each other.

This leads to the most profound understanding of the origin of religion: We look in vain when we search for the source of religion purely and solely in terms of *man's need for religion*. The argument from appetite can go to seed in this way. The theologian pushes the issue more ultimately by asking the question as to the nature, character, and intention of God. It needs to be said again that on matters of fact, particularly those which elucidate the functional processes of human life as it is lived, nothing will do but empirical observation. This observation must be existential as well as scientific. Any statements in the name of faith pretending to explain and elucidate these processes which are not at the same time ready to do the work of examining, observing, validating, and testing of hypotheses are certainly misguided. However, the function of faith in relation to psychology is to give clues, to value presuppositions, and to insist that questions be asked because of their importance and not because of the methods by which they may be studied.

Therefore, the question as to the nature, character, and purposes of God must be asked in any discussion of the origins of religions. The Christian revelation of God in Jesus Christ both raises and answers the question in such a way that the fellowship of discussion, inquiry, and personal encounter is stimulated and sustained rather than shut off and stifled to death. Psychologists of religion have too long lived compartmentalized lives in the name of a false kind of scientific allegiance which avoids asking distinctly theological questions about the results of their surveys, questionnaires, case histories, or autobiographies. Nor can we ask these questions in such a way as to shut off discussion, in an *ex cathedra* fashion, so to speak. For the interaction between psychology and religion has been first a soliloquy of religion and then one of psychology. A deep reciprocity of methodology such as has been suggested here should make an active dialogue of the relationship.

NOTES FOR CHAPTER VI

1. For example, a few of these are the following: Wilhelm Wundt, *Ethics: An Investigation of the Facts and Laws of the Moral Life,* trans. E. B. Titchener; Sigmund Freud, *The Future of an Illusion;* John Dewey, *A Common Faith;* Carl G. Jung, *Modern Man in Search of a Soul* and *Psychology and Religion;* Knight Dunlap, *Religion: Its Function in Human Life;* Gordon W. Allport, *The Individual and His Religion.* (Documentation for these books will be found in the Bibliography.)
2. *A Theological Word Book of the Bible,* "Religion," ed. Alan Richardson (New York: The Macmillan Company, 1952), p. 188.
3. Karl Barth, *The Doctrine of the Word of God* (New York: Charles Scribner's Sons, 1936), p. 38.
4. Morris Jastrow, *The Study of Religion* (New York: Charles Scribner's Sons, 1902), pp. 100-101, 153.
5. Rudolf Otto, *The Idea of the Holy: An Inquiry into the Non-Rational Factor in the Idea of the Divine and Its Relation to the Rational,* 2d ed., trans. John Harvey (London: Oxford University Press, 1950).
6. Göte Bergsten, *Pastoral Psychology* (New York: The Macmillan Company, 1951), pp. 106-107.
7. John Calvin, *Institutes of the Christian Religion,* trans. John Allen, Book III, Vol. II (Philadelphia: Presbyterian Board of Publication, 1909), p. 140.
8. Edwin D. Starbuck, *The Psychology of Religion: An Empirical Study of the Growth of Religious Consciousness* (New York: Charles Scribner's Sons, 1900), p. 403.

9. Gardner Murphy, *Personality: A Biosocial Approach to Origins and Structure* (New York: Harper & Brothers, 1947), pp. 490-491.
10. *Ibid.*, p. 925.
11. Sigmund Freud, *The Future of an Illusion* (London: Hogarth Press, 1943), p. 42.
12. *Ibid.*, p. 52.
13. Karl Marx, *Capital: A Critique of Political Economy*, trans. Moore and Aveling, Vol. I (Chicago: Charles H. Kerr and Co., 1921), pp. 91-92.
14. Albert Schweitzer, *Civilization and Ethics* (London: A. & C. Black, Ltd., 1929), pp. xiii-xiv. American edition copyrighted by The Macmillan Company, New York under title of *The Philosophy of Civilization*.
15. *Ibid.*
16. William Ernest Hocking, *The Meaning of God in Human Experience: A Philosophic Study of Religion* (New Haven, Conn.: Yale University Press, 1922), pp. 49-50. Used by permission.
17. Fyodor Dostoevsky, *The Idiot* (New York: Brentano's, 1887).
18. Albert Schweitzer, *The Philosophy of Civilization*, "Civilization and Ethics," trans. Campion, American ed. Used by permission of The Macmillan Company, copyright 1929.
19. Gilbert Murray, *Five Stages of Greek Religion* (Boston: Beacon Press, 1925). Used by permission.
20. Max Muller, *Lectures on the Origin and Growth of Religion* (London: Longmans, Green and Co., 1878), pp. 20, 21, 24.
21. *Ibid.*, p. 48.
22. Martin Buber, *Between Man and Man* (London: Routledge and Kegan Paul, Ltd., 1947), p. 132. Copyright held by The Macmillan Company, New York.
23. Blaise Pascal, *Pensées* (New York: Modern Library, 1941), p. 42.
24. Hocking, *op. cit.*, p. 50.
25. Friedrich Schleiermacher, *The Christian Faith* (Edinburgh: T. & T. Clark, 1928), pp. 126, 17.
26. Paul Tillich, *Systematic Theology*, Vol. I (Chicago: University of Chicago Press, 1952), p. 82.
27. *Ibid.*, p. 166.
28. *Ibid.*, pp. 192-197.
29. *Ibid.*, p. 201.
30. Johannes Pederson, *Israel: Its Life and Culture*, Vols. I-II (London: Geoffrey Cumberlege, 1940), p. 263. Used by permission of Oxford University Press, London, in conjunction with Branner og Korchs Forlag of Copenhagen.
31. W. Robertson Smith, *Lectures on the Religion of the Semites* (London: A. & C. Black, Ltd., 1894), p. 55.
32. Emile Durkheim, *The Elementary Forms of the Religious Life* (London: G. Allen and Unwin, Ltd., 1915), p. 419.
33. *Ibid.*, p. 418.
34. Sigmund Freud, *The Complete Psychological Works*, trans. James Strachey, Vol. XIII (London: Hogarth Press, 1955), pp. 140ff.
35. Sigmund Freud, *Group Psychology and the Analysis of the Ego* (London: Hogarth Press, 1948), pp. 43, 51.

36. Martin Buber, *I and Thou* (Edinburgh: T. & T. Clark, 1937), p. 45.
37. *Ibid.,* p. 65.
38. Martin Buber, *Between Man and Man,* trans. R. G. Smith (London: Routledge and Kegan Paul, Ltd., 1947), pp. 40 ff. Copyright held by The Macmillan Company, New York.
39. Søren Kierkegaard, *The Sickness unto Death* (Princeton, N. J.: Princeton University Press, 1941).
40. Paul Tillich, *The Courage to Be* (New Haven, Conn.: Yale University Press, 1952).
41. Gordon W. Allport, *Becoming: Basic Considerations for a Psychology of Personality* (New Haven, Conn.: Yale University Press, 1955), p. 94.
42. Gordon W. Allport, *The Individual and His Religion* (New York: The Macmillan Company, 1950), pp. 8, 11, 26.
43. *Ibid.,* p. 98.
44. Gordon W. Allport, *Personality: A Psychological Interpretation* (New York: Henry Holt & Company, Inc., 1937), p. 558.
45. Buber, *Between Man and Man, op. cit.*
46. *Ibid.,* p. 65.
47. Aristotle, *Politics,* I, v. 1-3, trans. H. Rackham (Cambridge, Mass.: Harvard University Press, 1944).
48. Aristotle, *De Anima,* Book I, Chapter 5, Section 411.
49. Derrick Sherwin Bailey, *The Mystery of Love and Marriage* (New York: Harper & Brothers, 1952), pp. 43 ff.
50. A. R. Johnson, *The Vitality of the Individual in the Thought of Ancient Israel* (Cardiff: University of Wales Press, 1949), pp. 7-8.
51. Prescott Lecky, *Self-Consistency: A Theory of Personality* (New York: Island Press, 1945), pp. 80-81. Copyright by Kathryn Lecky.
52. Gordon W. Allport, "The Roots of Religion," *Pastoral Psychology,* May, 1954, pp. 13-24.
53. E. B. Tylor, *Primitive Culture: Researches into the Development of Mythology, Philosophy, Religion, Language, Art and Custom,* Vol. I (New York: Henry Holt & Company, Inc., 1889), pp. 428 ff.
54. Henri Bergson, *The Two Sources of Morality and Religion* (New York: Doubleday & Company, Inc., 1954), p. 129.
55. *Ibid.,* p. 122.
56. *Ibid.,* p. 131.
57. *Ibid.,* p. 211.
58. *Ibid.,* p. 212.
59. *Ibid.,* p. 214.
60. Anton T. Boisen, *Religion in Crisis and Custom* (New York: Harper & Brothers, 1955).
61. Anton Boisen, *The Exploration of the Inner World* (New York: Harper & Brothers, 1952).
62. Andras Angyal, *Foundations for a Science of Personality* (New York: The Commonwealth Fund, 1941), p. 178.
63. Emil Brunner, *Man in Revolt: A Christian Anthropology,* trans. Olive Wyon (Philadelphia: Westminster Press, 1947), p. 83.
64. Gordon W. Allport, *The Individual and His Religion* (New York: The Macmillan Company, 1950), p. 4.

65. *Ibid.*, p. 9.
66. Felix Mainx, "Foundations of Biology," *International Encyclopedia of United Science*, Vol. I, Part 2 (Chicago: University of Chicago Press, 1955), pp. 641-642.
67. H. A. Overstreet, *The Great Enterprise* (New York: W. W. Norton & Company, Inc., 1952), p. 167.
68. *Ibid.*, p. 167.

CHAPTER VII

RELIGIOUS DIMENSIONS OF THE DEVELOPMENT OF PERSONALITY

THE DEVELOPMENT OF HUMAN PERSONS has intrigued the imagination of both theologians and psychologists. Sharp differences of opinions among and between them have arisen over their interpretations of religious experience in the light of conflicting theories of human development. In fact, one's basic conception of human nature itself is at stake in his understanding of personality development. In theological terms, both the nature and the destiny of man are brought into vivid focus in any working conception of the process of human development.

PRESCIENTIFIC INSIGHTS INTO HUMAN DEVELOPMENT

The Greek philosopher, Heraclitus, who lived about 500 B.C., was one of the first semireligious contemplatives to sense the reality of movement, change, and growth in human existence. He said, "You cannot step twice into the same river; for fresh waters are ever flowing in upon you." * [1] Heraclitus felt that the multiple changes of human life and the universe moved pro-

* Notes and credits for this chapter begin on page 169.

gressively through strife between opposing forces and felt that this tension was "the father of all and the king of all." [2] Heraclitus also believed in a dependable law of change and growth to which he gave the name "logos." Everything changes, but the way in which everything changes remains constant. This is the logos. Here we find an early intuition of the fact of lawful process in human experience.

When we look into the New Testament, we find that the parables of Jesus are filled with insights into the dynamic, developmental nature of Christian experience. Probably the parable of the sower (Matthew 13:1-9; Mark 4:1-9; Luke 8:4-8; 5:1-3) gives the most concrete recognition to the importance of rootage and growth. The seed of the Gospel does not even take root in some lives. In others, it has no depth of soil. Other seeds fall upon thorns and are choked out as the thorns grow up. Still others fall on good soil and bring forth good fruit. Apparently one of the secrets of the kingdom of heaven is the awareness of rootage, growth, and fruitage. It takes a person with ears to hear such a truth as this.

The Fourth Gospel, at the same time it sets forth the fact of the new birth into the kingdom of God, also relates faith in Christ to "the power to become the sons of God" (John 3:1-14 and John 1:12-13). Furthermore, as will be seen later in the discussion on maturity as one of the spiritual goals of man's becoming, the apostle Paul, in his discussion of Christian love, persistently relates it to growth in the spiritual life. The whole atmosphere of the Hebrew-Christian conception of God and man is imbued with a conscious awareness of the developmental character of the relationship between the people of God and the covenant-making father-God. A poignantly beautiful example of this is found in Hosea's words:

> When Israel was a child, then I loved him, and called my son out of Egypt. . . . I taught Ephraim also to go, taking them by their arms; but they knew not that I healed them. I drew them with

cords of a man, with bands of love: and I was to them as they that take off the yoke on their jaws, and I laid meat unto them.[3]

Just as this figure of speech gathers up the parental concern of God for the growth of the spiritual abilities of his children, so also do the words of Isaiah accept a distinctly maternal symbol of the developing relationship between God and man:

Shall I bring to the birth, and not cause to bring forth? saith the Lord: shall I cause to bring forth, and shut the womb? saith thy God. Rejoice ye with Jerusalem, and be glad with her, all ye that love her: rejoice for joy with her, all ye that mourn for her: That ye may suck, and be satisfied with the breasts of her consolations; that ye may milk out, and be delighted with the abundance of her glory. For thus saith the Lord, Behold, I will extend peace to her like a river, and the glory of the Gentiles like a flowing stream: then shall ye suck, ye shall be borne upon her sides, and be dandled upon her knees. As one whom his mother comforteth, so will I comfort you; and ye shall be comforted in Jerusalem." [4]

Here, in these two passages, are found symbolic references to two of the great developmental tasks of human life, walking and feeding.

Augustine

The Christian theologian who saw the human person most steadily and completely in terms of the total, unfolding life process of the spiritual pilgrimage of man was Augustine. He had the courage to see and record the process of human development in all its religious dimensions in his own autobiographical study, *The Confessions*. Augustine delved into the depths of his own being, but *The Confessions* are not a soliloquy. They are a dialogue between Augustine and God. Furthermore, *The Confessions* represent the autobiographical approach to the understanding of the intimacies of religious experience. He uses the technique of reminiscence to call "to mind his past," "reviewing the very bitterness of his remembrance," that he may "deepen his fellowship with God." As he pushes his remembrance to the uttermost, Augustine gives a thoroughgoing developmental understanding of his own religious experience. He moved from that time when he was "torn apiecemeal, turned from the one good God, lost among the multiplicity of things" [5] to the time in which he could with unity of heart and being worship God and live securely among men. One of the basic contributions, it seems to me, that Augustine made to the understanding of the religious dimensions of personality becomes apparent in his shift from the static nondevelopmental point of view of the Neo-platonists and Manichaeans to the dynamic, developmental, and depth point of view of the Hebrew-Christian view of life.

Bernard of Clairvaux

Another distinctly theological contribution to the understanding of the development of personality was written by Bernard of Clairvaux in A.D. 1126. In his treatise, *On the Love of God*,[6] Clairvaux delineates four progressive degrees of life. The first level of love is that degree "whereby a man loves himself for his own sake." The natural desires of man are "at the service of the author of nature." The second stage or degree of love is that in which a person "now loves God, then, but still for a while for his own sake and not for Himself." This is the love of God for what God can do for one. "From the occasion of frequent necessities God must be approached by man with constant appeals," and his petitions become a way of expressing his love to God. He loves God for his own sake and not for the sake of God himself. The third stage in the development of the spiritual life of love, according to Bernard, is that in which man loves God, not for his own necessity, but loves God for God's sake: "He . . . gives praise to the Lord, not for that He is good to him, but for that He is good, he truly loveth God for Himself and not for his own sake. . . . This is the third degree of love by which God is now loved for His very self." [7]

But, says Bernard, "there is even a fourth stage of maturing love. This is the stage in which man loves himself for the sake of God, and does not even love himself except for the sake of God." However, even at this stage of maturity, love is not perfected because the perfection of love does not belong even to those who are blessed before the resurrection. Bernard takes into consideration the fact that finitude and humanity are always characterized by an incompleteness of the power to love. Whereas Bernard does not give any elaborate and detailed outline of the development of personality, he has taken seriously the fact of growth and development in the dynamic character of Christian love. As we shall see later, the Christian concept of perfection and the psychological concept of maturity are both discussed in the context of love whether one consults the New Testament concept of *agape* or the contemporary psychological literature on maturity.

John Bunyan (1628–1688)

The English preacher and author, Bunyan, with quaint but uncanny precision depicted the long and arduous pilgrimage of development within the spiritual life of a Christian. Bunyan, in his book, *Grace Abounding*, wrote an autobiographical account of his own spiritual pilgrimage. He delved, as did Augustine, into the depths of his own being through the process of recall and remembrance until he encountered a meaningful pattern of God's providential dealings with him in the course of his own development. His increasing awareness that he was in face-to-face encounter with God brought him into a more acute knowledge of his own selfhood. This knowledge took the form of a confessional experience concerning the whole direction, meaning, and purpose of his life. He said that he was as one bound who felt himself shut up into the judgment to come, that the grace and love and mercy of God abounded to him as the testing and maturing temptations went from one stage of intensity to another.

When he reached the point that the Lord Jesus Christ enabled him to break out of his loneliness into a "longing for the company of some of God's people," he said, "I could scarce lie in my bed for joy and peace and triumph through Christ."

Bunyan's remarkable life story describes his religious experience in terms of his life history and personal development. This same motif is followed in his description of the Christian life, *Pilgrim's Progress.* His book outlines the ten stages of the Christian's pilgrimage from the City of Destruction to the Celestial City. The Christian life is portrayed, not as a static realization of a transactional type of salvation, but as a jagged and uneven, but forward moving, development from one level of spiritual achievement to another through temptation. Spurts of progress are often met by doldrums of despair, indifference, and vanity. Bunyan, himself, describes this in his own reaction to the Bible. He says that sometimes he sees "more in a line of the Bible than I could well tell how to stand under." He says also that another time "the whole Bible hath been to me as a dry stick, or rather, my heart hath been so dead and dry unto it that I could not conceive the least dram of refreshment, though I have looked it all over." [8] M. Esther Harding, in her book, *Journey into Self,* [9] introduces analytical psychological concepts alongside Bunyan's magnificent allegory. She, an analyst, feels that Bunyan reveals useful case material for the psychological study of the inner life of man.

Søren Kierkegaard

Probably the most detailed discussion of the development of personality from a religious point of view is given by Søren Kierkegaard, who was born in 1813 and who died at a relatively early age in 1855. Kierkegaard perceived himself as a psychologist of the Christian life. He saw life as being rooted in values and valuation. He used the term *stages* of life in the same sense that we use the term "ways of life."

The stages on life's way which he identified do not represent inevitable, evolutionary phases of personality development. The idea of a continuous process of development is actually irrelevant and inapplicable to Kierkegaard. Rather, the stages on life's way are qualitatively different ways of life. A personality in transition cannot by a mere process of reflection move from one to the other, nor can he merely trust to time that he will grow inevitably from one to another. The change from one sphere to the other, says David F. Swenson, "is never necessary but always contingent; if it presents itself as possible, it also presents itself as possible of nonrealization. Whenever the transition from one stage to another does take place, it always comes to pass through a 'leap of faith' and requires divine assistance through a true, creative act of God within the framework of a pre-existent creation." [10] Granting this, that it is impossible to reach one stage from another by mere development, it can be said that in the thought of Kierkegaard, the stages on life's way have a positive relationship to each other. They are successive steps on the way toward a more nearly perfect and richer life. However, they cannot be realized without the leap of faith and the creativity of God.

Kierkegaard lists three stages of life. They are the aesthetic, the ethical, and the religious stages of existence. The aesthetic stage is that of pleasure. "Only an immediate relationship concerns aesthetics." [11] The person who lives the aesthetic way of life avoids the necessity, yea, is not aware of the necessity, of making decisions and choosing between alternatives. "He rushes down into the manifold of life, . . . he dashes himself against a solid dam." [12] The aesthetic way of life is essentially a sensual way of life, embodying the satisfactions of the senses. The main threat to the aesthetician is boredom. The aesthetic man lives neither in hope nor in recollection, and the threat of the future and the impingement of the past jeopardize the tranquillity and charm of the moment.

The second stage on life's way is the ethical stage. This phase of life is characterized by the primacy of duty. For the ethical man "the chief thing is, not whether one can count on one's fingers how many duties one has, but that a man has once felt the intensity of duty in such a way that the consciousness of it is for him that assurance of the eternal validity of his being." [13] Furthermore, the ethical stage is characterized by an acute awareness of time and the necessity of decision. Not to make a decision is to make a decision! The ethical man comes into collision with sin as a fact which he is quite incapable of assimilating. The ethical man fulfills himself in this encounter with sin which in turn demands a "dialectical leap and appeals to the transcendency of the religious." [14]

The third stage or way of life, according to Kierkegaard, is the religious stage. Here, the ethical situation confronting man becomes an issue, not merely of what is right and wrong, but of existing as a self before God. The consciousness of being "before God" comes somewhat preliminary to the transition from the ethical to the religous stage. As Kierkegaard says in his book, *The Sickness unto Death,* the measure for the self always is the way in which in the religious stage of existence man becomes aware of "the eternal qualitative difference between him and God." Self-consciousness, in the sense of being a self before God, and God-consciousness are coterminous in the religious stage. Man falls into despair as he becomes a self before God. He may despair, in a pseudofashion, in not willing to become a self. Or, he may despair at having willed to become a self and failed. Or, in the third place, he may despair at having willed to become a self and having succeeded. In the latter phase of despair he may become a self not before God but over against God.

But religion is essentially a passive relationship to the divine, accompanied by suffering and a sense of guilt. This kind of religion Kierkegaard calls Religion A. He distinguishes it from

Religion B which is a transcendent experience of religion. The individual's eternal destiny is threatened, the sense of guilt is transformed into a sense of sin. The continuity between the actual self and the ideal self, the temporal self and the eternal self, is broken. The self is made free from the law of God by the simple confession of the fact that it is unable to comply with the demands. The totally invalidated personality recognizes itself to be so, and God manifests himself as love in time outside the individual in an intimate personal encounter of acceptance.

Two salient features characterize the Kierkegaardian conception of stages. He gives a depth and qualitative understanding of the movement of the self as it actualizes its potentialities, thereby rejecting a purely temporal conception of the development of personality. In the second place, he gives a vertical as well as horizontal interpretation of the relationships involved in the achievement of selfhood. He interprets the self in relation to God as well as in its dialogic relationship to itself and to its community.

Horace Bushnell

Another theologian who dealt with the problem of personality development and religious experience was Horace Bushnell (1802–1876). In 1860 he wrote his book, *Christian Nurture,* which was reprinted in June, 1953, by the Yale University Press. This book is a prophetic document in the field of the development of personality in much the same way that the writings of Walter Rauschenbusch were prophetic in the field of social relationships. Contrary to much popular opinion, Bushnell assumed the corruption of human nature, but felt that it was wisest to undertake the remedy of the corruption at once in the very earliest stages of human life. He felt that it was never too early for good to be communicated and that the spirit of truth need not wait for the child's ability intellectually to understand before it began to operate. He likened the development of a child to the parable of Jesus in which he said that the kingdom of heaven is as a grain of mustard seed. In an essay written in 1844, as early as that, he proposed a constructive alternative to the spiritually sterile revivalism which waited until a person was an adult and then sought to convert him to Christianity. The essence of this essay is as follows:

> We hold that children are, in a sense, included in the faith of their parents, partakers with them in their covenant, and brought into a peculiar relation to God, in virtue of it. On this ground they receive a common field of faith with them, in their baptism; and God on his part, contemplates, in the right, the fact that they are to grow up as Christians, or spiritually renewed persons. As to the precise time or manner in which they are to receive the germ of holy principles, nothing is affirmed. Only it is understood that God includes their infant age in the worn book of parental culture, and pledges himself to them and their parents, in such a way, as to offer the presumption, that they may grow up in love with all goodness, and remember no definite time when they became subjects of Christian principle. Christian education then is to conform to this view, and nothing is to be called Christian education which does not.[15]

Bushnell felt that the overemphasis upon conversion of adults, which implied the free moral agency and personal responsibility of children was a subtle way of parents absolving themselves from the responsibility for the moral and religious character of their children. He concentrated, therefore, on the organic unity of the family, seeing it as a body of interpersonal relationships exerting power over character which is more than just influence. Because this power is both unconscious and undesigned, children are spiritually transformed or, as the case may be, malformed through the personal holiness, or lack of holiness, of parents in relation to their children. Bushnell believed that qualities of education, habit, feeling, and character have a tendency always to grow in a family and by long continuance can become thoroughly inbred in this stock. He affirmed not only the inheritance of original sin but also the transmission of righteousness.

Through such teachings as these, Bushnell laid the theological groundwork for an intense development, in the field of the psychology of religion and religious education, of nurture approaches to religious experience. Although he dealt with the problems of parent-child relationships, theologically and cross-sectionally, he nevertheless opened the way for later religious educators to work out highly refined schemes of the development of personality and other religious consciousness. We turn now to evaluate some of these.

Hall, Starbuck, James, and Sherrill

The twentieth century marks a vast amount of vital activity among the psychologists of religion. The monumental studies of G. Stanley Hall on adolescence set the empirical framework for questionnaire analysis done by E. D. Starbuck and others. The major contribution of these works seems to be that of identifying conversion as a typically adolescent phenomenon and interpreting religious experience in terms of this particular state of personality development. An over-all emphasis is apparent, particularly in the work of E. D. Starbuck, which insists that religious experience is an intensification of process of maturation. For instance, a teen-ager goes through a normal process of storm and stress, doubt and rebellion. The experience of guilt also emerges. Under religious influences the teen-ager undergoes a rapid growth process which telescopes and intensifies these encounters in his developing selfhood.

William James, in his classical book, *The Varieties of Religious Experience,* also interprets conversion in terms of a dynamic growth process. He identifies it as that process, gradual or sudden, whereby a person who has been consciously inferior, divided, and unhappy becomes consciously superior, unified, and happy by reason of his firmer grasp upon spiritual realities. He inserts the time factor in his definition of conversion by saying that it may be "gradual or sudden."

But probably the most comprehensive synthesizer of all the foregoing insights, as well as those which will follow in the contributions of contemporary developmental psychologists and psychotherapists, is the late Professor Lewis J. Sherrill of Union Theological Seminary, New York City. In his book, *The Struggle of the Soul*,[16] Sherrill identifies the religious life as a pilgrimage in which the merging dynamic self of an individual is called out of one stage of development into another by faith. He is challenged to move out, not knowing where he goes, and not shrink back and thereby "lose his soul," to use a concept from Hebrews. Using biblical concepts and elevated poetic imagery, Sherrill discusses the growth of the human person in infancy, childhood, adolescence, adulthood, and later maturity. He points out that this developmental process may, according to the spiritual meaning that is attached to it, be to the individual a saga, a treadmill, or a pilgrimage. He draws heavily on the New Testament, especially the book of Hebrews, to identify the larger spiritual context of the faith pilgrimage of the individual in the Christian community.

THE DEVELOPMENTAL INSIGHTS OF THE PSYCHOLOGISTS
OF PERSONALITY AND PSYCHOTHERAPISTS

Gesell and His Associates

As we turn from the distinctly theological and more or less prescientific conceptualizations of the development of personality, the first major contribution we need to consider is that of Arnold Gesell, Francis Ilg, and Louise Ames. These research persons are interested primarily in the description of child behavior. Working with a highly selected group of children, they have carefully observed the behavior of their test group from infancy through adolescence. They have recorded their findings in four monumental studies: *The Infant and Child in the Culture of Today*,[17] *The First Five Years of Life: The Pre-School Years*,[18] *The Child from Five to Ten*,[19] and *Youth: The Years from Ten to Sixteen*.[20] These works describe the growth gradients of children in a series of stages or degrees of maturity by which the child progresses toward a higher level of behavior. However, these books seek only to present the frames of reference which can "be used to locate the stage of maturity which a child has reached in any given field of behavior." [21] Whereas these books present primarily a description of what behavior is like at different stages, Francis Ilg and Louise Ames have written another book entitled *Child Behavior* [22] which not only tells how behavior develops, but also gives specific advice on what to do about the many child behavior problems that appear at different developmental stages in the life of the growing individual.

In Gesell's conception of the development of personality, there are seven stages of development: (1) the embryo stage, 0-8 weeks; (2) fetus, 8-40 weeks; (3) infancy, birth to two years of age; (4) pre-school, 2-5 years of age; (5) childhood, 5-12 years of age; (6) adolescence, 12-20 or 24 years of age; (7) adulthood. It is important to note that the chronology or rapidity of appearance of these different stages is not nearly so important as the order of their appearances. Gesell and his associates worked out "behavior profiles" for each six-month period after two and each week period before two. They described the process of growth as a paradoxical mixture of creation and conservation. Each achieved stage is consolidated and conserved into the creation of new growth at the next stage. The achieved results of a given stage are the grounds upon which the individual stands in order to grow into the next.

Gesell and his associates make a great deal of the fact of individuality in children. Individuality of a child appears in the "growth pattern" whereby he temperamentally handles his own stage of development as it appears. They emphasize the importance of not standardizing and stereotyping behavior responses of children but seeking to understand the individuality of a given child.

One of the most important factors in the Gesell studies is their working hypothesis that the stages of growth are not evenly related to each other. There is a *jagged rhythm* of growth. There will be a spurt of growth and activity, a time of breaking out and vigorous expansion, a time of inwardized-outwardized, troubled, and confused behavior, and a time of rounded, balanced, smooth, and consolidated behavior. Ilg and Ames outline this in a rhythm pattern of the typical growth of children: [23]

2 years	5 years	10 years	Smooth, consolidated
2½	5½-6	11	Breaking up
3	6½	12	Rounded, balanced
3½	7	13	Inwardized
4	8	14	Vigorous, expansive
4½	9	15	Inwardized-outwardized, troubled "neurotic"
5	10	16	Smooth, consolidated

Two specific notes need to be made here as to the distinctly religious dimensions of the development of personality as the schemata have been set forth by Gesell and his associates. First, parents tend to interpret the behavior of children as being good or bad in terms of the spurts of growth and the periods of quiescent consolidation. The growth is considered to be times of difficulty, badness, and unmanageableness. Great moral and spiritual trepidations fill the hearts of parents during these times. On the other hand, the times of quiescence and consolidation are likely to be identified with goodness, virtue, and perfection in behavior. But the wisdom of growth is deeper than the wisdom of mothers and fathers who yearn for one good night's sleep, or for a little peace and quiet in the house!

The second observation that needs to be made is that Gesell

and his associates have taken seriously the expected and typical, religious, ethical, and philosophical attitudes of a child at each stage along the developmental cycle at which an individual child may be found. Each of the behavior profiles as recorded in these studies has a descriptive section on what parents, teachers, and pastors may expect in terms of religious ideation coming from the child at a given age level. Such problems as death and deity, time and space, belief and magic, Santa Claus are discussed in detail.

Some specific objections have been raised by the use of Gesell's research to the exclusion of other types of information and insight. One of them is that these facts which he presents are relatively misleading unless they are set within the context of an understanding relationship on the part of the parent. To use a figure of speech, they are like the words of a song without the music. The interpersonal relationship supplies this added dimension. Also, Margaret Mead, in her book, *Male and Female,* without naming Gesell at all, gives a fairly specific criticism of his methodology. She says:

> We . . . find it important to re-emphasize the fact that whatever the adults say, or feel, or repress, the child does have a body . . . the child is not only a *tabula rasa,* but a vigorous, maturing organism with modes of behavior appropriate to its own age and strength. But it is not maturing organism in a glass box, or in a consulting room. The artificialities of the world-lit cubicle in which a child can be photographed from six angles are useful ways of getting an abstract picture of the behavior pattern the child has developed as it grows up among other human beings. The other human beings may be subtracted for the moment, and the child viewed as a developing organism pushing its way towards adulthood, but in the whole of human experience this never happens. . . .[24]

Psychoanalysis and Personality Development

Probably the most influential theory of personality development in contemporary life is the psychoanalytic concepts set forth originally by Sigmund Freud and developed in larger detail by Karl Abraham. The psychoanalytic conception of personality is based on several postulates which must be understood as integral to the point of view. The first postulate is the theory of narcissism, or the attachment of the undifferentiated powers of life known as the libido to the self itself. Cathexis is the second postulate which means that the libido is attached to an object, ordinarily a meaningful person in one's life. The third postulate is regression, which means the resistance of the organism to a forward movement into life through the transfer of the libido to a loved person other than the self.

Or, regression more usually means the need of the organism to return to the totally parasitic, irresponsible, and completely cared-for life of the intra-uterine existence of the individual. This happens particularly when the organism is subjected to undue stress. The fourth postulate is that of fixation. This means the arresting of libidinal development at an immature level of growth, resulting in a fixed pattern of reaction to life at a given point.

The stages of development according to Freud and Abraham are as follows: (1) the dependent, or oral, stage of development which is usually associated with feeding and weaning; (2) the aggressive, or anal, stage of development which is usually associated with toilet training, bowel and bladder control, and the need for cleanliness and order; (3) the genital, or the oedipal, stage of development, which is characterized by activated needs for identification with the parent of the same sex and competition with the parent of the same sex for the warmth and tenderness of the parent of the opposite sex; (4) the latency, which is characterized by intense intellectual activity, closeness to the same sex, development of gangs; (5) puberty, or genital maturity, which is characterized by the development of the reproductive capacities at the biological level and the choice of a person of the opposite sex as a mate at the psychosocial level.

Karl Abraham, in his selected papers on psychoanalysis,[25] correlates these stages of personality development with what he calls character formation. He develops a typology of personality particularly as it appears in neurotic persons, on the basis of each one of these different stages of personality development. A more highly detailed psychoanalytic personality typology based on these stages of development is described in Leon Saul's book, *Emotional Maturity.*[26] But probably the most widely read and clearly written statement of these stages has been worked by O. Spurgeon English and G. H. J. Pearson in their book, *The Emotional Problems of Living.*[27]

As one reads these books, beginning with Freud, he sees a movement from the poetic insight of Freud to a carefully detailed and almost fixed developmental determinism in a book like that of English and Pearson. One of the basic criticisms of this conception of personality development is that personality itself is seen almost purely in terms of the longitudinal, early childhood skills development of the person. The vocational strivings of the individual are reduced to these explanations. Room for cultural and class variations in the various experiences of feeding, toilet training, masculine and feminine role taking, is squeezed out in the narrow confines of this fixed theory. Some of the larger issues in parent-child relationship, such as basic acceptance and rejection, are overlooked in preoccupation with these biological functions.

Harry Stack Sullivan. Harry Stack Sullivan has done much to offset some of the basic fallacies of these too rigid conceptions of the development of personality. At the same time, the basic values of classical psychoanalysis are retained. Sullivan, instead of using a "libido" concept, used the much more commonly understood concept of "experience," by which he meant an "undifferentiated life striving at birth" which begins to differentiate into several different "modes of experience." These modes are threefold in terms of the *speech history* of the individual:

1. The prototaxic mode of experience, which occurs before speech develops and encompasses the nonverbal experience of the individual.

2. The parataxic mode of experience, which refers to experience characterized by symbols used in a private or autistic way, such as an infant's babbling, or a mental patient's delusional conversation.

3. The syntaxic mode of experience is such experience as a person is able to communicate to another through the use of language and other types of symbolic expression.

Sullivan, on the basis of this fundamental emphasis upon communication, goes on to outline the stages in the development of personality:

> *Infancy* extends from a few minutes after birth to the appearance of articulate speech, however uncommunicative or meaningless. *Childhood* extends from the appearance of the ability to utter articulate sounds of or pertaining to speech, to the appearance of the need for playmates—that is, companions, co-operative beings of approximately one's own status in all sorts of respects. This ushers in the *juvenile era*, which extends through most of the grammar-school years to the eruption, due to maturation, of a need for an intimate relation with another person of comparable status. This, in turn, ushers in the era that we call *preadolescence*, an exceedingly important but chronologically rather brief period that ordinarily ends with the eruption of genital sexuality and puberty, but psychologically or psychiatrically ends with the movement of strong interests from a person of one's own sex to a person of the other sex. These phenomena mark the beginning of *adolescence*, which in this culture (it varies, however, from culture to culture) continues until one has patterned some type of performance which satisfies one's lust, one's genital drives. Such patterning ushers in *late adolescence*, which in turn continues as an era of personality until any partially developed aspects of personality fall into their proper relationship to their time partition; and one is able, at *adulthood*, to establish relationships of love for some other person, in which relationship the other person is as significant, or nearly as significant, as one's self. This really highly developed intimacy with

another is not the principal business of life, but is, perhaps, the principal source of satisfactions in life; and one goes on developing in depth of interest or in scope of interest, or in both depth and scope, from that time until unhappy retrogressive changes in the organism lead to old age.[28]

The spiritual dimensions of Harry Stack Sullivan's developmental conceptions are great enough to capture the imagination of the serious theologian who will take the time to master Sullivan's insights. For instance, Sullivan shifts the emphasis from a biological determinism of personality development and makes the experience of communication and a search for a meaningful community central in the distinctive development of the human being. The negative counterpart of community and communication is isolation and loneliness. Sullivan gives a penetrating understanding of the intensity of loneliness in the lives of spiritually isolated people. The alienation of a person from those whose approval he considers most worth while, from the nourishing associations of those who should love him and affirm his worth, makes of him an alien, a stranger, and a pilgrim on the earth. The overcoming of this barrier by a love that knows no barrier characterizes man's redemption.

Furthermore, Sullivan's understanding of the development of personality gives the religious educator and the theologian insight into the approximate meaning of theological truth to the growing person. Sullivan enables us to beam our message of reconciliation and redemption to the growing person at the level of every day's quietest need.

The infant receives the atmosphere of worship through touch and tone, through being held and handled securely, firmly, and gently.

The child learns the religious dimensions of life through his mastery of the words of the religious community, the names of religious places, persons, things, smells, and sounds, colors and lights.

In the juvenile era, religion becomes meaningful in terms of the child's relationship to his playmates. Being a Baptist is not nearly so important to him as being able to play on schedule with his Catholic neighbor friend. He prefers the church where his playmates go. Religion is spelled out to him in terms of the other children of his age throughout the world. This is a wonderful time to teach him the how and why of the lives of children of other races, other religions, and other social differences.

In the preadolescent phase of personality development, religious experience becomes meaningful to the growing person in terms of the close intimate relationship he has with one friend. This is the "chumship" stage. He is more likely to be influenced profoundly by that person of his own sex and comparable status to whom he would rather be near than to anyone else he knows. This "Jonathan and David" knitting of the soul together provides the child with an inner serenity with people his own age that becomes the ground upon which he stands as he moves out to people of the opposite sex. The uncanny experiences of religious awesomeness and wonder of the earlier years of life are overcome at this stage with a growing understanding of the friendship and closeness of God and Christ.

Adolescence is characterized by the revelatory power of the encounter between the different sexes. Religious experience becomes the quest for the freedom of the surging powers of creativity in sex, coupled with the questioning of one's ability to control the unleashed powers of life. The conflictual storm and stress of this period raises many ethical questions producing high idealism and corresponding discouragement in the adolescent period.

Late adolescence is that era of personality development in its religious dimensions in which the vocational, marital, and philosophical portions of the individual's existence are brought into reconciliation with each other and pointed up toward the long-term goals of life. This is the era of consolidation. Here religious experience becomes a systematizing and ordering of life. Family rituals become extremely important at this stage of development.

Finally, *adulthood* represents the religious encounter of bondage and freedom: the bondage of older immaturities that hinder one from establishing relationships of attention, considerateness, and care for other persons; the freedom to let oneself go in abandon and devotion without the hindrances of fear. Here it is that "perfect love casts out fear."

Robert J. Havighurst and Developmental Tasks

Another comprehensive and flexible conception of human development is that of Robert J. Havighurst. He calls the things a person must learn, if he is to be judged and to judge himself to be a reasonably happy and successful person, "developmental tasks." In a sense human development is a vocation, a calling; and the different encounters with the demands of maturity are "tasks." Havighurst defines these as follows:

> A developmental task is a task which arises at or about a certain period in the life of the individual, successful achievement of which leads to his happiness and to success with later tasks, while failure leads to unhappiness in the individual, disapproval by the society, and difficulty with later tasks.[29]

These developmental tasks of the individual are presented to him when he faces the new demands and expectations from society around him upon his having received new physical and psychological powers through the normal process of growth. For instance, when a child's legs grow larger and stronger and he is enabled to walk, the society expects this task of him. Furthermore, these developmental tasks arise also from the cultural pressure of society. For instance, learning to read is a part of the culture, and societal pressures tend to demand this of the individual. But more than this, Havighurst points out that the "personal values and aspirations of the individual, which are part of his personality, or self, . . . increasingly [are] a force in [their] own right in the subsequent development of the individual." [30]

Whenever a developmental task is presented to an individual, he is open to the educational efforts of his community. As Havighurst puts it, "when the body is ripe, and society requires, and the self is ready to achieve a certain task, the teachable moment has come." [31] These "teachable moments" are the "fullness of time" for the learning of a given skill for living, purpose of life, adjustment to reality, and discovery of a richer selfhood.

One of the fuller aspects of Havighurst's point of view is its emphasis upon the total life span of an individual from birth through childhood into maturity and even into old age. It is not biased in the direction of the purely infantile aspects of personality development. Likewise, Havighurst's concern is fundamentally an educational as well as therapeutic concern. He sets himself to deal with the broad range of the guidance as well as the more narrow range of the treatment of people. His point of view, therefore, is a larger context into which to place some of the findings of research persons who have drawn most of their insights from the study of neurotic or even more seriously ill persons.

SOME RELIGIOUS IMPLICATIONS OF CONCEPTIONS
OF PERSONALITY DEVELOPMENT

A synoptic view of the preceding theological and scientific analyses of the development of personality reflects several important religious implications.

The inseparability of redemption from development. In both the classical theological interpretations of the spiritual pilgrimage of man and the scientific conceptions of the personality development of man, the redemption of man from sin and the emergence of a free self in man, respectively, are inseparably tied up with a struggle of the soul in the process of time and becoming. When one draws upon the categories of revelational theology, he thinks in terms of regeneration and sanctification, whereby the Christian is born into a new life and brought to the fullness of the stature of Christ. In secular conceptions of the development of personality, brought out more recently in scientific pursuits, the teleological striving of individuals toward maturity is pictured through the process of growth. Therefore, the use of the method of correlation will reveal that the scientific conception of maturity today is in a sense a secularization of the religious conception of perfection and eschatology.

The developmental character of a dynamic ethic. John Bunyan saw that the spiritual life and growth of the Christian is not a smooth and easy path. It had many jagged turnings in the way to him. Likewise, Gesell, in his highly detailed descriptive psychology of personality development, underlines the fact that growth and development are not smoothly accomplished. They are filled with many spurts and jags. The over-all patterning of behavior is more important than the immediate lag or doldrum of outward growth. Likewise, the very darkest and foreboding developmental task may not only be threatening as a task but also promising as a "teachable moment."

Furthermore, the qualitative evaluation of a given kind of behavior changes from stage to stage of human development. For instance, homosexual thoughts and activities may be qualitatively and ethically different thoughts and activities in the life of a person at the age of 10 or 11 from what the same acts or thoughts would be at the age of 35 or 40. Likewise, the ethical life of an individual is gauged meaningfully in terms of the added difficulty of ethical living which unsolved developmental tasks create in the life of a person who, nevertheless, is facing newer tasks every day. For the psychologist of religious experience who attends to the confessional needs of parishioners before God in prayer, this insight into the meaning of temptation, as such, becomes an indispensable one for effective pastoral care and counseling. The person who has mastered, for instance, Havighurst's conception of developmental tasks and teachable moments has an unusually deepened appreciation of the weight of some of the burdens that people carry.

Theories of development and dramas of redemption. Contemporary psychologists and psychotherapists have evolved varied theories of development as has been seen in the foregoing descriptions. Within the temporal confines of the life of man these research people have given detailed analyses of both vicissitudes and the potentialities of man. The more they chart the developmental process of man's becoming a self, the more they encounter the necessity of evaluating the ultimate goals of man's being. This is why, apparently, psychologists of personality are becoming more and more concerned with the broader aspects of culture and personality. Likewise, it is why religious concern is apparent as a given research man's explorations in personality development themselves mature. Gordon Allport and Erich Fromm are cases in point.

Just at this stage the theologians themselves have made a basic contribution to a psychological understanding of the development of personality. The apostle Paul, St. Augustine, Bernard of Clairvaux, Søren Kierkegaard, and John Bunyan, themselves, encompassed many of the realities of the development of personality in the dramas of spiritual redemption which have been reviewed above. However, they are unique in their contributions at several points: First, they had the courage to interpret spiritual development in terms of their own personal autobiography. (Interestingly enough, Sigmund Freud did this himself in his book on *The Interpretation of Dreams.*) They developed symbolic or mythological patterns for conceptualizing the spiritual pilgrimage of man. At one important point, though, these theologians transcend the conceptions of the developmental psychologists. They seek the ultimate goal and not merely the proximate goal of man's becoming. Another way of stating it, is that they interpret the spiritual pilgrimage of man in terms of his essential nature and his infinite destiny rather than in terms of his obvious nature (which can be observed) and his finite destiny.

This pinpoints the essential contribution that the theologians have made to the understanding of the development of personality. Søren Kierkegaard, in his conception of the stages on life's way, repudiates the idea that personality development is automatic progress and that if left alone and given proper conditions, a personality will inevitably develop. Although this idea is not set forth in any great dogmatic way by the developmental psychologists, nevertheless it is a tacit assumption that can be all too easily drawn from what they say. Kierkegaard, to the contrary, saw the stages on life's way as essentially valuational stages. He saw personality development as occurring through radical transformation when a person, through faith, encounters God and thereby is enabled to take "the leap" from one stage to another through an activated decision to grow.

When we have taken into account and given full credence to all the nourishing factors in personality development, we still come face to face with the quiet reality that we are not quite able to avoid; namely, man decides upon faith whether or not it is *better* for him to grow or to *remain as he is!* This is a decisive evaluation in the presence of any developmental task. Such a decision arises from his inmost depths and is made basically upon the transcendent ultimacy or the handy expediency in the measure of reality the person grasps. When, therefore, we say that a person is in touch with reality, the theologian immediately goes to work to evaluate the kind of reality with which he may be in touch. Is it a proximate or an ultimate concern that fosters his growth?

Personality development and Christian eschatology. Focusing the proximate concerns of man with his ultimate is a major problem in personality development of both the individual and the group. The proximate concerns of man are always in tension with his ultimate concerns, whether he knows it or not. This tension in personality is essentially an eschatological tension. Biblical theology, as such, grapples with *the meaning* of this tension between the temporal and the ultimate for the perfection of the saints, the edification of the Body of Christ, and the consummation of the Christian community at the set end of the age.

John Marsh discusses the whole problem in the light of the meanings of *chronos* (measured time, duration) and *kairos* (time of opportunity and fulfillment). He very aptly says that "biblical conception of time is not that of evaluation or progress, or even of chronological succession." In biblical realism *kairos* is at bottom a time of promise (prophetic and historical) and fulfillment, and essentially "history consists of times bringing opportunities, the basic time and the decisive opportunity being that of the coming of Jesus Christ. . . ." [32]

Personality development in such an understanding of time and growth would not be the result of the mere passage of time, or of inevitable progress. Rather, growth hinges upon decisions made at given redemptive moments in life. Personality is conditioned but not determined by circumstances and chronological age. The self is the accrued results of its faith responses to the decisive grace of God revealed in opportune moments of life. Eternal life breaks through in the *kairos,* involving man in anxious confrontation of the necessities of his finitude and the free possibilities of God's grace. These are decisive moments, proximately in man's hands by reason of the response of faith, but ultimately in God's hands. Oscar Cullmann defines *kairos* thus:

> *Kairos* in secular usage is the moment in time which is especially favorable for an undertaking; . . . it is the fixed day, which, in modern jargon, for example is called D day. . . . The New Testament usage with reference to redemptive history is the same. Here, however, it is not human deliberations but a divine decision that makes this or that date a *kairos,* a point of time that has a special place in the execution of God's plan for salvation. Because the realization of the divine plan of salvation is bound to such points of *kairoi* chosen by God, therefore it is a redemptive *history.* [33]

This conception of time reasserts the difference between mere chronological maturity and spiritual maturity. Kierkegaard was being faithful to the biblical realism of time when he interpreted movement from one stage of life to another as a decisive change of "ways of life," not as the automatic growth of a plant if given enough time and the right conditions. Decision, which he called a leap of faith, was necessary for growth.

Apart from this understanding, personality development becomes simply a process of adjustment to the least common denominator of the meaningless process of history into which we are born. The creative break-through in a decisive moment of time of portents of another age is not possible. All that *is* is a direct result of what has been.

Contemporary conceptions of personality development have in too many instances (although most certainly not in all instances) been posited upon the scientific optimism characteristic of the age of enlightenment. Man's tension between the proximate and ultimate concerns of life has been settled in terms of a proximate understanding of reality. Thus reality has been defined in "common sense" terms as to what is appropriate to time, place, and utilitarian function in society as it is. Adjustment becomes the goal of personality. When we ask, What is reality? we get this "common sense" definition. Consequently, the struggle of the soul to respond to the decisive break-through of the ultimate concerns of an individual about his existence are relegated to a realm known as fantasy or illusion. The research of Boisen reflects the chaotic, undisciplined, and pride-ridden concern of psychotic patients as to the ultimate end of their existence as well as that of the world as a whole.

My whole point here is that Christian eschatology (which may be defined as the study of the relation of the ultimate destiny of the universe to the ordering of the proximate situation of man in society) is reciprocally related to our understanding of personality development. Our eschatology shapes the goals of our personal strivings, whether we know it or not. These goals, in turn, specifically determine our interpretation of the developmental pilgrimage of the individual personality. These two ideas are so rarely seen as being in relation to each other that I hesitate to mention them together lest I fail utterly to communicate what I mean. However, I draw much comfort from the writing of Ray Petry who has said that the eschatological, cataclysmic conception of life is held to have no rapport with the more developmental conception. The "cataclysm of the Gospels and the more developmental conception of modern times are held to be in necessary conflict. Yet, there may be evolution and growth within cataclysm; and cataclysm may take place within process." [34] Often lost in the semantic confusion of today is the direct connection which Jesus always made in his parables between the growth and cataclysm in God's redemption of man and society between the "fulness of time" of the coming of the Kingdom, on the one hand, and the expectant growth necessary for that *kairos,* on the other hand.

Stages of personality development and the communication of religious reality. One of the greatest truths that have come to us through the developmental study of personality is that religion is communicated differently at different stages of the development of a person. Religious concern manifests itself with different meanings at different levels of spiritual growth. This is the insight which Bushnell intuitively discerned long "before his time." The grasping of the ultimate reality of God is seen by persons like Lewis Sherrill to be mediated through the proximate relationships of parent to child, and the whole religious quest consists of opening the doors of childhood to the incursions of the Eternal. When a specific human relationship closes in upon a growing child, the shutter of his soul is closed to the light of God. At length the picture of God that he gets is a distorted one, but on the other hand, an open relationship of parent to child can more and more turn the child away from the parent himself to a direct relationship to God. However, one of the contributions that the theologians have made to our understanding of the development of personality is that God himself is capable of breaking through some of the distortions of interpersonal relationships and establishing direct encounter with the person himself. This is often done through other redemptive personalities or communities around the individual. The mystic and the contemplative religious person clings rather tenaciously to the quiet conviction that God may reveal himself directly to the individual apart from other types of interpersonal relationships. To say that God *usually* manifests himself to a growing person through his significant field of interpersonal relationships is a very different thing from saying that God *cannot* manifest himself in any other way!

Great theological battles have been fought back and forth over the terrain on which developmental psychologists are working today. The same basic issues, for instance of Pelagianism and Augustinianism, have tended to emerge again in the controversial discussions of contemporary psychologists of personality. However, they emerge in a distinctly secular semantic framework and seem to be new problems to those who have either remained uninformed about historical theology or have rejected these categories as representatives of a kind of authority which they could not tolerate. Nevertheless, the same basic issues remain, and in a sense religious concern goes on, although it has been pushed underground.

NOTES FOR CHAPTER VII

1. Fragment 91-b, trans. by John Burnette, *Early Greek Philosophy* (London: A. & C. Black, Ltd., 1930), pp. 133 ff.
2. Fragment 44, *ibid.*
3. Hosea 11:1, 3-4.
4. Isaiah 66:9-13.
5. *The Confessions of St. Augustine,* trans. E. B. Pusey (Mt. Vernon, N. Y.: The Peter Pauper Press, first published in 1838), p. 28.
6. *The Book of St. Bernard on the Love of God,* ed. and trans. Edmund G. Gardner (New York: E. P. Dutton & Co., Inc., 1915), p. 87.

7. *Ibid.*, p. 97.
8. John Bunyan, *Grace Abounding*, Tercentenary edition, pp. 103-104, 128.
9. New York: Longmans, Green & Co., Inc., 1956.
10. David Swenson, *Something About Kierkegaard*, rev. ed. (Minneapolis, Minn.: Augsburg Publishing House, 1945), pp. 162-163.
11. Søren Kierkegaard, *Stages on Life's Way*, trans. Walter Lowrie (Princeton, N. J.: Princeton University Press, 1945), p. 413.
12. Søren Kierkegaard, *Either-Or*, Vol. I, trans. David and Lillian Swenson (Princeton, N. J.: Princeton University Press, 1949), p. 83.
13. *Ibid.*, Vol. 2, p. 223.
14. Regis Jolivet, *Introduction to Kierkegaard*, trans. W. H. Barber (London: Frederick Muller, Ltd., 1950), p. 140.
15. Horace Bushnell, *The Kingdom of Heaven as a Grain of Mustard Seed*, "The New Englander," II (October, 1844), pp. 600-619. Quoted by H. Shelton Smith, *Changing Conceptions of Original Sin: A Study in American Theology Since 1750* (New York: Charles Scribner's Sons, 1955), p. 142.
16. New York: The Macmillan Company, 1951.
17. New York: Harper & Brothers, 1944.
18. New York: Harper & Brothers, 1940.
19. New York: Harper & Brothers, 1946.
20. New York: Harper & Brothers, 1956.
21. *The Infant and Child in the Culture of Today, op. cit.*, p. 26.
22. New York: Harper & Brothers, 1955.
23. *Child Behavior, op. cit.*, p. 14.
24. Margaret Mead, *Male and Female: A Study of the Sexes in a Changing World* (New York: William Morrow & Company, Inc., © 1949), p. 145. Used by permission.
25. Karl Abraham, *Selected Papers*, trans. Douglas Bryan and Alix Strachey (London: Hogarth Press, 1948), pp. 370 ff.
26. Leon Saul, *Emotional Maturity* (Philadelphia: J. B. Lippincott Company, 1947).
27. O. Spurgeon English and G. H. J. Pearson, *Emotional Problems of Living: Avoiding the Neurotic Pattern*, rev. and enlarged edition (New York: W. W. Norton & Company, Inc., 1955).
28. Harry Stack Sullivan, *The Interpersonal Theory of Psychiatry*, eds. Helen Swick Perry and Mary Ladd Gawel (New York: W. W. Norton & Company, Inc., 1953), pp. 33-34. Used by permission.
29. Robert J. Havighurst, *Human Development and Education* (New York: Longmans, Green & Co., Inc., 1953), p. 2.
30. *Ibid.*, p. 4.
31. *Ibid.*, p. 5.
32. John Marsh, "Time," *A Theological Word Book of the Bible*, ed. Alan Richardson (New York: The Macmillan Company, 1952), p. 263.
33. From *Christ and Time* by Oscar Cullmann, Copyright, 1950, by W. L. Jenkins, The Westminster Press. Used by permission.
34. Ray Petry, *Christian Eschatology and Social Thought* (New York: Abingdon Press, 1956), p. 44.

CHAPTER VIII

RELIGION AND THE STRUCTURE
OF PERSONALITY

PERSONALITY TAKES STRUCTURAL FORM through the process of development. The structure or form which personality takes in and of itself has certain distinctly religious dimensions. The patterning of personality has always been of primary concern to the theologian, and has been of more recent empirical interest to the psychologist of personality.*

THE STRUCTURE OF PERSONALITY AND
A CHRISTIAN DOCTRINE OF MAN

Whereas the psychologists of personality usually discuss architectural descriptions of human personality under such categories as "the structure of personality," theological discussions usually think of the same basic reality from a different perspectival frame of reference under the category of the Christian doctrine of man or Christian anthropology.

The Christian doctrine of man, in turn, is deeply rooted in the Old Testament conception of the human person.

* Notes and credits for this chapter begin on page 195.

John A. T. Robinson

In both the Old and New Testament conceptions of man we find a theocentric understanding of the totality of man. Of this understanding John A. T. Robinson has written:

> The Hebrews did not think about the body for its own sake. They were not interested in the body as such. All questions of the interrelation of its different parts and functions were entirely subordinated to the question of the relation of the whole man, as part of the solidarity of creation, to God. All Hebrew thinking was done, as it were, in this vertical dimension of man's relatedness to God as a creature and as a fallen creature.[1]

In fact, A. R. Johnson says that this awareness of totality "is the 'open sesame' which unlocks the secrets of the Hebrew language and reveals the riches of the Israelite mind."[2] The oneness and individuality of personality, the corporate character of personality, and the distinctly theocentric relationship of man as a total creation to God as a supreme and personal creator are distinguishing characteristics of the holistic understanding of personality in both the Old and the New Testament.

As has been said before, John A. T. Robinson sees in the New Testament word *soma* "the nearest equivalent to our word personality."[3] *Soma* does not mean something external to man himself. Man does not have a body; he is a body. Likewise, the body is "that which joins all people, irrespective of individual differences, in life's bundle together."[4] Robinson goes on to point out how the doctrine of the resurrection of the body and the importance of the Christian community as "the body of Christ" are doctrinal expressions of the inherent indivisibility of personality and its cohesive totality and of the essentially interpersonal or communal character of personality. The body—personality, that is—is characterized by infirmity or weakness, mortality or finitude, and death. Death is man's destiny; it exercises its dominion over man in sin, and the law is the instrument of sin. In the body of Christ death, sin, and the law are overcome; and, in the promise of resurrection and through the power of faith working through love, this victory can be gained by the individual believer. The whole drama of redemption in Christ, according to Robinson's interpretation of Paul, is quite accurately seen to be the transformation and preservation of the totality of man's purposive being in Christ.

When one in Western Christendom says that he believes in the resurrection of the body, he always has to ask himself if he has really faced up to the questions which Plato solved to his own satisfaction and to that of many Christian theologians, when he set forth his idea of immortality that man sloughs off the body as being nonintegral to his being. He is also asked by modern Christians: "Do you mean this *literally?*" What I mean when I say this, is that the integrity, the identity, and the durable significance of our persons is *somehow* sustained by God. I believe this as an act of faith, and I believe that death does not separate us from the love of God which he has made known to us in Christ. But the nature of the body is of God's own choosing, just as he has fearfully and wonderfully made us as we are in this aspect of our existence.

This is a succinct statement of the Hebrew-Christian view of the structure of personality. It is fairly generally conceded today that the contemporary Christian view of man has been heavily influenced by Hellenistic sources of the understanding of man. The inveterate stamp of Greek modes of thinking upon contemporary interpretations of the structure and function of personality cannot be genuinely understood apart from a brief look at Platonic, Aristotelian, and Neoplatonic conceptions of personality.

Plato

We find a very different frame of reference from the Hebrew-Christian perspective when we read Plato as he said that "we should conceive of the double nature which we call the living being." Although he saw the necessity of the relationship of the body and the soul being "healthy and well balanced," he also said that "there is no symmetry or want of symmetry greater than that of the soul to the body." He said, too, "There are three kinds of soul located within us, each of them having their own proper motion." These three kinds of soul are roughly correlative with plant, animal, and human life.[5] Plato's doctrine of the immortality of the soul even more radically dissociated the soul from the body. He speaks of the "body which is moved from without"[6] as being soul. He symbolized the relation of the body and the soul with the allegory of the pair of winged horses and the charioteer.

> Now the winged horses and the charioteer of the gods are all of them noble, and of noble breed, while ours are mixed; and we have a charioteer who drives them in a pair, and one of them is noble and of noble origin and the other is ignoble and of ignoble origin. . . . The soul or animate being has the care of the inanimate, and traverses the whole heaven in diverse forms appearing;—when perfect and fully winged she soars upward, and is ruler of the universe; while the imperfect soul loses her feathers and drooping in her flight at last settled on the solid ground—there finding a home, she receives an earthly frame which appears to be self moved, but is really moved by her power; and this composition of soul and body is called the living and mortal creature.[7]

Plato's conception of immortality presents the soul as pre-existing and postexisting the body and as being highly separable from the body. He laid the groundwork for later Neoplatonic thought of Plotinus, which considered the body to be basically evil, of darkness, and as essentially antagonistic to the soul. In fact, Plotinus would not even admit that he had a body!

Contemporary Christians are little aware of how much of our thinking concerning personality is distinctly Platonic in nature. The neat separation of body and soul, the speculative concern for the pre-existence of the soul and for its immortality without consideration of the radically redemptive character of the resurrection of the Christ have been blended into the Christian tradition, often without appreciation or criticism of the Platonic origin of these interpretations of personality.

Aristotle

In the conceptions of Aristotle, we find a much more unified understanding of man. He emphasized the inseparability of body and soul:

> Some hold that the soul is divisible, and that one part thinks, another desires. If, then, its nature admits of its being divided, what can it be that holds the parts together? Surely not the body; on the contrary it seems rather to be the soul that holds the body together; at any rate, when the soul departs, the body disintegrates and decays. If, then, there is something else which makes the soul one, this unifying agency would have the best right to the name of the soul, and we shall have to repeat for it the question: Is *it* one or multipartite? If it is one, why not at once admit that "the soul" is one? [8]

Aristotle described the functional aspects of the soul in a threefold nature: the nutritive soul is the minimal soul, which exists in plants and animals alike. In this sense all living entities are "besouled" beings. The sensitive soul exists in all animals. Functions of the sensitive soul are those such as sensory experience, perception, feelings of pleasure and pain, desiring. The outgrowths of the sensitive soul are imagination, and memory, and appetite. The third type of soul is the rational soul, which Aristotle says is "just what it is and nothing else" and is the highest nature of man.

Although Aristotle insisted that the soul was what held the body and all the constituent parts of personality as such together; nevertheless, he did insist that the reason exists before the body into which it enters from without as something divine and immortal.[9]

Although both Plato and Aristotle may genuinely be considered as theists and believers in the immortality of the soul, Sterling P. Lamprecht is right when he says that Plato in particular is the historical source of the humanistic tradition in Western culture. This tradition has a twofold thesis that "the highest good of man lies in the fulfillment of his natural potentialities and, second, that the only sound method of achieving those potentialities is the use of man's natural powers of reason to improve himself. This is a very different frame of reference from the perspective of the Hebrew conception of personality in which man is considered to be a creature of God, a unified whole from birth throughout eternity, and as a fallen creature who needs radical redemption which he cannot effect for himself. However, these two traditions merged into one known as the Western Christian tradition.[10]

Augustine

Augustine (A.D. 354–430) effectively synthesized several earlier philosophical traditions. He is one of the prime movers of the Western Christian tradition to which we have just referred. Although in his earlier writings he was severely influenced by Neoplatonism and Manichaeism, nevertheless, the Hebrew-Christian theism of the Old and New Testaments, especially from Paul, gained precedence in his thinking. He based his understanding of personality upon a trinitarian view of God as a person who reveals himself in direct encounter with man. This God reveals man to himself as a sinner, and radically redeems him from his sin through faith in Christ. This Augustine believed, having wrought it out through the struggle of his own soul. The heavenly things of God, the Father and Son and Holy Spirit, are, then, the moving presuppositions of all that Augustine says about the constitution of human personality.

In his treatise, *De Trinitate*, Augustine, having talked to great extent about the character of the Trinity, turns then to the image of that trinity in man. He refers to it as

. . . that inadequate image, which yet is an image, that is, man; for our feeble mind perhaps can gaze upon this more familiarly and more easily.[11]

As Augustine plumbs the depths of the image of God in man, he becomes aware of his own selfhood as a triad of being, intelligence, and purpose. This triune character of selfhood is known mediately by man and is communicated to him by God. Man has a basic existence, an intuitive knowledge of that existence, and the capacity to rejoice in this existence and knowledge. Augustine says:

> We both exist, and know that we exist, and rejoice in this existence, and this knowledge. In these three, when the mind knows and loves itself, there may be seen a trinity, mind, love, knowledge; not to be confounded by any intermixture, although each exists in itself and all mutually in all, or each in the other two, or the other two in each.[12]

Whereas the structure of personality is definitely triune in character, Augustine further insists that "in these three," we can "discern . . . how inseparable a life there is, one life, one mind, and one essence; how inseparable a distinction and yet a distinction." [13] The personhood of man, therefore, is an interinvolvement of rich intracommunication or dialogue. Man, though he feels lonely, is always in encounter with himself. The more he presses this dialogue of the self, the deeper he goes into the self itself. Sooner or later, he encounters the totally Other within the self. This is a radical departure from the sharp cleavage between the subjective and the objective world which one finds in classical idealism. There is an inner reality which is as surely objective as any outer reality. Augustine puts it this way: "You will now be able to apprehend God more clearly than a brother; more clearly because more directly, more immediately, and more certainly." [14]

However, this apprehension of God, which is clearer than that a brother could do for one, does not come to pass through any process of scanning the skies or studying the intricate nature of the external world. Augustine says:

> Don't go outside yourself, return into yourself. The dwelling place of truth is in the inner man. And if you discover your own nature as subject to change, then go beyond that nature. But, remember that, when you thus go beyond it, it is the reasoning soul which you go beyond. Press on, therefore, toward the source from which the light of reason itself is kindled.[15]

Augustine, furthermore, underscores both the finite and the fallen nature of man as a creature. He refuses to attribute this finitude and fallen character either to the spirit or to the body, setting them over against each other in a Neoplatonic sense. Thereby, he undermines the conception of the immortality of the soul, bequeathed to us by Plato, which makes the soul co-eternal with God. Also, he undercuts the fallacy of the omnipotence of reason, whereby man is able to improve himself *ad infinitum* by the exercise of his natural reason. Augustine himself says that we indeed "recognize in ourselves the image of God," but that it is not "equal to God." [16]

Although elements of the Augustinian conception of personality which were more indigenous to the classical tradition of Platonism have been vitally active in the Western Christian tradition ever since Augustine lived, Cochrane is right when he says that Augustine radically broke with classicism and provided for us "a fresh foundation for what we have called the values of personality." [17] He bequeathed to us an existential view of man as a person in dynamic encounter with himself and with the person of God. Just as, in our understanding of the development of personality, we saw that Augustine interpreted religious experience in terms of his own developmental pilgrimage in *The Confessions,* so here in the discussion of the structure of personality we see that he interpreted this problem in the light of the being of God. In a very real sense he gave us a theology of personality. In doing so he has made the realistic-interpersonal and unified-diverse understanding of the structure of personality native to the New Testament available to the Western Christian tradition.

Otherwise, the massive influence of humanistic rationalism in interpreting personality would have had full sway. As it stands, the classical tradition has exerted profound influence on contemporary theories of personality structure. The easy division of personality, for instance, into compartmentalized "functions" of reason, volition, and passion has come down to us in the faculty psychology approach to personality. It is derived principally from the classical tradition. Its genealogy is so easily attributed to Plato, Aristotle, Thomas Aquinas, Descartes, and/or Kant that we do not know just whom to hold responsible for this tripartition of personality. It would be closer to the truth to say that wherever we find a glorification of human reason, we shall find a faculty psychology. Wherever we find this kind of psychology, we find a conglomeration of absurdities when it comes to the interpretation of the nature and destiny of man. The understanding of the poignant desperation and suffering of man is bypassed for speculative systems. And the development of ways and means for relieving man's distress and bringing to him a message of redemption of his whole being is left to secularists. Likewise, we can be sure that we are out of touch with both the main stream of the Hebrew-Christian understanding of personality and the holistic emphases of contemporary conceptions of personality. (For example, note the absurdities which arise in the psychology of preaching when we try to classify sermons as "intellectual," "moralistic," and "emotional" sermons. Likewise, note the disintegration in the self-concept of the college student who says that he does not know whether his problem is "psychological," "spiritual," or "just sex.")

The repudiation of such a faculty psychology which conceives of personality as being neatly tripartitioned calls for a clearer and more dynamic alternative to its confusion. Contemporary theorists in personality have developed what they call "working" or "theoretical" models of personality. A careful review of these conceptions of the structure of personality will, I think, give us a vaster perspective and appreciation of the Hebrew-Christian view of man and at the same time help us to fill in some of these badly needed details for our understanding from the empirical researches of the psychologists of personality.

CONTEMPORARY THEORETICAL MODELS OF PERSONALITY

Sigmund Freud

The pervasive influence of the psychoanalytic structuralization of the human personality calls for first attention. Sigmund Freud describes this conception in his book, *The Ego and the Id*.[18] In his studies of hysteria, he discovered a vital, dynamic, "opposing force" by which ideas in question can be removed from consciousness. This opposing force is repression. And, Freud says, "We obtain our concept of the unconscious . . . from the theory of repression." This is the first and most important part of personality, Freud says. He says that "there are two kinds of unconsciousness—that which is latent but capable of becoming conscious." This he calls the preconscious. "The other kind of unconscious is that which is repressed and not capable of becoming conscious in the ordinary way." Add to this the clear level of awareness, which Freud called the conscious, and you have the first threefold description of the "anatomy of personality" set forth by Freud. The residual contribution of this point of view is that Freud thereby articulated a dynamic conception of personality, a depth view of man, and set this over against surface rationalisms of his day.

Freud let his whole case for his conception of personality stand or fall upon the dynamic character of the unconscious. He arrived at this through several channels of observation: He observed the posthypnotic behavior of persons who had been hypnotized. He saw the evidences of an unconscious life in the dream life of his patients. He could observe patterns of meaning and the common slips or errors of speech, memory, and action of everyday life. He deduced it from the small amount of one's environment that can be held in consciousness at any one time in comparison with the total contents of the mind. But probably his most vivid source of observation was the mental and physical symptoms that are found to be meaningful when one becomes deeply acquainted with a disturbed mental patient.

Later, Freud revised his conception of the division of the constitution of mental life into a more precise tripartition. The second division of theory was not intended to supplant the other, but to give an even more dynamic insight into the nature of personality. In this second revision of the mental life, Freud saw three aspects:

1. *The ego.* The ego is a coherent organization of mental processes, which includes consciousness and controls action. It is the institution in the mind which regulates all its own constituent processes and accommodates the total organism to reality. It is that which goes to sleep at night, though it continues to exercise some censorship upon dreams. Through its encounter with the ego, a part of the ego may become repressed. Nevertheless, the ego is that part of the basic desires of man which has been modified by the direct influence of the external world acting upon it through what Freud called the *reality principle.*

2. *The id.* The id is the unknown, unconscious aspect of mental life. The ego is not sharply separated from the id but it operates on a quite different principle from the reality principle of the ego. The id is controlled by the pleasure principle which reigns supreme in all that is contained in the id. The id contains the passive passions. Freud says that "we shall not look upon the mind of an individual as an unknown and unconscious id, upon whose surface rests the ego . . . more or less as the germinal air rests upon the ovum." [19]

3. *The super ego.* There is a differentiating grade within the ego which may be called the ego ideal or the super ego. The super ego is a record of past object identifications, that is, persons with whom the individual has identified, like whom he has become, and whose approval he values and fears. The origin of the super ego is in the Oedipal stage of personality development hitherto referred to and it is formed through identification with the parent of the same sex.

Freud says: "The broad general outcome of the sexual phase governed by the Oedipus complex may, therefore, be taken to be the forming of a precipitate in the ego, consisting of these two identifications in some way combined together. This modification of the ego retains its special position; it stands in contrast to the other constituents of the ego in the form of an ego ideal or super ego." [20]

Freud goes on to point out that the super ego is not merely a "deposit left by the earliest object choices of the id." The super ego is also a negative reaction formation opposite these choices. The super ego is the combined set of prohibitions which control the personality, a more primeval guiding image which directs its path. The "thou shalt nots" and the "thou shalts" are epitomized in the super ego. Freud derived this tripartition of personality from his work with badly disturbed mental patients and the fragmentation of their selves was acutely apparent in what they said to Freud as their physician. However, Freud does not restrict this understanding of personality to sick people. He universalizes it into a comprehensive explanation of the structure of personality.

However, one hastens to say that Freud himself did not conceive of his system as a "complete" psychology, although he was wedded to the psychological method, as such. He felt that he had the grimy task of cutting the stone from the quarry and getting it out the best that he could. The completion of a system, the development of a consistent edifice of personality theory he perceived as being the task of those who followed him.

C. G. Jung

C. G. Jung introduced some significant variations in his conception of the structure of personality from that of Sigmund Freud. One of the basic variations was the shift of emphasis from a more or less realistic interpretation of the sexual needs of the person to a more psychological-symbolic interpretation of the same processes. But the most important contribution of C. G. Jung is in his extension of the personal psyche beyond the mere individual unconscious to what he called the collective or racial unconscious. In this collective psyche, primordial "universally human images" reside.

> The collective psyche represents a certain part of the mental function which is fixed and automatic in its action. It is inherited and, being present everywhere in man, is universal and therefore 'super personal' or 'impersonal.' [21]

The individual not only has a personal history, but by reason of his membership in the human family, Jung felt that the individual also has inherited potentialities of the human imagination in the historical background of the psyche. Therefore, the psyche has three "levels": (1) consciousness; (2) the personal unconscious, which is part of the collective; and (3) the collective unconscious.

Jung felt also that the collective unconscious participates in human existence according to certain primordial themes known as archetypes which are precipitants of the experience of the race with all its latent potentialities. Whereas he accused Freud of attributing evil impulses to the unconscious, he, himself, chose to emphasize the positive, creative, and redemptive aspects of the unconscious life of the individual. As Jung's interpreter, Jacobi puts it:

To open the store to one's psyche, to wake it to new life, and to integrate it with consciousness, means therefore nothing less than to take the individual out of his isolation and to incorporate him in the eternal cosmic process.[22]

The task and duty, yes, even the vocation, of the individual is, therefore, the apprehension of the deepest sources of power latent within the unconscious.

With this picture of personality in mind, it is important to get Jung's concept of complexes, which is really his explanation of how personality is shattered and divided. He calls these complexes "psychological parts split off from the personality, groups of psychic contents isolated from consciousness, functioning arbitrarily and autonomously, leading a life of their own in the dark sphere of the unconscious in which they can at every moment hinder or further conscious acts."[23]

Harry Stack Sullivan

The theoretical formulations of Harry Stack Sullivan are becoming a ground for synthesis of the lasting results of other contemporary theorists in personality. In his understanding of the structure of personality, Sullivan does not present a neat tripartition of the human psyche. One has difficulty getting a diagram from him. Rather, he begins with the basic premise of the dynamism of the self-system. He interprets the structure of personality in terms of this self-system. The dynamism of the self-system is accrued through experience of the alertness to approval, tenderness, and disapproval which one encounters in his significant field of interpersonal relationships. The self is built out of approbation and disapproval, out of reward and punishment. Disapproval creates anxiety.

"The self-system thus is an organization . . . called into being by the necessity to avoid or to minimize incidents of anxiety." By anxiety Sullivan means a basically negative experience of disjunctive tension. In this encounter with one's meaningful sphere of interpersonal relationships, Sullivan observed "through aspects of interpersonal co-operation." Each of these aspects of interpersonal co-operation are incorporated into the individual's self-system. They are as follows:

1. The experience of interpersonal co-operation "in which satisfactions have been enhanced by rewarding increments of tenderness," in other words acceptance. As these experiences become organized into the self-system, they become the "good-me" which is, the ordinary topic of discussion about "I."

2. A second kind of interpersonal experience becomes organized in which "increasing degrees of anxiety are associated with behavior" which is "forbidding," that is, rejected. When this organization of experience becomes personified within the self-system of the individual, it becomes the "bad-me." It becomes the rejected sphere of interpersonal relationships.

3. Both the "good-me" and the "bad-me" are "a part of the communicated thinking of the child," the accessible insight of the adult. But many aspects of a growing child or adult's experience are basically incommunicable both to himself and to those in whose interpersonal experiences he is involved. This kind of interpersonal encounter is most conspicuous in dreams while we are asleep, in severe mental disorders, and is "made up of poorly grasped aspects of living which will presently be regarded as 'dreadful' and which still later will be differentiated into incidents which are tended by awe, horror, loathing, or dread." [24] Whereas the "good-me" is associated with feelings of acceptance, the "bad-me" with feelings of rejection, the experiences we have just been describing are called the "not-me" and are associated with feelings of uncanniness.

In discussing this theoretical model of personality, Sullivan insists that it is "enormously important" to understand that he is talking about a *dynamism*. He does not want this to be understood as an "explanatory conception." He says that it is "not a thing, a region, or what-not such as super egos, egos, ids, and so on." Rather, "these personifications are not adequate descriptions of that which is personified." Sullivan vehemently rejects any attempt to correlate the various theoretical systems of personality. He says that he has "not found anything but headaches in trying to discover parallels." [25]

Much of the organization and disorganization of personality goes on outside of the realm of awareness of the self. Some of these processes are easily acceptable to awareness when called to the attention of a person. But they must be called to the attention of the person in some particular way. These processes are said to be "selectively inattended." On the other hand, there are processes whose existence, even if the person has them called to his attention, he will deny and even become angry. The self refuses to grant awareness. These are not necessarily "abnormal," but they are "dissociated," in the conceptions of Harry Stack Sullivan.[26]

Prescott Lecky

Prescott Lecky, in a small but provocative volume, *Self-Consistency: A Theory of Personality*,[27] strikes out in a fresh direction. He rejects the rigid determinism of nineteenth-century science and especially scientific psychology, because they were "committed to a causal program in which behavior was determined solely by two sets of factors, environmental and hereditary." He rejects this either-or dichotomy and pronounces something of a curse on both houses. He says that "psychoanalytic theory . . . is really a theory of psychohydraulics as a stimulus-response psychology is a theory of psychotelephonics." He says that in the one case, repressed motives or instincts are thought of as liquids under pressure exerting an outward stress. And he says that in the other instance, stimuli are "thought of as separate and haphazard incoming messages entering an automatic telephone system." [28] He, himself, is more completely interested in the "total organization" of personality as it is implied "in the use of such terms as character, style of life, or personality." Then in a particularly penetrating remark, he says:

> It is our view that behavior is usually "in character" not because the separate acts are related to one another, but because all the acts of an individual have the goal of maintaining the same structure of values. Our position is that predictability is a function of stability and therefore of the basic need for consistent self organization.[29]

Lecky conceives of personality as being unified by a single purpose, namely, ". . . the organism's attempt to maintain its own organization." Therefore, he sees the personality structure of an individual in terms of the valued goals toward which the organism is moving. Conflict occurs when these goals are challenged. Learning becomes "essentially a means of resolving conflicts" and "a conflict must always be present before the learning can occur." In applying this theory, he criticizes behavioristic and deterministic types of psychology by saying that "behaviorism must give up the habits, therein frankly recognize the organism as a problem solver before it can consistently explain its own experiments." [30] And in another connection, Lecky says that man's behavior must be "interpreted in terms of action rather than reaction, that is, in terms of purpose." [31] Therefore, he conceives of a single principle of "the unity or self consistency" of personality as the purpose of its existence and he conceives of "the personality as an organization of values which are felt to be consistent with one another." [32]

The upshot of all of Lecky's thinking seems to be summarized in an essentially valuative conception of the organization of personality into "a single system, the preservation of whose integrity is essential." He says that the total personality is organized around the nucleus of

> the individual's evaluation of himself. . . . Any value entering the system which is inconsistent with the individual's evaluation of himself cannot be assimilated; it meets with resistance and is likely, unless a general reorganization occurs, to be rejected.[33]

Thus the need for unity is the prime mover of human behavior, and the dynamic encounter with challenges to first one unification and then the other of the personality is a conflict which creates a crisis in the life of the person. "There is thus a constant assimilation of new ideas and the expulsion of old ideas throughout life." And the individual's conception of himself is the central axiom of his whole life's style, theory, pattern, or organization. Here is modern psychology. Here is a reaffirmation of the Hebrew awareness of totality and the striving toward the maintenance of the oneness of life in purpose of existence.[34]

Gardner Murphy

Gardner Murphy approaches the whole problem of the structure or organization of personality in terms of the movement of the human personality through three developmental stages of organization. The first stage is that of a homogeneous, undifferentiated, global mass; the second is that of a differentiation, a cleavage between qualitatively distinct parts or ingredients of the personality; and the third stage is the establishment of functional relations between the differentiated parts of the total personality so as to constitute an organized system.[35] He notes how the analytical approaches to personality, characteristic of certain attempts to understand the structure of personality, sometimes lose the "clue to the structural whole." Accordingly, it is necessary for all psychologists of the personality "to look more closely at wholes as wholes—*to study structure*." [36] Murphy insists that the terms "organization" and "structure" are properly used to point "to the interrelatedness of organic responses and to the dangers inherent in what the biologists call 'isolation experiments.'" Moving from Gestaltist presuppositions, Murphy interprets the organization of personality structure as a *"tension system."* The interdependence of the various parts of personality draw their meaning, balance, direction, and functional connections from the total over-all organization and patterning of the personality.

Carl R. Rogers

Carl R. Rogers synthesized much of the research just reviewed in his theory of personality and behavior upon which he bases his client-centered therapy. He sets forth a patterned continuity of propositions concerning personality. These are so coherently organized that a thorough reporting is necessary:

> Every individual exists in a continually changing world of experience of which he is the center. . . . The organism reacts to the field as it is experienced and perceived. This perceptual field, is for the individual, reality . . . the organism reacts as an organized whole to this phenomenal field. . . . The organism has one basic in striving—to actualize, maintain, and enhance the experiencing organism. . . .
>
> Behavior is basically the goal-directed attempt of the organism to satisfy its needs as experienced in the field as perceived. Emotion accompanies, and in general facilitates, such goal-directed behavior, the kind of emotion being related to seeking versus the consummatory aspects of the behavior, and the intensity of the motion being related to the perceived significance of the behavior for the maintenance and enhancement of the organism. . . .
>
> The best vantage point for understanding behavior is from the internal frame of reference of the individual himself. . . . A portion of the total perceptual field gradually becomes differentiated as the self. . . . As a result of interaction with the environment, and particularly as a result of evaluational interaction with others, the structure of the self is formed—an organized, fluid, but consistent conceptual pattern of perceptions of characteristics and relationships of the "I" or the "me" together with values attached to these concepts. . . . As experiences occur in the life of the individual, they are either (a) symbolized, perceived and organized into some relationship to the self, (b) ignored because there is no perceived relationship to the self structure, (c) denied symbolization or given a distorted symbolization because the experience is inconsistent with the structure of the self. . . .
>
> Most of the ways of behaving which are adopted by the organ-

ism are those which are consistent with the concept of the self. . . .
Behavior may, in some instances, be brought about for organic
experiences and needs which have not been symbolized. Such behavior may be inconsistent with the structure of the self, but in
such instances, the behavior is not "owned" by the individual. . . .
Psychological maladjustment exists when the organism denies to
awareness significance, sensory, and visceral experiences, which
consequently are not symbolized and organized into the Gestalt
of the self structure. When this situation exists, there is a basic or
potential psychological tension. . . .

Psychological adjustment exists when the concept of the self is
such that all the sensory and visceral experiences of the organism
are, or may be, assimilated on the symbolic level into a consistent
relationship with the concept of the self. . . . Any experience which
is inconsistent with the organization or structure of self may be
perceived as a threat, and the more of these perceptions there are,
the more rigidly the self structure is organized to maintain itself.
. . . Under certain conditions, involving primarily complete absence
of any threat to the self structure, experiences which are inconsistent with it may be perceived and examined, and the structure
of the self revised to assimilate and include such experiences. . . .

When the individual perceives and accepts into one consistent
and integrated system all his sensory and visceral experiences, then
he is necessarily more understanding of others and is more accepting of others as separate individuals. . . . As the individual perceives and accepts into his self structure more of his organic experiences, he finds that he is replacing his present value system—
based so largely upon interjections which have been distortedly
symbolized—with a continuing organismic process.[37]

This rather lengthy quotation of propositions with reference to
personality is exceptionally important because it summarizes the
thinking of many different research people. Likewise, it embodies
a humanistic conception of the wholeness of personality, the
purposiveness of personality, the ways in which personality is
thrown into inconsistency and conflict, the need for reconciliation, the ways in which the human self is relaxed in its defensiveness and enabled to explore its own nature and inconsis-

tencies, and the ways in which one set of values is exchanged for a new set of values.

THE RELEVANCE OF PERSONALITY STRUCTURE HYPOTHESES FOR THE RELIGIOUS QUEST

The reader who has patiently borne with the preceding detailed description of theories of personality structure has already begun to ask the question about the practical relevance of these data for the religious quest. Likewise, he has been able to discern certain persistent themes of religious dimensions which are apparent to the careful eye.

Practical Theology and the Structure of Personality

In practical religious living it is imperative that a person take seriously his understanding of the structure of the human person. For instance, Dr. Billy Graham, when preaching in the author's home city, referred often to conversion as being an act of the will and not of the emotions. This represents basic confusion as to the New Testament and Old Testament conception of the wholeness of personality and the totality of the religious decision. Or, take another example to which reference has already been made. A layman asked his minister to preach on the first commandment of all the commandments. He was referring to Jesus' injunction in Mark 12:30, "And thou shalt love the Lord thy God with all thy heart, and with all thy soul, and with all thy mind, and with all thy strength: This is the first commandment." The layman asked his minister to preach on "loving the Lord *with all thy mind.*" Wisely the pastor said that Jesus was not setting the mind apart as a separate portion of the human person but, by emphasizing all these expressions of the total human person, he was calling for a total commitment of the whole person to the Lord our God. Another practical example of the confusion that can arise from misconceptions of personality is the assumption that man *has* a soul rather than that man *is* a living soul, having been made so as a creature by God the Creator. This confusion is especially evident in the ministry to the dying in which a minister is expected to "deal with the soul" and the doctor is expected to "deal with the body."

We have seen in both the Hebrew-Christian tradition concerning human personality and the movement of the scientific study of personality, that Dr. John A. T. Robinson is right when he says that "man does not have a body, he is a body. He is a flesh-animated-by-soul, the whole conceived as a psychophysical unity." [38] The scientific revolution moved the discussion of the nature of man into the orbit of the empirical, naturalistic, descriptive studies of the scientific psychologists. The more the scientists have studied, the more their conceptions of personality have moved, as is so clearly illustrated in the comments of Lecky, away from a mechanical determinism to a meaningful purposivism, and away from a fragmentary atomism to a dynamic understanding of the search of the self for wholeness.

Christian Ethics and the Structure of Personality

This latter observation vividly accents the indispensable relevance of values for the structure of personality. Personality is organized in terms of moral and ethical structures. This is obvious even in the terminology of Sullivan, for instance, who describes the three types of interpersonal co-operation as the "good-me," the "bad-me," and the "not-me." The preoccupation of Freud with ethical issues, and his structuralization of the super ego in his anatomical description of human life certainly moralize and ethicize personality. The fact that the whole ethical evaluational system of contemporary thought has been so profoundly influenced by these schemata of personality is often overlooked by the classroom theologians who teach our practicing ministers.

Likewise, the secular theorists of personality, such as Erich

Fromm, are being heard today on pressing ethical issues in ways in which professors of Christian ethics are not even known, much less heard. Not only are the apologetic foundations of the Christian faith as a revelational experience of grace from a triune and personal God being challenged, but also the ethical conceptions of the nature and destiny of man are being reformulated by scientists of personality. However, it is heartening to see that the more they work at the problem of the structure of personality, the more the basic validity of the nonreflective and existential Hebrew-Christian understanding of the wholeness of man is reconfirmed.

Demythologization and Remythologization of the Doctrine of Man

A great deal has been said in theological circles recently about the demythologization of the Gospel. This point of view had been set forth most specifically by Rudolf Bultmann. He contends that the language of the New Testament is the language of mythology. This, he says, is a hindrance to the conversion of modern man. Therefore, Bultmann concludes:

> The kerygma is incredible to modern man, for he is convinced that the mythical view of the world is obsolete. We are, therefore, bound to ask whether, when we preach the Gospel today, we expect our converts to accept not only the Gospel message, but also the mythical view of the world in which it is set. If not, does the New Testament embody a truth which is quite independent of its mythical setting? If it does, theology must undertake the task of stripping the kerygma from its mythical framework of "demythologizing" it.[39]

This need of modern man as he searches for a soul, to use Jung's phrase, to have the Gospel stripped of its mythical character, must be re-examined in the light of what is occurring in the field of psychotherapy and the contemporary view of man. The over-all impression of a book such as Patrick Mullahy's *Oedipus: Myth and Complex* is that a rather conscious process of remythologization is taking place. Various myths are being re-enacted in the light of their psychodynamic meaning. This is obviously true of Freudian use of Greek mythology. The ways in which concepts of field theory, borrowed from physics, are being used by the psychologists of personality to describe the tension systems of the human organism are additional evidence. Man must have a picture with which to think, it seems. The destruction of one set of myths does not guarantee that another mythology will not take its place. The preceding pages reflect that the Trinitarian conception of St. Augustine has been stripped from our discussions of the structure of personality. Platonic and Neoplatonic mythology has striven with the symbolic attempts of Augustine to express the ineffably difficult-to-express nature of the soul's inner relationships to itself. Analytical descriptions of the super ego, the id and the ego, and of the collective unconscious have become the common coin of conversation.

The essential religious dimensions of the structure of personality emerge most clearly at the asking of the crucial question about man's conflict: How can it be reconciled without raising the deeper conflict that man has over his own finitude, weakness, and the ultimate character of his self-condemnation? Likewise, the religious dimension appears also in the question: What is the nature of that Being within man which is not himself but an ultimately Other with whom he finds himself in dialogue as did Augustine in *The Confessions?* When answers to these questions come, then man has a new point of departure for reformulating his whole understanding of the nature of personality on the basis of his discovery of the nature of God. The one is the presupposition of the other.

NOTES FOR CHAPTER VIII

1. John A. T. Robinson, *The Body: A Study in Pauline Theology* (Chicago: Henry Regnery Company, 1952), pp. 15-16. Used by permission.
2. A. R. Johnson, *The Vitality of the Individual in the Thought of Ancient Israel* (Cardiff: University of Wales Press, 1949), pp. 7-8.
3. Robinson, *op. cit.*, p. 28.
4. *Ibid.*, p. 29.
5. *The Works of Plato,* trans. B. Jowett, Vol. 4, p. 372 ff. *The Timaeus* (New York: The Tudor Publishing Company).
6. *Ibid., The Phaedrus,* p. 403.
7. *Ibid.*, p. 404.
8. The Basic Writings of Aristotle, *De Anima,* Book I, Ch. 5, Lines 5-12.
9. Friedrich Ueberweg, *A History of Philosophy from Thales to the Present Time,* trans. George S. Morris, Vol. I (New York: Scribner, Armstrong and Company, 1871), p. 168.
10. Sterling P. Lamprecht, *Our Philosophical Traditions: A Brief History of Philosophy in Western Civilization* (New York: Appleton-Century-Crofts, Inc., 1955), p. 53.
11. *De Trinitate,* Book IX, Ch. 2, Sec. 2.
12. *Civitas Dei,* Book XI, Ch. 26. Also *De Trinitate,* Book IX, Ch. 5, Sec. 8.
13. *The Confessions,* XIII, xi, 12.
14. *Soliloquies,* i, 6. 12 and 13.
15. *De Vera, Relig.* 39. 72.
16. *Civitas Dei,* XI, 26.
17. C. N. Cochrane, *Christianity and Classical Culture* (New York: Oxford University Press, 1944), p. 410.
18. London: Hogarth Press, 1947.
19. Sigmund Freud, *The Ego and the Id* (London: Hogarth Press, 1947), p. 28.
20. *Ibid.*, p. 44.
21. Patrick Mullahy, *Oedipus: Myth and Complex; A Review of Psychoanalytic Theory* (New York: Hermitage Press, 1948), p. 145.
22. Jolan Jacobi, *The Psychology of Jung,* trans. K. W. Bash (New Haven, Conn.: Yale University Press, 1943), p. 47.
23. C. G. Jung, *Modern Man in Search of a Soul* (London: Kegan Paul, Trench, Trubner and Co., Ltd., 1933), p. 90.
24. Harry Stack Sullivan, *The Interpersonal Theory of Psychiatry,* eds. Helen Swick Perry and Mary Ladd Gawel (New York: W. W. Norton & Company, Inc., 1953), pp. 162-163.
25. *Ibid.*, pp. 166-167.
26. Mullahy, *op. cit.*, pp. 299-300.
27. Prescott Lecky, *Self-Consistency: A Theory of Personality* (New York: Island Press, 1945, copyright by Kathryn Lecky).
28. *Ibid.*, p. 5.
29. *Ibid.*, p. 19.

30. *Ibid.*, p. 55.
31. *Ibid.*, p. 80.
32. *Ibid.*, p. 82.
33. *Ibid.*
34. *Ibid.*, pp. 82, 150.
35. Gardner Murphy, *Personality: A Biosocial Approach to Origins and Structure* (New York: Harper & Brothers, 1947), p. 619.
36. *Ibid.*
37. Carl R. Rogers, *Client-Centered Therapy* (Boston: Houghton Mifflin Company, 1951), pp. 481-522. Used by permission.
38. John A. T. Robinson, *op. cit.*, p. 14.
39. Rudolf Bultmann, *New Testament and Mythology*, "Kerygma and Myth: A Theological Debate," ed. Hans W. Bartsch (London: S.P.C.K., 1953), p. 3.

CHAPTER IX

THE RELIGIOUS DIMENSIONS
OF THE DESTRUCTION
OF PERSONALITY

HUMAN PERSONALITY BECOMES STRUCTURED and organized. This structure and organization is, to some extent, observable. Andras Angyal, in likening the personality structure to the trunk and branches of a tree, says the growing edge of personality is most plastic at the "terminal branches," and that "the structure becomes increasingly rigid as the branches move back to the trunk." However, to carry his figure of speech further, "runaway growths," or pathological structures of personality do arise, and these may become fragmentary forces in the total structure of the personality. They become parasitic growths, drawing strength from but not contributing to, the total personality. They may become parasites upon the total personality; they may even dominate the total personality.*

The foregoing discussion of the structure of personality has laid the groundwork for a further discussion of the twisted, distorted, or fragmented personality. A consuming fear of "going

* Notes and credits for this chapter are found on pages 216 and 217.

to pieces" grips many people today. A quiet sense of desperation causes many people to say to themselves that they are going to have to "pull themselves together." These are so many colloquial ways of saying that personality does become fragmented, that it faces the threat of destruction.

The fear of destruction today is just as intense as it was in the days of Jonathan Edwards. However, it expresses itself not so often in the fear of death and of hell as it does in the fear of disease and of mental illness. The old lion has turned into a thousand mice of which to be afraid! Whereas attention is given to the processes whereby personality destruction takes place and is explained, the reader should not lose sight of the fact that these actually are processes of death. A more formal discussion of the fact of death appears in Chapter XI, but this chapter emphasizes the harsher reality that we do not die all at once, but a bit at a time. The fragmentation of personality often occurs when the whole of life is jeopardized in order that a part may survive, or vice versa.

Redemption from destruction is more than a passing fancy. What are some of the historical and contemporary ways in which the fragmented personality has been described? What are the spiritual dimensions of this shattering of the structure of personality? These are some of the issues to which we need to address our attention now.

DEMONISM AND PERSONALITY

The New Testament

Although a great many absurd things have been said in attempts to superimpose contemporary psychotherapeutic concepts upon the New Testament teachings concerning demonism, nevertheless serious students of religious experience and psychology of personality cannot overlook the intuitive insights of the biblical conceptions of demonism. These conceptions are intensely relevant to our understanding of the fragmentation of personality. As Edward Langton, in discussing the teachings of the New Testament concerning demonology, says, "the different 'psychic states' or 'splits of personality' or 'fragmentary selves,' as they are variously called can assume the guise of different personalities, and act as the individual they are supposed to be, in the most lifelike manner." [1] Langton assumes that one of the main factors, although not the only one, accounting for demon possession as portrayed in the Gospels is the existence of pathological "psychic states which can assume the appearance of individuality." [2]

Professor S. Vernon McCasland has studied the Gospels in the light of the contemporary Hellenistic civilization in which the New Testament was written. He draws upon the forms of thought in the situation that was existent in New Testament times and correlates these insights with contemporary psychotherapeutic information. He says that

> . . . physicians in our time call disorganizations of the mind neurosis or psychosis; the ancients called the same phenomenon demon possession . . . the modern vocabulary refers to compulsions arising from the *id* or from *complexes* or from the *super-ego* which are so strong that the normal self, the *ego*, is unable to retain its rational sovereignity. Disorganization sets in and personality loses its integration.[3]

Some transversal conceptions run throughout the biblical account concerning the dynamics of the fragmentation in a personality. First of all, the basic relationship between God and man is an intensely personal encounter between the Creator and the creature. This Creator-creature relationship is a transforming one in which the creature is "changed into the same image" of the Creator (II Corinthians 3:18). The creature is a partipotent person as over against the Creator who is an omnipotent personality. When the creature seeks to serve and worship himself or another creature more than the Creator, he breaks from reality and "changes the truth of God into a lie" (Romans 1:25).

That finite creature which man places in the stead of the Creator becomes an organizing center for a separate, rebellious, runaway, and isolated portion of his personhood. Soon this portion rises up and rules the whole personality. Or, the victory may be incomplete; and this portion simply makes periodic, predatory raids on the total personality. This is what Plato defined as sin, namely, the rising up of a part of the soul against the whole. This is what Paul Tillich describes as "the absolutizing of the finite." That which one has substituted for God "possesses" the total person, and exerts "demonic" power over self. Leslie D. Weatherhead has pointed out that Jesus makes no reference to devils (though the conversations around him were full of reference to them) apart from the context of disease and the possible exception of the storm on the lake.[4] Nevertheless, Jesus did insist repeatedly that no man could serve two masters; and purity of heart, the priority of the vision of God, oneness of devotion were all related to the maintenance of the integrity of the total person. Likewise later persons, captured by the singleness of heart of obedience to Christ, could say that a double-minded man is unstable in all his ways.

It is beyond the scope of this treatise to deal with the elaborate literature on the history of demonology, witchcraft, and exorcism. However, this has been carefully studied by Gregory Zilboorg in relation to the way in which a restless surrender of both the church and medicine to doctrines of demonology made of medical psychology "a part of codified demonology, and the treatment of the mentally ill became for the most part a problem of legal procedure. The darkest ages of psychiatry set in." He also points out in another connection that the vast fear of demons contributed to what he calls "epidemics of insanity produced by moral contagion."[5]

The two Dominican Inquisitors, Henry Kramer and James

Sprenger, wrote their legal handbook [6] for the diagnosis and punishment of persons who are possessed of witches, possessed of demons and evil spirits. The fact that many elaborately detailed discussions of what today would be considered psychiatric disorders appear in the work of these men is ample evidence to validate Zilboorg's statement.

SCIENTIFIC FORMULATIONS OF THE FRAGMENTATION OF PERSONALITY

Psychoanalysis

Scientific observers have been quick to evaluate the profound psychological dimensions of the religio-legal conceptions of demonology. A process of reinterpretation of these phenomena was initiated by Sigmund Freud. In a paper written in 1923 Freud says:

> . . . despite the somatic idealogy of the era of "exact" science, the demonological theory of these dark ages has in the long run justified itself. . . . What in those days were thought to be evil spirits to us are base and evil wishes, the derivatives of impulses which have been rejected and repressed. In one respect only do we not subscribe to the explanation of these phenomena current in mediaeval times; we have abandoned the projection of them into the outer world, attributing their origin instead to the inner life of the patient to whom they manifest themselves. [7]

Freud goes on to interpret the possession of the soul of the demoniacally possessed patient of whom he had a record from 1669, in terms of his basic presupposition that the "Devil" was "chosen as a substitute for a father figure." He assumes that God and the Devil "were originally one and the same, a single figure which was later split in the two bearing opposed characteristics." [8] He also says that

> If the benevolent and righteous God is a father substitute, it is not to be wondered at that the hostile attitude, which leads to hate, fear

and accusations against him comes to expression in the figure of satan. The father is thus the individual prototypable God and the Devil.[9]

However, a real philosophical question needs to be raised about the "easy" solution to a difficult problem which Freud has given us. He rightly challenges the naïve projection of evil and base wishes (which have been rejected and repressed) upon the outer world, which is certainly obvious in acutely disturbed mentally ill people. Particularly is this true of the paranoid schizophrenic who externalizes the conscious and reads it back into himself in persecution. However, the more we seek to plumb the illimitable depths of the self, the more we ask the question about Freud's neat distinction between the inner and outer worlds. Is that which is objectively real only that which is on the outside of our geographically definable self? Is, as Gardner Murphy queried, our skin the dividing line between that which is subjective and that which is objective? Obviously, Augustine was much closer to the truth when he affirmed the reality of a Self other than the self within the self.

Analytical Psychology

Carl G. Jung challenges the easy solipsism of Freud without question at this point. He says:

> . . . no, the unconscious is anything but a capsulated, personal system; it is the wide world, and objectivity as open as the world. *I* am the object, even the subject of the object, in a complete reversal of my ordinary consciousness, where I am always a subject that has an object. There I find myself in the closest entanglement with the world, so much a part of it that I oft forget all too easily who I really am. "Lost in oneself" is a good phrase to describe this state. But this self is the world if only a consciousness could see it. That is why we must know who we are.[10]

Jung epitomized this objectivity within the self in his concept of "archetypes" which he says derives from Augustine and is a term which may be used as "an explanatory paraphrase of the Platonic eidos." [11] As was seen in the discussion of the structure of personality Jung gave a place of separateness and independence to complex organizations of the personality which exist apart from consciousness and have a life of their own. This particular conception is unusually relevant to the discussion of the fragmentation of personality. As Jung says:

> . . . whatever else may be taking place within the obscure recesses of the psyche—and there are notoriously many opinions as to this matter—one thing is certain: it is first and foremost the so called complexes [emotionally toned contents having a certain amount of autonomy] which play an important part there. The expression "autonomous complex" has often met with opposition, although, as it seems to me unjustifiably. The active contents of the unconscious do behave in a way I cannot describe better than by the word "autonomous." The . . . complexes . . . come and go as they please. . . . They have been split off from consciousness and lead a separate existence in the unconscious, being at all times ready to hinder or reinforce the conscious intensions. [12]

In fact, Jung points out that the archetype of the anima, for instance, takes us into the realm of the gods and is itself endowed with a numinous quality. It is just one of the many archetypes of the unconscious. It is chaotic life urge. It confronts us in our most personal life "as our most personal and bitter misunderstanding." It has demonic character.

> When, for instance, a highly honored scholar in his seventies deserts his family and marries a twenty year old, red haired actress, then we know that the gods have claimed another victim. It is thus that demonic supremacy shows itself to us. (In the middle ages it would have been much easier to do away with the young woman as a witch.) [13]

Jung goes on to say that "a man's unconscious is feminine and personified by the anima." Similarly it could be said that a woman's unconscious is masculine and is personified by the animus. In both instances the "other" stands for evil itself all too frequently. Jung translates this symbolically into a discussion of the Trinity. He says that "the Christian Godhead is One in Three Persons. The fourth person in the heavenly drama is unquestionably the devil." He posits a quaternity rather than a trinity in the Godhead. Jung goes on to interpret this in terms of ethics:

> according to moral valuation he [the Devil] is man's sin; therefore a function belonging to him and hence masculine. The femininity in the Godhead is kept a secret and to say that the Holy Ghost is Sofia counts as a heresy . . . The fourth function is contaminated with the unconscious and, when it is made conscious, draws the whole unconscious in its train. Then we come to a settlement with the unconscious and must attempt to bring about a synthesis with the opposites. But first of all that breaks out the violent conflicts that would beset any reasonable man when it became evident that he must swallow the absurd superstitions.[14]

In the light of these concepts Carl G. Jung emphasizes the importance of our doctrine of original sin and the inveterate way in which man reformulates and restates this doctrine when his conscious rationalism has made him too sophisticated to accept it intellectually.

However, from a distinctly theological point of view, we must be wary of the gnostic connotations of the preceding doctrine. Jung does not come to grips with the ontological problem and in his remythologization of the unconscious, he imputes as "real" a kind of reality to the devil as he does to God. He does not bring them under the criticism of the categories of created and uncreated beings nor does he make note of the essentially counterfeit kind of apparent reality, barred from a higher source, and vaunting themselves as being "on an equality with God." Victor White presents it in this way:

> . . . finally, it must be made clear that we do not of course contend that "devils" and "complexes" are altogether synonymous and interchangeable terms. When the theologian says that somebody is af-

flicted by the devil, he is describing his situation in relation to God. When the psychologist says he is suffering from a nonassimilated autonomous complex, he is describing an inherent functional disorder. He speaks a different language; each describes an observed occurrence from a different point of view, or as the scholastics would say, in a different *ratio formalis qua*. Our contention is that the meanings of the two sets of terms (the theological and the psychopathological) are, however, not mutually exclusive; and we would offer for expert consideration the suggestion that, while the meanings are different, each term may be, and commonly is, referable to the selfsame phenomenon or occurrence.[15]

We can, therefore, discern broad overlapping areas between the prescientific discussions of the fragmentation of personality and the more recent psychotherapeutic mythologies concerning structural concepts of the personality such as have been set forth by C. G. Jung, Sigmund Freud, and others.

Morton Prince

Another important set of clinical observations was published much earlier by Morton Prince in his book on *The Dissociation of Personality*.[16] He made a biographical study in abnormal psychology of a certain "Miss Christine L. Beauchamp" in whom several different and distinct personalities developed. Her personality would change from time to time, often from hour to hour, and with each change her character would become transformed and her memories altered. Prince says:

> . . . in addition to the real, original or normal self, the self that was born and which she was intended by nature to be, she may be any one of three different persons. I say three different, because, although making use of the same body, each, nevertheless, has a distinctly different character; a difference manifested by different trains of thought, by different views, beliefs, ideals, and temperament, and by different acquisitions, tastes, habits, experiences, and memories. Each varies in these respects from the other two and from the original Miss Beauchamp. Two of these personalities have no knowledge of each other or of the third, excepting such informa-

tion as may be obtained by inference or second hand, so that in the memory of each of these two there are blanks which correspond to the times when the others are in the flesh. All of a sudden one or the other wakes to find herself, she knows not where, and ignorant of what she has said or done a moment before. Only one of three has knowledge of the lives of the others, and this one presents such a bizarre character, so far removed from the others in individuality, that the transformation from one of the other personalities to herself is one of the most striking and dramatic features of the case. The personalities come and go in kaleidoscopic succession, many changes often being made in the course of twenty-four hours. And it so happens that Miss Beauchamp, if I may use the name to designate several distinct people, at one moment says and does and plans and arranges something to which a short time before she most strongly objected, indulges tastes which a moment before would have been abhorrent to her ideals, and undoes or destroys what she had just laboriously planned and arranged.[17]

Prince, who at that time was professor of diseases of the nervous system at Tufts College Medical School and physician in the same field at Boston City Hospital, says that a correct term for designating such a personality is the "disintegrated personality." He uses this term because each "secondary personality is a part only of a normal whole self." [18] Other such cases of the fragmented personality have been observed and recorded, representing varying degrees of complexity of organization and independence from personalities. These have been observed in hypnotic phenomena by such persons as Pierre Janet, and in trancelike states of psychical media through the use of hypnosis and other forms of suggestive treatment. Prince observed this person over a period of seven years from 1898 to 1904 inclusive.

Prince concludes that the mental cohesion of a person "necessarily yields to the disintegrating effects of the strains of life." After having recorded carefully over five hundred pages of clinical material concerning this one conglomerate personality, he felt that the circumstances of her life were such that it was impossible for her to have the freedom from care, anxiety, and responsibilty as well as the mental and physical strains attached to these that a unified person should have. Through an extended process of therapy, Miss Beauchamp would appear again as herself. She could talk freely about herself as two of the three "other selves," B I and B IV. But she never was able to integrate her life, her doings as "Sally," except indirectly.

The insights of Harry Stack Sullivan concerning the intracommunication systems of the organized and disorganized self dynamism throw vast light on the report of Morton Prince. The good-me, the bad-me, and the not-me were obvious. "Miss Beauchamp" had access to the first two through association, but the "not-me" was inaccessible, uncanny, and horrible to her.

As a chaplain on the wards of a state hospital, I observed the multiple personality fairly frequently. On one occasion a patient greeted me when I asked her name by saying, "My name is Legion, for we are many." She was in a semi-state of consciousness lying curled in an intra-uterine position on the floor. Beyond this remark she was completely noncommunicative. Likewise, I have made clinical note of the way in which separate self-concepts tend to emerge in the pattern of voice of a person. One particular counselee had at least three distinctly different voices in which she talked. The tonal quality, the vocabulary, the pitch, and the concomitant emotions and facial expressions were obviously distinct from each other. One was that of a curt, professional woman. Another was that of a tender, mothering, caring, helping person. The other voice was that of a tiny three- or four-year-old child amounting to a wail accompanied by profuse tears. And a fourth voice was that of a harsh, bitter competitor with other inferior women. This is reminiscent of what Plato said about demons. He said that "demoniacs do not use their own dialect or tongue, but that of the demons who have entered into them."

Anthropology

Spencer L. Rogers records the story of an eighteen-year-old boy in the Banks Islands. His report is very similar to the instance found in Mark 5:2-9:

> . . . he (the boy) complained of a headache. He went to sleep and awakened in a state called "possessed." He was extraordinarily strong, about eight men most of whom were powerful fellows, endeavoring vainly to hold him. In the intervals of these violent paroxysms he spoke, certainly in a voice quite unlike his own. A compatriot, staring into his eyes said to him, "What is your name?" "We are many," replied the possessed boy. "Is it so and so in you?" to which the possessed replied "yes" or "no" till it was ascertained who were in him (various dead relatives, some of whom were known to the writers).[19]

In the same context Rogers also calls attention to the fact that "occasionally a distinction is made" between types of spirits responsible for possession. He says that the peoples of Southern India

> . . . recognize two classes of potentially possessing spirits which may cause insanity. One type of demon is the spirit of an ancestor who has been slighted through failure to show him the proper ceremonial respect. The other type of demon takes in a large class of local supernatural beings. A competent exorcist is able to drive out either type and thus cure madness.[20]

This particular theory set forth by these primitive tribes, has a remarkable relevance to certain psychoanalytic concepts of interpersonal relationships. In the first place, the spirit of a departed and dead loved one—or hated one—or both—certainly is introjected in the experience of bereavement. Even in more sophisticated cultures one sees a severely bereaved person taking on the mannerisms, the voice, and even following the habits of a dead member of their family. Likewise, the residual results of the long years of identification with a person now dead tend to come forth, in the experiences of stress in the process of grief.

Another psychoanalytic insight is obvious in Rogers' account in that through the process of transference, the basic identifications of a person with his earlier parent figures can be shifted to other highly esteemed persons within the community whose spirits, after they are dead, live on as "local supernatural beings." But one has only to read Shakespeare's *Hamlet* to see the possessing and demonic power of departed spirits upon the lives of those who remain. These insights are extremely relevant to the dynamics of bereavement, and the research of Lindemann and others on grief accentuate the psychological relevance of the primitive beliefs on demonic spirits. (A survey of this material is to be found in Chapter 3 of my own book, *Anxiety and Christian Experience*.[21]

However, we do not have to go to primitive society for insight into the fragmented personality. The multiplicity of selves is starkly apparent in the following autobiographical report of Thomas Wolfe:

. . . in Paris I couldn't sleep at all—I walked the streets from night to morning and was in the worse shape I have ever been in my life. All the pent up strain and tension of the last few months seemed to explode and I will confess to you that there were times there when I really was horribly afraid I was going mad—all the unity and control of personality seemed to have escaped from me—it was as if I were on the back of some immense rackety engine which was running wild and over which I had no more control than a fly. I came home to my hotel one night—or rather at daybreak one morning—tried to get off to sleep—and had the horrible experience of seeming to disintegrate into at least six people—I was in bed and suddenly it seemed these other shapes of myself were moving *out* of me—all around me—one of them touched me by the arm—another was talking in my ear—others walking around the room—and suddenly I would come to with a terrific jerk and all of them would rush back into me again. I can swear to you I was not asleep—it was one of the strangest and most horrible experiences I have ever had. There were about three days of which I could give no clear accounting—and loss of memory of that sort is to me one of the worse things that can happen.[22]

Andras Angyal

Andras Angyal describes such experiences as this one through which Wolfe passed with the term "bionegativity." He proposed this term to offset some of the loose generalizations that have been made, even by authors referred to in this present discussion, and which he termed "confusing ballast of hazy connotations." By the term bionegativity he means "a personality constellation in which one or more part processes disturb the total function of the organism." He says also that bionegative constellations occur not only when a "poorly integrated part function disturbs the total function." They also happen when some part-function which is essential for the total function is damaged or lacking. This latter distinction removes some of the neat moral rejection from the spiritual realities we have been describing. Just because a portion of the self may be considered as other than the self does not *necessarily* mean that it is evil. In fact, it may even mean that the creative, redemptive, and wholesome necessities of life in a given individual are being denied, thwarted, and ruled out of existence. For example, Socrates interpreted the *daimonion* as the guiding voice of his life to which he listened! The creative writing of Thomas Wolfe may even have been burgeoned out of the suffering which he described. In fact, he thought that it was.

SOME RELIGIOUS IMPLICATIONS OF THE
DESTRUCTION OF PERSONALITY

The foregoing discussion has revealed extensive overlapping in the discussion of biblical, historical, and contemporary beliefs in demons, on the one hand, and the scientific statements concerning mental illness on the other hand. Some basic clarifications are needed here. This *is* an overlapping, but we find confusion *ad infinitum* when the overlapping is taken to be an exact equation or identity. For instance, periodically popular interpretations of the story of the Gadarene demoniac appear in sermons, both spoken and written. Jesus is likened to "the world's greatest psychiatrist," the treatment he gives to the demoniac is likened to shock therapy, the prefrontal lobotomy, tranquillizing drugs, or whatever happens to be the current discovery in the treatment of mental illness. Such absurdities miss the depth dimensions both of contemporary psychiatry and of the message inherent in the situation-that-was at the time of Jesus' encounter with the demoniac. On the other hand, one gets the impression that similar absurdities appear when attempts are made to equate contemporary diagnostic categories of mental illness with the few threads of information about the actual disorders of persons in the biblical stories. In both these instances the overlapping nature of the prescientific and scientific descriptions of the similar phenomena is turned into an exact equation. This accounts for many of the sheer absurdities which we get back from this process of thinking.

Equally misleading are the exclusivistic attitudes of both contemporary psychotherapists on the one hand and the fundamentalistic religionists on the other hand. Some psychotherapists would reject the whole discussion of demonology as irrelevant to contemporary psychotherapy and would not take the anthropological point of view of Spencer L. Rogers, for instance. They would feel as Zilboorg does, namely, that this is simply to encourage a return of the Dark Ages. They do not forget the inquisitional and legalistic treatment of mentally ill patients. Kramer and Sprenger not only believed in demons as an "article of support" for the supposed infallibility of their interpretations of the Bible. They also believed in them as a diagnostic hypothesis for the actual treatment (or mistreatment) of people.

Merrill Unger of Dallas Theological Seminary represents a literalistic belief in demons to the exclusion of correlation with psychiatric information of today. He says that "the gospels prove conclusively that demons are purely spiritually beings" and have "the specific attribute of . . . immateriality, incorporeality." [23]

In the same context he feels that there are instances where the human will is overwhelmed and overborne by an irresistible power which is supplied with strength by a demonic agency, such as in the case of the alcoholic or the suicide.[24]

This kind of literalistic thinking today is largely what might be called "ivory-tower" thinking. Rarely does one find people who hold such views today and act upon them when one of their own family members becomes mentally ill. One asks the question, for instance, What would Unger believe and think if someone whom he loved very much should attempt suicide or become an alcoholic? Would he develop a program of exorcism for that loved one? Does he have clinical records to substantiate the actual therapy of alcoholics by demonic exorcism? If he had a loved one who developed an acute schizophrenic illness, would he call for an exorcist, or would he seek to have that patient hospitalized and call psychiatric help?

Although I do not know Professor Unger, I do know many people who have held opinions similar to his who, when the press of an actual existential situation is upon them, do not even think of their biblical exegesis, much less attempt to put it into effect. Rather, they turn to contemporary medical specialists in the field of psychiatry or some other speciality which is in keeping with the disease they presume the person to have. For instance, the parent of an epileptic child would certainly go to a neurologist for help and would be quite dependent upon his guidance even though his defense of the authority of the Scriptures included a literalistic belief in demons.

This discussion of the fragmentation of personality accents again the importance of the insistence of Rudolf Bultmann upon demythologization of New Testament truth. Paul Tillich speaks pointedly to both the relevance and the hazards involved in the handling of the concepts of the demonic. He says that "demonic" is decisive for his "interpretation of history."

It is one of the forgotten concepts of the New Testament, which, in spite of its tremendous importance for Jesus and the apostles, has become obsolete in modern theology. The thing responsible for this neglect was the reaction of philosophers of the Enlightenment against the superstitious, abominable use of the idea of the demonic in the Middle Ages and in orthodox Protestantism. But abuse should not forbid right use. The idea of the demonic is the mythical expression of reality that was in the center of Luther's experience as it was in Paul's, namely, the structural and therefore inescapable power of evil. The Enlightenment, foreshadowed by Erasmus's fight with Luther and by theological humanism says only the individual acts of evil are dependent upon the free decisions of the conscious personality. It believed in the possibility of inducing the great majority of individuals to follow the demands of an integrated personal and social life by education, persuasion, and adequate institutions. But this belief was broken down not only by the "Storms of Our Times" . . . but also by the new recognition of the destructive mechanism determining the unconscious trends of individuals and groups. Theologians could reinterpret the badly named but profoundly true doctrine of "original sin" in the light of recent scientific discoveries. The powerful symbol of the demonic was everywhere accepted in the sense which we had used it, namely, as a structure of evil beyond the moral power of good will, producing social and individual tragedy precisely through the inseparable mixture of good and evil in every human act. None of the concepts by our interpretation of history has found as much response in religious or secular literature as has the concept of the demonic. This response may be interpreted as a symptom of the general feeling for the structural character of evil in our period. If evil has no demonic or structural character limiting individual freedom, its conquest can come only by the opposite, the divine structure, that is, by what we have called a structure or "Gestalt" of grace.[25]

We can genuinely say that there is a wrestling going on within the self and that it is against principalities and powers and kingdoms of darkness. The dialogue which the self carries on within itself, as Reinhold Niebuhr has said, is certainly "more complex than understood in classical philosophy." Likewise Tillich and Niebuhr are appealing for an approach to the self which is both therapeutically adequate for pathological aberrations of the selfhood and capable of comprehending the real problems of the self on either the political or the religious level. The end result is a dynamic encounter between contemporary psychotherapy and modern theology, but no advocation of either by puerile attempts at equating the two. The points of meeting are also points of departure at intersections of common concern. However, as Niebuhr again has said, "Depth psychology has uncovered many of [the] complexities" of the dialogue which the self carries on within itself.[26]

Modern psychology has gone far in the rediscovery of the intuitive depths and contradictory cries for deliverance from the "powers of darkness" which have been obscured by easy rationalistic kinds of thinking. As Emil Brunner says, modern psychology "is in the act of re-emphasizing certain truths of mythical thinking which had been 'written off' by the Enlightenment."[27] However, not all the discussion of man's self-destructiveness in either the biblical view of man or contemporary psychology is set in mythological terms by any means. Nor is the discussion of the "powers of darkness" which invade and destroy men's integrity always cast in terms of a "three-story" universe.

Much to the contrary, the drama of man in the biblical and revelational understanding is not a "still" picture of man with a fixed "anatomy of personality," to use Freud's terms. It is a moving picture of man in conflict with himself, of man as a wrestler with an inner law of his mind, crying for deliverance from his own destruction of himself. Equally so, the contemporary psychotherapist, Menninger, speaks of man being against himself in an ingenious swerve toward self-destruction.[28] This struggle is not with "flesh and blood" but with the powers of darkness. The real bondage comes in the worship of gods that are "no-gods," the elevation of the self to live "in distance" from God and neighbor, and the deification of a self-chosen part of life as if it were the whole of life.

On these diagnoses, the phenomenological and the theological descriptions of the destruction of human personality are remarkably at home with each other. They begin to diverge from each other at the point of the proximate or ultimate nature of the deliverance from bondage and self-destruction. Whereas the psychotherapists have rejected the neat rationalism of the Enlightenment in their empirical descriptions of man's contradictoriness and self-destructiveness, they still operate within the hope of human reason, self-affirmation, and causal readjustment for man's redemption from his plight. They dedicate their books, as one of them did:

> To those who would use intelligence in the battle against death— to strengthen the will to live against the wish to die, and to replace with love the blind compulsion to give hostages to hatred as the price of living.

This is all well and good if set within the larger context of the meaning of the Christian gospel in its radical redemption of men from the power of death through an historical act of love in Jesus Christ. This act was one of redemptive suffering which works objectively for us, accomplishing for us what we cannot do for ourselves, thus affirming our weakness and limitation; it works subjectively for us in that we are called to a life of redemptive suffering, whereby we take up our cross, shoulder the burden of anxiety, and find meaning in suffering which transforms it into Christian experience. The Perfect Love casts out fear, and that suffering which, in the unredeemed mind, was seen to be punishment is now seen to be a challenge which the person is enabled to meet creatively by means of the "comfort wherewith he has been comforted of God."

The theme of redemptive suffering is by no means absent entirely from the reflections of contemporary psychotherapists, as will be evident in later chapters where the work of Victor Frankl, Gotthard Booth, and others will be reviewed. But it needs to be said that the empirical exploration of the therapeutic relevance of the vocation of suffering, previously written off as "masochism," or "repressed hostility," is yet to be done by psychotherapists.

All that we have been saying in this chapter on the richness and complexity of the inner structure of personality, both in its serene and its chaotic manifestations, points up some realities, however, which still need to be considered. N. P. Jacobson has rightly said that "the individuating tendencies of a complex culture drive a wedge deep into the internal life of every personality." He talks of our having been "delivered over into the power of gigantic integrations that leave the inner life unexpressed, indeterminate, and alone." He interprets the gospel of grace found within the Christian tradition as a search "to free the inner self that lurks in solitary confinement, furtive, incommunicable, and unconfessed mind and within the particular organization of sensitivity and response that we embody when the socializing and falsifying process has done its work." [29]

However, Jacobson's remarks have only to accentuate three basic questions which we are yet to address ourselves: "Are the ways in which the self is fragmented empirically discernible, and what are the dynamics of this shattering process?" And, in the second place, "What are the spiritual dimensions of the goals of man's becoming a whole person rather than a self-destroying civil war with two legs?" And, finally, "What are the unique insights which identify the Christian understanding of personality?"

The succeeding chapters will discuss these three questions in detail.

NOTES FOR CHAPTER IX

1. *Essentials of Demonology: A Study of Jewish and Christian Doctrine, Its Origin and Development* (London: Eppleworth Press, 1945), p. 155.
2. *Ibid.*

3. S. Vernon McCasland, *By the Finger of God: Demon Possession and Exorcism in Early Christianity in the Light of Modern Views of Mental Illness* (New York: The Macmillan Company, 1951), p. 26. Used by permission of The Macmillan Company.

4. Leslie D. Weatherhead, *Psychology, Religion, and Healing* (London: Hodder and Stoughton, Ltd., 1951), p. 99.

5. Gregory Zilboorg, *A History of Medical Psychology* (New York: W. W. Norton & Company, Inc., 1941), pp. 142-143.

6. Henry Kramer and James Sprenger, *Malleus Maleficarum* (London: The Pushkin Press, 1948).

7. Sigmund Freud, "A Neurosis of Demoniacal Possession in the 17th Century," *Collected Papers*, Vol. IV, trans. Joanne Riviere (London: Hogarth Press, 1949), pp. 436 ff.

8. *Ibid.*, p. 450.

9. *Ibid.*, p. 451.

10. C. G. Jung, *The Integration of Personality*, ed. Stanley Del (New York: Farrar and Rinehart, 1939), p. 70. Used by permission of Routledge & Kegan Paul, Ltd., © 1948.

11. *Ibid.*, p. 53.

12. C. G. Jung, *Modern Man in Search of a Soul* (New York: Harcourt, Brace and Co., 1933), p. 91. Used by permission.

13. C. G. Jung, *The Integration of Personality, op. cit.*, p. 80. Used by permission of Routledge & Kegan Paul, Ltd., © 1948.

14. *Ibid.*, pp. 156-157. Used by permission.

15. Victor White, *God and the Unconscious*, Foreword by C. G. Jung (London: Harvill Press, Ltd., 1952), p. 189. Used by permission.

16. New York: Longmans, Green & Co., Inc., 1913.

17. From *The Dissociation of a Personality* by Morton Prince by permission of Longmans, Green & Co., Inc., 1913.

18. *Ibid.*, p. 3.

19. Spencer L. Rogers, "Early Psychotherapy," *Ciba Symposia*, Vol. IX, Nos. 1, 2, April-May, 1947, pp. 604-605.

20. *Ibid.*

21. Philadelphia: Westminster Press, 1955.

22. *The Letters of Thomas Wolfe*, ed. Elizabeth Nowell (New York: Charles Scribner's Sons, 1956), p. 438. Used by permission.

23. Merrill Unger, *Biblical Demonology* (Wheaton, Ill.: Van Kampen Press, 1952), pp. 62-63, 65.

24. *Ibid.* p. 40.

25. *The Protestant Era* (Chicago: University of Chicago Press, 1948), pp. xx, xxi. Used by permission.

26. Reinhold Niebuhr, *The Self and the Dramas of History* (New York: Charles Scribner's Sons, 1955), p. 11.

27. *Christian Doctrine of Creation and Redemption* (Philadelphia: Westminster Press, 1952), p. 270.

28. Karl Menninger, *Man Against Himself* (New York: Harcourt, Brace & Company, Inc., 1938).

29. N. P. Jacobson, "Religion and the Fragmentation of Man," *The Journal of Religion*, Vol. XXXII, January, 1952, pp. 22, 24.

CHAPTER X

SOME SPIRITUAL LAWS
OF PERSONALITY

ONE OF THE FOCAL PREMISES UNDERLYING this whole discussion is that an autonomous self both exists and becomes the stackpole of personality. The self is in dialogue with itself but, as Reinhold Niebuhr says, "There are not two distinct selves in this internal dialogue . . . the healthy self is always one self, no matter how much it engages in a perpetual internal dialogue." * [1] One of the main tasks of the self, therefore, is to stay in touch with itself and to maintain its central directions.

However, the destruction of the self into many warring selves represents the fact that the self does lose touch with itself; the intracommunication of the self-system breaks down. The total interpersonal context of the individual self becomes a necessary part of the dramatic tragedy of this inner loss of communication within the self. Sometimes the people in the interpersonal field of relationships become merely an audience to what is going on within the self. Sometimes they are whispering prompters on the edge of the drama. Sometimes they are pressed into service as actual representatives of the portions of the self which have been

* Notes and credits for this chapter begin on page 246.

banished and exiled. But always, the inner dialogue of the self with itself is carried on in the arena of the interpersonal field of relationships.

The inner communication of the self with itself obeys dimly discernible spiritual laws. I say "dimly discernible" because *the self as subject is always the one doing the discerning!* Therefore, its observations of the laws themselves occur according to the laws. In other words, the fragmentation of personality happens lawfully, but even our descriptions of these laws are fragmentary. We know in part, and we prophesy in part. The poets and prophets have discerned the ways in which the self either loses touch with or gets in touch with itself. With profound sensitivity and laconic wisdom, they have described how fearfully and wonderfully we are made and have observed how deceitful is the human heart. The psychologists of personality have, with the help of empirically devised methodology, sought to classify and codify these spiritual laws of the dynamic self. These research men have identified such laws as "mechanisms" or "dynamisms" of personality. An extensive and detailed study, for example, is found in the book by William Healy, Augusta F. Bronner, and Anna Mae Bowers, *The Structure and Meaning of Psychoanalysis as Related to Personality and Behavior.*[2] Another valuable treatment of the same subject is found in Karl Menninger, *The Human Mind.*[3] Here Menninger classifies this discussion under the subject of "motives." He uses a mechanical figure of speech and says that motives are the "sources and distribution of the power that drives the machine." Another discussion of the laws of which we have been speaking here is found in Chapter 8 of the book by Donald Snygg and Arthur W. Combs entitled *Individual Behavior: A New Frame of Reference for Psychology.*[4]

One may ask: "Why do you call these spiritual laws?" In these formulations of contemporary psychologists we find the kind of wisdom of the serpents necessary for all true discipleship. In addition to the sturdy theological tests of the spirit set forth in

I John, we have in these laws operational hypotheses for trying the spirits that prompt men to say and do many of the things they do. When these seemingly negative statements of spiritual laws are applied with the full thrust of honesty and love which the Holy Spirit "sheds abroad" in the human life, they become the laws whereby we confess our faults one to another and enter the reconciliation characteristic of the forgiving fellowship of Christians. For, as II Timothy says: "God hath not given us a spirit of fear, but of power and of love and of a sound mind." [5] These psychologists perceive the phenomenal self as being constantly under the threat of divisive inconsistencies. They interpret these laws of personality under the concept of "techniques of dealing with threat." Harry Stack Sullivan deals with this same set of laws under his concept of "the Theorem of Escape" and the definite inventions which he calls "security operations." This is found in his book, *The Interpersonal Theory of Psychiatry*. [6]

Two basic principles of personality organization and functioning must be understood for any clear appreciation of the dynamics of personality. The first one is *regression*. This principle is contingent upon the process of development in personality. It refers to that process whereby a person returns to an earlier stage of satisfaction, security, and development when put under the pressures of a more adult demand of life. When this happens, various types of reaction may occur, such as will be discussed in the description of different dynamisms of personality. For instance, the person may make up for the difference between the stage of maturity to which he regressed and that which is demanded of him by his interpersonal field of relationships by rationalization, a reaction-formation, or other behavior.

The next concept which is prerequisite to understanding the dynamics of personality is that of *fixation*. As Karl Menninger puts it, "Instead of normal or super-normal progress . . . the action may be interrupted. . . . The play never moves on . . .

and . . . same acts are repeated over and over with slight changes." [7] Instead of returning to an earlier stage, in the instance of fixation, the personality never leaves a given stage of emotional maturation, but remains there. As the individual becomes chronologically older, he more and more often responds to the maturing demands of life with first one and then the other of the dynamisms which we shall discuss shortly.

Both these concepts are potentially relevant to our understanding of the religious dimensions of personality. For instance, earlier, intuitive theological insights into personality have formulated various ways of describing "backsliding" in the spiritual pilgrimage of a person. Furthermore, they have symbolically discussed immature expressions of religion in terms of the mold of maturity and perfection which is set for man's becoming. The following discussion of the dynamic laws of the spiritual life of man becomes more and more abstract apart from an understanding of regression and progression. Here we are handling formulations of modern psychologists which have been generally accepted by psychologists of personality. They are mechanisms of self-enhancement and self-defense. They have become a part of everyday conversation and are dependably called "laws," "hypotheses," or "theorems" of personality in action.

A DESCRIPTION OF SOME OF THE SPIRITUAL LAWS

The Law of Identification

Identification is an unconscious relationship of positive feeling of one individual for another, in such a way that the "ego of the one becomes like the other, one which results in the first ego behaving itself . . . in the same way as the second; it imitates it, and as it were, takes it into itself." [8] This is not a conscious process of imitation, but one which goes on through the unconscious attachment of the energies of a growing person to another.

Identification and personality development. The first appearance of this dynamism in actual life is in the feeding experience of the child. The mother first imprints his character. The second phase of this identification is in the development of a child's aggressive and passive traits in which he becomes civilized in ratio to the "civilization" of his parents. But the most important phase of identification in personality development, according to Freud, is during the Oedipal period of life. The individual takes into himself the masculine or feminine characteristics of the parent with whom he identifies. Normally, he adopts the role and gender of the parent of his same sex. If he is not able to do this safely by reason of the fear between him and the parent of the same sex, he is likely to develop an inverted conception of himself as to gender. This makes sexual adjustments in adolescence exceedingly difficult.

As has already been said, identification is primarily unconscious and works in terms of love or fear. It is not a conscious process wrought out in oral transmission and/or moralistic instruction. The intuitive depths of the parent-child relationship provide the nourishment or present the deprivation out of which the selfhood of the individual is made. The child learns, for instance, to curb his aggressions in order to keep from feeling alienated from his parents; he absorbs their character traits as it were in his mother's milk and his father's pipe smoke. This is the child's natural way of learning what the real world is like.

From a religious point of view, these early identifications are the first experiences a child has with an object of worship. As Freud says: "When we were little children, we knew these higher natures, we admired them and feared them; and later took them into ourselves." [9] Anton Boisen reverses the interpretation of Sigmund Freud. He says that the parents draw their own reality as "higher beings" from God rather than God being dependent upon man for his projection of himself into human life. Likewise, Ruel Howe in discussing man's need and God's action, speaks of the "language of relationships" and underscores the profoundly interpersonal character of the communication of God to the child through the parent. This is not to say that God *necessarily* works through parents. God is capable of dealing autonomously with the individual soul even apart from his parents. To describe God's usual way of acting is not to set limits upon what he can and cannot do. However, God *ordinarily* manifests himself to children through the intimate encounters of the parent-child relationship. The law of identification, therefore becomes the first rudiment of worship. Walt Whitman expresses this idea in his poem, "There Was a Child Went Forth":

> There was a child went forth every day,
> And the first object he looked upon and received with
>   wonder, pity, love or dread, that object he became,
> And that object became part of him for the day or a
>   certain part of the day, or for many years, or
>   stretching cycles of the years . . .
>
> His own parents
> He that fathered him, and she that conceived him in her
>   womb and nursed him,
> They gave this child more of themselves than that, they
>   gave him afterward every day—they and of them
>   became part of him . . . These became part of their
>   child who went forth every day, and who now goes and
>   will always go forth every day.

Identification, worship, and idolatry. The process of identification lies at the heart of the worship experience. The character of the individual becomes like the object of its admiration. In a sense, "we are changed from glory unto glory" into the same image of the object of our worship (II Corinthians 3:18). The admired ideal of our God is incorporated into our behavior patterns. A look at the process of identification from a theological point of view reveals the dynamics of the principle of incarnation. This is not simply an extraneous spirit entering into a capturing body. Far from it. It is a whole personality being transformed into the same likeness. Every Christian loves Christ as his ideal and feels himself united with other Christians by the tie of identification. This is a normative view of the social function of religion which leads to an understanding of the importance of religious leadership in the molding of the character of society. For instance, in education the law of identification accentuates the futility of abstract, legalistic, oral transmission as a means of changing personality. This is like giving a hungry man a menu or passing out recipes during a famine. This not only does not feed people's spirit; it also increases their symptoms! The hailstones of crystallized theological dogma, to change the figure, can bounce off the tops of people's minds and never water the depths of the spirit that are musty from having been closed off. The mere inscription of intellectual formulations in the people's thinking may or may not enter the vast unconscious areas of their basic identifications. Through a fundamental identification of people with a dependable and trustworthy leadership, lives are changed, guilts removed, and powers released for creative work.

But, on the other side of the ledger, the law of identification also gives us an empirical basis for understanding the dynamics of idolatry. The autonomous self hits the limits of its growth quickly when one chooses a restricted, finite, creature as the ultimate center of his identification. The worship of the creature is exchanged for the worship of the creator. The Reformation insistence upon the sovereignty of God becomes intensely relevant to the dignity and maturity of the human person. Said John Calvin, "Whatever belongs to the Deity, should not be transferred to another. This shows how pure religion differs from idolatry." [10] But long before this Jesus said, "Call no man your father on earth, for you have one Father, who is in heaven" (Matthew 23:9). In the same context, he disparaged overidentification with rabbis, masters, and the like. The experience of redemption, release, often amounting to radical regeneration of adult lives, normally involves the "casting down" of every "high thing" that exalts itself against the knowledge of God. Many fixated relationships have to be broken and re-established as "brother-to-brother" rather than idol-slave relationships. Religious conversion should always include this "calling from the idols."

THE LAW OF REPRESSION

"The essence of repression lies simply in the function of rejecting and keeping something out of consciousness." [11] Repression also is an unconscious process, "very different from a conscious condemning judgment." It is the prevention of an idea or an impulse to act in a certain way from becoming conscious and not a known restraint of an act itself. This is a master dynamism of personality. All the other dynamisms are related to it. For instance, the positive identification of a growing person with another admired person calls for the exclusion of certain acts and thoughts from consciousness and behavior. These are held out of consciousness through repression. Harry Stack Sullivan uses a kindred but different way of describing the same reality. He emphasizes the fact that much of human experience and behavior occurs outside self-awareness. Some of these occurrences can very easily become the object of careful awareness. They may be called to our attention by a friend who points them out to us. Such processes are said to be "selectively inattended." They can be accepted by the self when called to attention. But other processes, when they are called to our attention, we deny vigorously. We may become tense and angry at the efforts of others to reveal them to us. We do not usually recall them under any circumstance. Sullivan names this process "disassociation." [12] This happens in all kinds of people. It may but does not necessarily refer to a pathological process.

Repression and moral judgments. The ethical and religious dimensions of repression are far reaching. Repression is something different from a moral judgment. Much loose talk has maintained that repression is at the root of every ethical consideration, that there is no such thing as rationality in moral behavior. Such surmising cuts the fact of discriminatory moral judgment out of the realm of ethics, and implies that there is no such thing as moral responsibility. But usually this is a popular distortion of the basic conception of repression. J. A. Hadfield would say that when the "complexes are recognized and are conscientiously inhibited from expression in conduct, we call it restraint; . . . when the process of inhibition is unconscious, we call it repression." [13] Also, William Ernest Hocking draws the same distinction between compulsive obedience and voluntary self-control.[14]

Hadfield differentiates between sin and moral disease in terms of the law of repression. The man who does a thing deliberately, as the Hebrews put it, with a "high hand," is said to be a sinner. The man who does the same thing not having rational and responsible control over himself is said to be morally diseased. The difference lies in the element of compulsion and repression involved. The noted English physician made this differentiation because he observed that the "sinner" is ordinarily otherwise healthy, whereas the morally diseased person is otherwise incapacitated and in need of a doctor. Hadfield's analysis lacks depth, however, in that it overlooks the integral relationship between conscious and unconscious motivation. His hypothesis is valuable and practical in everyday dealings with people, especially in the tempering of penal attitudes with a distinctly pastoral perception of people's motives. To say that all we can go by in judging people's behavior is their conscious, expressed motives is to take a distinctly pharisaical position in relation to morality. And one of the great contributions of the depth psychotherapists has been in the realm of ethical discernment of the motives for human behavior. This is in line with the wisdom of Jesus in shifting away from externalism to internalism in the ethical view of life.

Repression and repentance. Repression, furthermore, when seen in a theological context, involves some specific relevance for the doctrine of repentance. Repentance has too often been preached as a conscious condemnation of the self. Prayer in such a shallow view of personality becomes simply a "putting of one's best moral foot forward" and the deification of the distortions of a conglomerately put-together conscience. The end result of this is the deification of human will power. Changing one's own behavior calls for exploring the deeper reasons for one's behavior. This issues in self-affirmation as a basis of personality change. Repentance is taken out of this legalistic trap by an understanding of repression.

Repentance begins with an experience of worship in which the person's spiritual sight is dilated. The light of God's truth is allowed to come through in its fullest possible expression. Through self-searching, one gains insight into himself. Repentance continues as a person accepts himself in the light of the insight he has received. The process verges upon the experience of forgiveness as the person realizes that God also accepts him as he is. The middle wall of partition which alienates a person from himself is repression. It is broken down through insight into one's self as a sinner, acceptance of one's self as a sinner, and a thrusting of the self upon the grace of God. The middle wall of partition that separates man from God is his elevation of the self that he knows against and above God. Karl Menninger evaluates prayer in the light of this process of repentance when he says that prayer can be a healthy, psychotherapeutic experience when it enables "strong, practicing believers to verbalize certain conscious introspective reflections and half conscious wishes under circumstances of intimacy and faith which rarely prevail in interpersonal relationships." [15]

Repentance, then, is epitomized in the prayer of the psalmist when he prayed: "Behold, thou desirest truth in the inward being; therefore teach me wisdom in my secret heart" (Psalm

51:6). Snygg and Combs, along with Carl Rogers, have re-emphasized the fact that the self does not really change when it merely conforms outwardly. When enough of the threat to the self-structure is absent, the self is enabled to experience "those things which are inconsistent with it, examine them, and revise the structure of the self to include such experiences." [16] This element of threat is removed in the climate of an accepting and nonthreatening relationship. Acceptance does not mean self-condonement, nor does it mean self-condemnation. It means seeing oneself as he really is and admitting that this is so! When a person can see himself as he really is, and make some decisions, he thereby transcends himself as he is. W. D. Chamberlain says that repentance is a mental metamorphosis in which a person accepts the realities of his inner self as true.[17] He sees himself in a new relationship to the Father. The self is transformed by a renewing of the mind (Romans 12:1 ff).

The Law of Sublimation

The process of insight reveals to a person selectively inattended and dissociated portions of his selfhood. These have been buried in a field of the negativity of life. This is what Angyal means by bionegativity. These unassimilated masses of experience must be meaningfully reintegrated into the whole of life somehow or other. Sublimation is one of the laws whereby this takes place. Freud defines sublimation as "a process that concerns the object-libido and consists in the instinct's directing itself toward an aim other than, and remote from, that of sexual (or aggressive) gratification." [18] In a word, sublimation is the *deflection* of a need from its natural aim. Here Freud's fundamental biological orientation is brought to light. He distinguishes between natural and artificial aims. The natural aim of any impulse would be immediate satisfaction; the artificial aim would be a delayed and differentiated satisfaction, somewhat deflected from the original aim. Lester F. Ward suggestively interprets this distinction:

> The dynamics of society is, in the main, the antithesis of the dynamics of animal life. The psychic element . . . supplants nature by art. If we call the biological processes natural, we must call the social processes artificial.[19]

This process estimates social aims above essentially hedonistic aims of immediate satisfaction. Society in a sense is a threat to the omnipotent desires of the individual. It is always deflecting the aim of the individual into conformity with the larger social needs of the community. Likewise, the longer-term purposes of the total life of the individual calls for a deferring of satisfaction and the exchange of short-term values for long-term values.

This is basically what was meant by the original statement of the law of sublimation. However, popular coinage of this concept or law has used this insight to reinforce ascetic views of life. Therefore, the concept of sublimation has trickled into the tributaries of religious psychology. Sublimation has too often been interpreted as a way of palliating the tremendous desires of adolescents whose sexual needs are being delayed from satisfaction. The highly competitive, professional-minded culture of which they are a part requires educational goals for them far beyond the time of their biological maturity.

To the contrary, sublimation is literally the socially acceptable expression of a basic desire rather than the total negation of it. For instance, the hostile aggressions of a religious group may become obvious in the tremendous zeal with which they build a building or conduct a prohibition campaign. Likewise, many basically destructive needs of a given personality, when disciplined and controlled in guided expression, become creative and useful to society. Freud makes the point that art, vocation, and religion as well as other manifestations of civilization are sublimated and refined expressions of what would otherwise be chaotic influences in society. For instance, a knife in the hand of a murderer is a very different thing from the knife in the hand of a surgeon. And yet, both of them are cutting operations.

The whole concept of sublimation as a law of personality has been challenged by some more recent investigation. Kinsey and his associates, upon the basis of their studies of the sexual behavior of the human male, concluded that it "still remains to be determined" whether or not sublimation is a valued law of personality or whether in the process of sublimation "nervous energy is shunted from one to another portion of the nervous system." [20] They further say that sublimation is "so subtle or so rare, as to constitute an academic possibility rather than a demonstrated actuality." [21] In fact, the hypothesis of sublimation has been the most popularly used law of personality as formulated by the depth psychotherapists, and at the same time it is the least definable and most deceptive in its application.

The Law of Reaction-Formation or Reversed Formation

This is that process whereby "psychic counter forces (feelings of reaction) . . . build up . . . psychical dams of disgust, shame and morality." [22] This is actually a "reversal of an impulse into its opposite." The polarities of personality are called into play here: If one side of the polarity, such as love, is completely repressed, failure of the repression is seen in the reversal of love into its opposite, namely, hate. The mother who has a profound sense of rejection for her child which she dares not face consciously reacts against this with an overweening overprotectiveness. The bizarre Don Juan is severely reacting against his uneasy feeling that maybe he is not really masculine after all. The term overcompensation, used by other psychologists, is apparently synonymous with the term reaction-formation.

Reaction-formation and pharisaism. The religious significance of this law of a reversed affect is profound. To state this law in biblical terms, the reaction-formation is the "whited sepulchre" reaction of pharisaism. Jesus stated the mechanism well when he said that the Pharisees may "clean the outside of the cup and of the platter, but within are full of extortion and excess" (Matthew 23:25). He also noted the compulsive reformer tendencies of those who "compass sea and land to make one proselyte" and when he is made they "make him twofold more the child of hell than" themselves (Matthew 23:15). Paul Scherer is undoubtedly aware of this law of the spirit when he says:

> There are those who find in hyper-orthodoxy an escape from the relentless ethical demands of this troublesome Christ. Whatever else the mind is, it is a highly formidable piece of compensating machinery. All moralists in the pulpit and out of it should make a diligent note of that.[23]

In the more obvious pathological states of the psychoneuroses, the reaction-formation seems to be one of the maintaining mechanisms of the compulsive obsession. For instance, handwashing compulsions signify reaction-formation against unconscious feelings of uncleanness; the *extreme* care in cleanliness, orderliness, and stinginess may well represent a reaction-formation against great quantities of aggression. The religious worker confronts the less specific form in the hyperreligiosity of the fanatic.

The Law of Projection

Projection is the law whereby an unbearable impulse is externalized in order to protect the self from pain. An internal perception is suppressed; its content undergoes a certain degree of distortion; it enters into consciousness as if it had come from outside the self. This is a thrusting forth, or a projection, of a feeling into the environment. What should have been felt internally is perceived externally.

Freud pointed out that the delusional misrepresentation of reality found in the persecutory reaction toward life of the paranoid schizophrenic person moves on the basis of the law of projection. But it appears not only in paranoid reactions to life, but in all normal people's psychological condition also. Three examples of this law in operation appear regularly in religious experience:

Projection and moral condemnation. Moralistic judgments are often predominated by projection. The person doing the judging, rather than seeing the mote in his own eye sees it magnified into a beam in his neighbor's eye. Judgment has its roots in personal bias and begins in the unconscious repressions of the critic. This seems to be the depth dimension of Jesus' words: "Judge not, that ye be not judged, for with what judgment ye judge, ye shall be judged; with what measure ye mete, it shall be measured to you again" (Matthew 7:1, 2). For instance, preaching by its very nature is autobiographical, and should by definition be a profound witness of the preacher to his people.

By the same token, preaching is a "morally perilous vocation," as Richard Niebuhr and his associates have said. It is morally perilous for the very reason that the preaching prophet tends to address himself to the problems of his people which are at the same time most real to him. Consequently, the quicksands of projection are ever a peril to the preacher. This is why the emotionally healthy prophet is distinguished from the emotionally sick prophet, Anton Boisen says, by the dimension of humility which arises from the healthy prophet's awareness that he "prophesies in part." Likewise, in all hypercriticism, the critic needs to be aware of the injunction of the apostle Paul which gathers up the law of projection in a biblical statement:

> Brethren, if a man is overtaken in any trespass, you who are spiritual should restore him in a spirit of gentleness. Look to yourself, lest you too be tempted.[24]

Projection and religious delusions. Still another manifestation of the law of projection is to be observed in the religious life, apparent in the projection of unbearable responsibility upon God. The bereaved person, faced with the necessity of accepting the inevitable reality of death, thrusts the responsibility for "taking" their loved one upon God. As one parent of a college student said when the girl died suddenly and unexpectedly, "If that's the kind of God you have, to hell with him! No God is fit to be God who would take a beautiful person like my daughter!" For fifteen years this man has carried a "grudge against God" for the death of his daughter. Another example is taken from the experience of a college student struggling with a severe temptation. When he succumbed to the temptation, he said, "Why would God let me do such a thing as this? I asked him to keep me from it."

Projection and the fear of homosexuality. Psychotherapists note a third expression of the law of projection in religious living evident in the sense of horror with which a college campus and a church fellowship can react with self-righteous indignation when a student or member is accused of homosexuality. The contemporary drama, *Tea and Sympathy,* portrays this without the religious connotations associated with the phenomenon. Not only did Freud associate the law of projection with the paranoid reaction to life, but he also correlated the high incidence of repressed or latent homosexual feelings in paranoid behavior and attitudes. Suspicion, jealousy, envy, backbiting, railings, and interpersonal panic within political and religious life often become tainted with accusations of this particularly tabooed behavior. All the doubts of adequacy of a whole community can be heaped upon the victim of such accusations, alleged or true. So much is this true that the occasion for the Group for the Advancement of Psychiatry study of homosexuality was in connection with the tension within the governmental agencies over accused and convicted cases of homosexuality.

The Law of Symbolization

Symbolization is "an unconscious process built upon association and similarity whereby one object comes to represent or stand for (symbolize) another object, through some part, quality, or aspect which the two have in common. But the essence of symbolization is in the displacement of emotional values from one object to another." [25]

Symbolization and personality development. Symbolization has its most obvious expression in the miracles of human language. The child soon learns that he can establish relationship with others by symbolizing his feelings in communication. As Harry Stack Sullivan says, "For all practical purposes all human behavior so purely and unquestionably manifests the organization of experiences into what are in effect signs—whether signals or symbols. . . ." [26] The naming of persons and objects, even as is symbolized in the dramatic story of Adam's naming of the different forms of creation in the presence of God, is one of the processes whereby the external and internal world of the individual and his field of interpersonal relationships become one.

Even more deeply than this, the naming of oneself as being this, that, or the other kind of person by reason of the agreed-upon evaluations of oneself given to him by those whose approval he considers most worth while becomes one's way of symbolizing the whole of his being. This is poignantly set forth in the experience of Thomas Wolfe. Once again we turn to him for insight into our basic meanings:

> I think I learned about being alone when I was a child about eight years old and I think I have known about it ever since. People, I think, mean well by children but are often cruel because of something insensitive or cruel in their own natures which they cannot help. It is not a good thing, however, for older people to tell a little child that he is selfish, unnatural and inferior . . . because a child is small and helpless and has no defense, although he is no worse than other children, and in fact is as full of affection, love, and good will as anyone could be, he may in time come to believe the things which are told him about himself, and that is when he begins to live alone and wants to be alone and if possible to get far, far away from the people who have told him how much better they are than he is. I can truthfully and sincerely say that I have no bitterness and nothing but pity for anyone who ever did that, but I can also say that the habit of loneliness, once formed,

grows on a man from year to year and he wanders across the face of the earth and has no home and is an exile, and he is never able to break out of the prison of his own loneliness again, no matter how much he wants to.[27]

The symbol, the name, which one "in time comes to believe" as being a picture of himself, therefore, is of lasting importance.

Symbolization and dreams. However, the less conscious aspects of symbolization are even more important than those we have just discussed. These appear most often in the dream life of an individual. The processes of repression, or selective inattention and dissociation, are often circumvented in the symbol-making experience of dreams. This is one of the reasons that Freud called dreams the "royal road to the unconscious." However, we do not need to depend upon Freud for the awareness of the depth and importance of dreams. As Erich Fromm observes, myths and dreams were among the most significant expressions of the mind of the people of the past, living in the great cultures of both East and West.[28]

Albert Meiburg has effectively demonstrated that an understanding of the dream as a means of self-revelation and divine revelation is part and parcel of the biblical revelation of God to man and that "symbolism is the special language of dreams. It is a picture language. . . . The symbols appear in twelve of seventeen dreams recorded in the Old Testament and these symbols embody themes which run throughout the Bible and are not restricted to the dream." [29] Man's defenses are so cleverly erected against insight into the meaning and purpose of God for his life, and his own needs for rebellion are so consistently maintained in his waking life that the only way God can get through to him is when he is asleep! Even then the messages of self-revelation, calling for a reordering of life, are masked in symbols.

Symbolization and prophetic acts. Lowered respect for the meaning of symbolism has been especially apparent in the process of abstraction through which religious experience crystallizes into theological dogma. Man attempts to turn his encounter with God into a science, known as theology, and tries to get away from symbols. All the time, nevertheless, he is simply pushed from one level of abstraction to another in symbolic expression. A time comes in the attempt to articulate and communicate our deepest experiences of God, however, that we can only point with the outstretched finger and with a hand over the hushed mouth, as Korzybski has so aptly said.

Probably the most necessary thing to say about symbolization, however, is that feelings, attitudes, and attentions which cannot be consciously expressed and for which no words can be found to describe, are often symbolized in acts. This is what I have chosen to call *symbolic acts*. The delinquent child, for instance, acts out his feelings, even as does his more socially acceptable playmate. Instead of *saying* something, even in a masked symbol, he *does* something.

The psychoanalysts have interpreted the otherwise meaningless behavior of the acutely disturbed person in handwashing compulsions, hysterical blindness, hysterical tremors, and much of the "organ language" of disease as symbolic expressions of the deepest and most dissociated portions of the real self of the patient. Freud even called them *private religious rituals*. That which one cannot say, not even to himself, is acted out blindly in the illness. Therefore, an over-all understanding of strange behavior requires a knowledge of the total patterning of the life style of the person. One needs to ask in all these instances: What is he trying to say with this behavior?

The communicative power of expressive signs, actions, and objects, has been thoroughly studied and depicted in the writing and photography of Jurgen Ruesch and Weldon Kees in their fascinating study, *Nonverbal Communication*.[30] They build their studies on the easily demonstrable assumption that a great deal of living is not objectively observable and cannot be put into words without much unnecessary complication of life's immediacy and meaning. This important dimension of life goes on without words. Hence, they magnify the importance of the unmediated communication of such experiences as movement, posture, clothing, grouping, and hundreds of other cues for perception of meaning and relationship. The way in which photography, television, movies, and the pictorial newspaper and magazine have taken over in the field of mass communication makes the teaching and learning of reading and writing, for instance, much less necessary, therefore, and much more difficult than previously.

In times of great social repression under authoritarian dictatorships, nonverbal communication of sign, symbol, and motion become all the more necessary for the deeper spiritual communion of people. This is one of the reasons that the Bible is so difficult for unimaginative and abstract-minded people to understand. Much of it was written under the stress of persecution and its writers could be beheaded, crucified, thrown to the gladiatorial lions, or at best exiled for what they wrote. Therefore, the prophetic meanings had to be symbolized, gestured, acted out, dramatized.

Long before life was punily segmented into "normal" and "abnormal," into "sacred" and "secular," and when all life was seen as a whole, the prophets of eighth century Hebrew life found it necessary to communicate their message through symbolic acts. These symbolic acts were at the heart of a prophetic nature.

For example, Jeremiah bought a potter's earthen bottle and took some of the elders of the people and of the elders of the priests and went to the Valley of Hinnom. There he broke the bottle in the sight of the men who went with him and said unto them, "Thus saith Jehovah of hosts: Even so will I break this people and this city as one breaketh a potter's vessel, that cannot be made whole again; and they shall bury them in Tophet, till there be no place to bury" (Jeremiah 19:10-11). Furthermore, through the symbolic act of buying a field, Jeremiah communicated the hope of the God of Israel to his people. He bought a field from Hanameel, subscribed the deed, sealed it, called the witnesses, weighed the money in the balances. He took the deed of purchase and delivered it unto Baruch in the presence of many witnesses. In doing so, he said: "For thus saith Jehovah of hosts, the God of Israel; houses and fields and vineyards shall yet again be bought in this land" (Jeremiah 32:9-15).

In the New Testament a similar symbolization of a prophecy is found in the story of a "certain prophet, named Agabus." The whole Christian community felt the great peril which the apostle Paul was facing in going to Jerusalem. They knew that he would fall into the hands of his enemies. Agabus felt the concern of the whole community and symbolized it in a dramatic act. He took Paul's girdle, and bound his own feet and hands and said: "Thus saith the Holy Spirit, so shall the Jews at Jerusalem bind the man that owneth this girdle, and shall deliver him into the hands of the Gentiles" (Acts 21:11). This, like other examples which can be multiplied one upon the other, depicts the role of symbolic acts in the communication of religious experience. We can find illustrations of it in contemporary life, but they are much rarer than they should be.

Contemporary religious groups are much more prone to prepare a resolution, appoint a committee, start a discussion group, or prepare a three-point sermon to be delivered at 11:00 o'clock on a certain day! However, a certain white minister in a small Tennessee town in which the white population had forbidden the Negro population to send their children to the local high school, chose to symbolize his feeling and prophetic vision in the whole situation by going into the Negro community and walking with the children to the high school. After having done so, he was accosted by a mob and given a beating. The editor of the town newspaper said that the situation had gotten beyond the point that words would do any good. Some act had to say it.

He said that the minister's action did it. The editor felt that this was the point of the turning of the tide from anarchy to a spiritually lawful way of handling the problem.

Rationalization as a Spiritual Law

The heart may have reasons that the mind knows not of, as Pascal has said. However, if this is true, the mind will think of some reasons. As someone has said, the human being is the most reasonable creature there is; he can think of a reason for anything he wants to do! These are rationalizations. Rationalization may be described as that process whereby the self selects those aspects of any given situation which are self-enhancing and ignores those which are not. Snygg and Combs give an example:

> He finds "good" reasons for the "real" reasons for his behavior. For instance, a woman goes shopping and finds two dresses in which she would be very attractive. She buys both dresses and thus achieves an enhancement of the self. When friends remark, "Oh, you bought *two* dresses," this may represent a threat to her concept of herself as thrifty and our shopper replies, "They are such a bargain, I couldn't resist them." Thus she achieves not only a disillusion of the threat but even an enhancement of the self as a thrifty shopper who knows how to take advantage of a bargain.[31]

Examples of rationalizations may be found on every side. A man buys a new car and says that the old one was beginning to use too much oil. To admit that he is comparing an $1800 investment with the necessity of buying 30 quarts of oil in a year's time would cause him to appear as an improvident and squandering person. The threat to his concept of himself as a smart businessman is too great. He rationalizes. Rationalization is the necessity everyone feels to have what may be called a theory of life, and particularly a theory of himself. It is actually our reality need to maintain self-consistency at any price. In the biblical account, we see the Pharisees "justifying" themselves. The lawyer who stood up to test Jesus, asking him what he should do to inherit

eternal life, answered Jesus' question with the twofold statement of the law of God, to love God and neighbor. When Jesus
commended him upon giving the right answer, he still "desiring
to justify himself" said to Jesus, "And who is my neighbor?" Then
Jesus told the story of the Good Samaritan (Luke 10:25 ff).

The legal catacombs through which religious conversations
often go represent vividly the processes of rationalization in religious experience. John Baillie, sensing the relationship of the
law of rationalization to men's failure to receive the revelations
God has for them, says:

> We are never such skilled logicians as when we are trying to find
> reasons for doing the things we want to do. We are never such elo-
> quent orators as when we are telling ourselves why we should not
> do the things we do not want to do. . . . How Sigmund Freud hu-
> miliated (and offended) us when he first began telling us that our
> subconscious rationalization of our prejudices far surpasses in elabo-
> ration the conscious use of our reason in the discovery of the truth.[32]

THE SPIRITUAL LAWS OF PERSONALITY
AND ENCOUNTER WITH GOD

The preceding list of some of the spiritual laws of personality is
incomplete. Purposefully the word "some" has been used. Many
other definitions of the devious workings of the human personality could be named, such as isolation, undoing, idealization,
condensation. However, these laws have been selected as most
illustrative. They have remarkable relevance for the interpretation of religion and personality. An over-all, comprehensive perspective of the religious dimensions of these empirically described laws of the inner communication of the self is in order
at this point. Some will raise the question as to why I have named
them "spiritual" laws. The word "spiritual" in the popular mind
has a "good" connotation. Many of these laws seem to be descriptions of what is not necessarily complimentary to human nature

and certainly not "good" in the moralistic sense of the word. This choice of words has been purposeful, however, and with the plain intention of underscoring the fact that even a demonic spirit is "spiritual" and that these laws, also, are no respecters of the just and the unjust. They are like the rain!

True and False Revelation

This points up the imperative necessity that the religious person "test the spirits" to see whether they are of God or not, for many false prophets are in the world. Contemporary psychological descriptions of the laws of self-enhancement, self-defense, and self-adjustment are indispensable tools in the hands of the religiously perceptive person. They may be instruments for evaluating the validity of many different kinds of experience, particularly intimately personal religious experiences. They may be methods of "testing the spirits" as to whether one is being moved toward or away from reality, as to whether or not one is being internally honest, or whether some important insight is being held out of the ken of consciousness and spiritual responsibility.

Every virtue espoused by religion has its counterfeit in the everyday life of so-called normal people. Its grotesque caricatures appear in the compulsions, obsessions, and delusions which plague the existence of man. Every prophecy from God can be counterfeited and made a time server for uncrucified, unredeemed, and unresurrected motives of men. The uneasy feeling dawns upon us that contemporary psychotherapists have discussed the dynamics or mechanisms of personality in ways that sound disturbingly like our theological discussions of revelation. David Roberts, out of the depths of his own personal experiences of revelation in psychotherapy, said,

> The structure of reality links misery and conflict to man's failure to reach a position where he can affirm his *whole* self; and it links beatitude to honesty and wholeness.[33]

Some theologians seem threatened when we say that there is a possibility of revelation of God throughout human experience as man seeks to get in touch with the buried and dissociated portions of his real selfhood. But, as Roberts infers, this could well be God working in us both to will and to do his own good pleasure and to reveal himself to us. Daniel Day Williams, in his discussion of revelation, observes very aptly, "Revelation . . . always comes to particular men in particular situations in history. It does not come as an abstract and universal truth out of history." [34] John Baillie puts it more pointedly when he says.

> It is clearly absurd to be pining for some grand revelation of God's will while we are refusing to attend to this or that small beginning of a revelation that is already unmistakably before us. It may only be "something telling me," as we say, that I am not using my money as I ought—not holding it in stewardship. It may be a recurrent doubt about the strict honesty of some habitual practice. It may be an uncomfortable feeling about a certain indulgence I have been allowing myself. It may even be a secret knowledge that my support of a particular political party or a particular system of philosophy has been grounded in motives of self-interest rather than honest conviction. I would *like* this or this to be true, and therefore I have been trying to persuade myself that it *is* true, instead of listening to the Truth and allowing it (or shall we not say Him— Him who is the Truth) to persuade me. It will perhaps cause no surprise if I confess that in the case of one such as myself, who have published books, one of the things that prevents me from listening to the Truth is my reluctance to revise opinions to which I have already committed myself in print.[35]

Subjectivity, Objectivity, and Revelation

The psychological study of the spiritual laws of personality is itself subject to distortion. Total objectivity of observation is impossible. The psychologist and theologian both are under and subject to the same laws they espouse. Therefore, *our descriptions* of the laws of the human self are colored by our own subjection to these laws. The knowledge of projection, rationalization, and the like *may* become an "avoidance procedure" in and of itself. Everything anyone does may become a "symptom of something else," and the self may never really "take a stand" with itself at any point. The person never says with decisive certitude: "This is who I really am, and I am going to act on this appraisal at this time until more light comes." In other words, the verbal formulation of the laws of personality *may* become "psychological swear-words" with which to avoid insight, protect a flimsy selfhood, and maintain an infantile state of irresponsibility. Fear-ridden, we erect defenses against the violent reordering of life required by the truth spoken from within and without in love. We "flee Him down the labyrinthine ways of the mind," and cast ourselves down with exhaustion as did Francis Thompson, as the objective reality of God hews our psychological "harness from us, piece by piece." And we cease to sabotage ourselves with subjectivity.

This sabotaging self-defeat is, it seems to me, the only possible final result of the naturalistic search to explain *everything* causally. The thrust of omnipotence in such an assumption is unmistakably present. Each leap of the mind becomes more and more of a "squirrel cage" of futility. Karl Barth describes such a situation:

> Here man obviously wants to get behind God, behind God as he really shows and gives Himself, and therefore behind what He is . . . it is a matter of making God an object . . . divine objectivity is absorbed by the human inquiring after a God who does not exist. Here also man finds himself, this time *via* mysticism, alone with himself in the end, in his own world.[36]

But when man begins to search beyond himself for the validity of his self-revelations, he does not necessarily arrive at the conclusion that they come from God. They may be felt to be quite objective but to have originated with Satan, and thereby to be rejected as evil. One of the most common deceptions of ourselves is to project our own unacceptable impulses upon the devil and thereby not of ourselves. Here objectivity becomes objectification of a portion of ourselves, the "not-me," as Sullivan calls it. But, as John Calvin again expresses it,

> The blinding of the wicked, and all the iniquities consequent upon it, are called the works of Satan, *the course of which is not to be sought in anything external to the will of man, in which the root of evil lies, and in which the foundation of Satan's kingdom, in other words, sin, is fixed.*[37]

On the other hand, my previous remarks that hidden revelations from the depths of the self may indeed be God himself "working in us," may be interpreted as an equation of the self with God. This is the accusation of immanentism leveled at some mystics who claim that the self is either obliterated and that they are co-equal with God, or that God is seen in pantheistic terms. This is exactly the kind of "headwind" the psychotherapist is always "bucking against" as he confronts the mystery of being in his patients in deeper therapy. This is why some of them are drawn to Oriental forms of mysticism as over against Protestant personalistic understandings of religion and the life of faith.

To the contrary, the search for the ultimate criterion of revelation calls for a concrete, historical, personalized, and objective revelation. The Christian cannot sit supinely and evaluate the *process* of revelation without at the same time defining the *content* of the revelation. The laws of personality functioning cannot be understood without some more comprehensive revelation of the nature of the reality in relation to which all their functioning operates. Otherwise, we are simply exchanging one set of rational categories for another, substituting the content of a particular system of psychotherapy for the older and more tested content of the Christian faith. But if the scribe can bring things both new and old from his good treasure, he is not forced to make this artificial choice. In both instances, as Richard Niebuhr says,

Human reason . . . is not only inadequate because it does not lead to knowledge and truth necessary to salvation; but it is also erroneous and deceptive.[38]

This applies to purely *process* interpretations of revelation and to purely *objective* interpretations as well. Both are rational hypotheses. Erich Fromm undercuts the fallacy of such "managed rationalism" when he says that "complete rational knowledge is possible only of things," not persons.[39] But even the "flower in a crannied wall" defies the fate of man's complete rational comprehension.

The objective content given to the revelation of the "knowledge of God and truth necessary to salvation" in the historical fact of the birth, life, death, burial, and resurrection of Jesus Christ and the coming of the Holy Spirit makes the difference in reality between an erroneous and a dependably true way of salvation. This must be entered as the first proposition of the Christian understanding of the spiritual laws of personality.

NOTES FOR CHAPTER X

1. *The Self and the Dramas of History* (New York: Charles Scribner's Sons, 1955), pp. 6-7.
2. New York: Alfred A. Knopf, Inc., 1938, pp. 192-261.
3. Karl Menninger, *The Human Mind* (New York: Alfred A. Knopf, Inc., 1945), pp. 265-362.
4. New York: Harper & Brothers, 1949.
5. II Timothy, 1:7.
6. New York: W. W. Norton & Company, Inc., 1952, pp. 190-199, 323-343, 346-363, 379-380.
7. Menninger, *op. cit.*, p. 306.
8. Sigmund Freud, *New Introductory Lectures on Psychoanalysis*, trans. W. H. J. Sprott (London: Hogarth Press, 1933), p. 90.
9. Sigmund Freud, *The Ego and the Id* (London: Hogarth Press, 1947), p. 47.
10. John Calvin, *The Institutes*, Book I, Ch. XII, 6th ed., trans. John Allen, Vol. I (Philadelphia: Presbyterian Board of Publication, 1902), p. 112.
11. Sigmund Freud, "Repression," (1915), *Collected Papers*, Vol. II (London: Hogarth Press, 1949), p. 86.

12. Patrick Mullahy, *Oedipus: Myth and Complex* (New York: Hermitage Press, 1948), p. 800.
13. J. A. Hadfield, *Psychology and Morals: An Analysis of Character* (New York: R. H. McBride and Company, 1925), p. 32.
14. William E. Hocking, *Human Nature and Its Remaking* (New Haven, Conn.: Yale University Press, 1923), p. 37.
15. Karl Menninger, *Love Against Hate* (New York: Harcourt, Brace & Company, Inc., 1942), p. 201.
16. Carl R. Rogers, *Client-Centered Therapy* (Boston: Houghton Mifflin Company, 1951), p. 517.
17. William D. Chamberlain, *The Meaning of Repentance* (Philadephia: Westminster Press, 1943), p. 37.
18. Sigmund Freud, "On Narcissism: An Introduction" (1941), *Collected Papers*, Vol. IV (London: Hogarth Press, 1949), p. 51.
19. Lester F. Ward, *Psychic Factors of Civilization* (New York: Ginn and Company, 1906), p. 135.
20. A. C. Kinsey, W. B. Pomeroy and C. E. Martin, *Sexual Behavior in the Human Male* (Philadelphia: W. B. Saunders Company, 1948), p. 207.
21. *Ibid.*, p. 213.
22. Sigmund Freud, *Three Contributions to the Theory of Sex,* trans. A. A. Brill (New York: Nervous and Mental Disease Monographs, 1930), p. 625.
23. Paul Scherer, *For We Have This Treasure* (New York: Harper & Brothers, 1944), p. 36.
24. Galatians, 6:1, RSV.
25. Healy, Bronner, and Bowers, *The Structure and Meaning of Psychoanalysis as Related to Personality and Behavior* (New York: Alfred A. Knopf, Inc., 1938), p. 206.
26. Harry Stack Sullivan, *The Interpersonal Theory of Psychiatry,* eds. Helen Swick Perry and Mary Ladd Gawel (New York: W. W. Norton & Company, Inc., 1953), p. 186.
27. *The Letters of Thomas Wolfe,* ed. Elizabeth Nowell (New York: Charles Scribner's Sons, 1956), pp. 370-371.
28. Erich Fromm, *The Forgotten Language* (New York: Rinehart & Company, Inc., 1951), pp. 7-8.
29. Albert Meiburg, *An Understanding of the Dream as a Means of Divine Revelation,* unpublished doctoral dissertation, Southern Baptist Theological Seminary, 1954, pp. 18-19.
30. Jurgen Ruesch and Weldon Kees, *Nonverbal Communication: Notes on the Visual Perception of Human Relations* (Los Angeles: University of California Press, 1956).
31. Donald Snygg and Arthur W. Combs, *Individual Behavior: A New Frame of Reference for Psychology* (New York: Harper & Brothers, 1949), p. 156. Used by permission.
32. John Baillie, *The Idea of Revelation in Recent Thought* (New York: Columbia University Press, 1956), p. 144. Used by permission.
33. David Roberts, *Psychotherapy and a Christian View of Man* (New York: Charles Scribner's Sons, 1950), p. 133.

34. Daniel Day Williams, *What Present-Day Theologians Are Thinking* (New York: Harper & Brothers, 1952), p. 66.
35. John Baillie, *The Idea of Revelation in Recent Thought* (New York: Columbia University Press, 1956). Used by permission.
36. Karl Barth, *The Doctrine of the Word of God* (New York: Charles Scribner's Sons, 1936), p. 439. Used by permission.
37. *The Institutes*, Book II, Ch. IV, Vol. I, p. 266.
38. H. Richard Niebuhr, *Christ and Culture* (New York: Harper & Brothers, 1951), p. 77.
39. Erich Fromm, "Man Is Not a Thing," *Saturday Review of Literature*, March 16, 1957, p. 10.

CHAPTER XI

---◆---

THE SPIRITUAL GOALS
OF MAN'S BECOMING

THE ULTIMATE GOALS TOWARD WHICH man strives, the "hill from whence comes his help," set both the nature and the direction of his search for redemption. These goals create man's understanding of himself and his world. Through self-projection and self-transcendence of his "thrown existence," as Heidegger calls it, man is able to envision relationships and intentions for his life that call him forth on a pilgrimage. This pilgrimage is a way of life for him. Contemporary scientists of personality have reinterpreted the ethical and spiritual ways of life through their research. They have rather unsystematically fallen upon certain ethical goals for mankind. The almost moral connotations of words like "meaning," "direction," "balance," "interpersonal," "maturity," "integration," certainly suggest this.*

For some psychologists these goals represent the humanization and secularization of all that remains necessary of religion. Others feel as Allport does, that "a psychology which impedes understanding of the religious potentialities of man scarcely deserves to be called a logos of the psyche at all."[1] Allport says

* Notes and credits for this chapter begin on page 274.

that these goals, unattainable as they are, nevertheless exert a powerful effect upon present conduct and "direct the course of becoming." [2] To overlook the shaping power of these goals is to shirk responsibility for dealing with what Allport calls the "dynamics of futurity." And, in the words of Nicolas Berdyaev, "the problem of the personality in general becomes that of the personality endowed with a *particular* vocation, with a goal in life, and with the creative power to achieve it." [3] The situation into which one is thrust gives vocation to man. The "city not made with hands" toward which his pilgrimage is set gives calling and requires faith of man. The interaction of vocation, calling, and faith sets the pattern of man ultimately as a person.

THE MAIN GOALS OF MAN'S BECOMING

Meaningfulness as a Spiritual Goal of Man's Becoming

Meaningfulness is a necessary goal of life. It nourishes man's will-to-life and sustains the forward movement of his existence. As Lewin has pointed out, these shape and fashion the behavior of a child. They enrich and hasten his growth. However, various theories of the development of personality are remarkably short on assessing the meaninglessness in the spiritual development of chronologically mature adults.

Adulthood and meaninglessness. One of the glaring differences between our age and that of any other previous age is that the life-expectancy of the average adult has been extended twenty years beyond that of 1900. The goal-structure of our psychologies of the development of personality and our religious values as well has been aimed at getting a child *to* adulthood, not *through* it! Our culture has become a child-centered culture that lays inestimable value upon youth and beauty. Adults are exhorted to understand children. But the possibilities of doing just this are slim apart from an understanding of their own adulthood.

At this point the psychologists and the theologians both have need for closer collaboration.

The draining of life of its meaning in adulthood may be associated with the increased life expectancy. The stepped-up success patterns made possible through technology and modern education have also added to people's spiritual weariness. Skills formerly were learned by working one's way up through the ranks of an industry, business, or profession through apprenticeships. Now they are often learned in a third of the time through technological education and internships. Men achieve places of responsibility, *and are expected by our culture to achieve these goals,* much earlier than they formerly did. At the age of thirty-five, forty, or forty-five, therefore, they are spoken of as "veterans." They become anxious in the dreadful situation of "having to hold their own" for the rest of their lives. The excitement of a new adventure has worn off. Boredom sets in. A nameless search for a deeper meaning for existence grips them. "*Now,* what am I going to do?" is their way of asking themselves, *Quo vadis?*

Therefore, the main disruptive experiences of life begin to appear in adulthood. "Somewhere inside," as Seward Hiltner puts it, an adult's "deeper self has begun to rebel at the increasingly prosaic character of his existence." [4] The disillusionment he feels roots in the fact that the goals he strove toward in the twenties and thirties now, "once achieved," are of "little value." The nice house, the new car, the two or three children, the social position—"all these he has attained. But they seem flat . . . he seems to be holding the line, fighting a defensive battle, or acting as an automaton to keep the wheels running." [5] Marital infidelity, alcoholism, psychosomatic disorders; the overbuying of "boredom toys" such as motor boats, racing cars, horses; and mental disorders, particularly depressions—all are symptoms of the emptiness and meaninglessness experienced by adults.

The psychotherapists have spoken to this situation. Gotthard Booth underscores the need for a *raison d'etre* when he says:

> It is beyond the competence of the psychiatrist to decide whether the health of a devout Christian or of a militant atheist is better, but he has theoretical and empirical reasons to believe that either one is healthier than the person who has found nothing in the world for which he wants to live and die.[6]

Carl G. Jung similarly states that the majority of his patients are not suffering from any clinically definable neurosis but from an existential condition of the sheer meaninglessness and purposelessness of their being.

Viktor Frankl has given the most thoroughgoing treatment of this kind of nameless anxiety in people. A Viennese psychiatrist, Frankl was captured by the Nazis and placed in a concentration camp. There he encountered the successive stages of shock, apathy, struggle for self-preservation, freedom fantasies, shattered vocational self-concepts, and abject futurelessness which plague prisoners in a concentration camp. As a doctor, he struggled to give his fellow prisoners "some content for their lives," to help them "find an aim and a purpose in their existence." He quotes Nietzsche who said: "Whoever has a reason for living endures almost any mode of life." Therefore, Frankl emerged with the conviction that psychoanalysis and other types of therapy would necessarily have to be augmented by what he calls "existential analysis." By definition this kind of therapy, Frankl says,

> aims at bringing the patient to the point of highest possible concentration and dedication. It is our business, then, to show how the life of every man has a unique goal toward which only one single course leads. . . . If the patient should object that he does not know the meaning of his life, that the unique potentialities of his existence are not apparent to him, then we can only reply that his primary task is just this: to find his way to his own proper task, to advance toward the uniqueness and the singularity of his own meaning in life.[7]

The search for meaning in and of itself can be a goal for living, in the absence of any clear sense of purpose and explicitly defined task.

The vocational heart of pastoral counseling. Pastoral counseling at its heart is concerned with the longer-reaching goals of the whole life rather than with tinkering in an amateurish fashion with the removal of this or that symptom. The process of pastoral counseling is participation in a pilgrimage-like search for the ultimate meaning of life. This is the "vocational heart" of pastoral counseling. The pastor believes in God, that he is, and that he is a rewarder of them that diligently seek after him. He joins upon a search with the seeker after life much more often than he gives pat "answers" to deep life issues, thereby relieving the person of the anxiety of asking and seeking. This shifts the pastor away from static conceptions of salvation to dynamic, meaningful ascendance from "faith unto faith," as the apostle Paul expressed it.

Direction as a Spiritual Goal of Personality

However, setting out on such a pilgrimage involves several vital spiritual necessities: freedom, choice of direction, and acceptance of responsibility. As Frankl again states it, *"Being human means being conscious and being responsible."* [8] The sense of direction is a necessary ingredient of the meaningfulness of existence, a qualitative and a distinctively spiritual dimension of personality. C. MacFie Campbell has said, "The essence of religious experience is seen in the search for the highest value of mental life; the personality of the 'religious type' is permanently directed to the creation of the highest and absolutely satisfying life experience." [9]

The setting of personality. The choice of a direction in a person has been concisely symbolized by Andras Angyal. He describes an attitude as the readiness of the organism to behave in certain specific ways. When this attitude becomes activated, he calls this a "setting" of the personality. Various "sets" of attitudes form a hierarchical organization, according to Angyal. Precedent sets determine the total direction of the personality, forming a system of axioms for behavior. Discordant personalities are those in which incompatibility of axioms throws the person out of balance. But, says Angyal, strong discordances may exist in even powerful personalities. However, "a good compatibility of axioms . . . is the main characteristic of the harmonious personality." [10]

The New Testament word *steridzo,* used to describe Jesus' choice of a direction for his life, reveals insight into the meaning of the spiritual goals of personality. Jesus did not perceive his sonship as an accomplished fact free of temptation or possibility of wrong decision. The freedom of decision was obviously his and the necessity of decision was a part of his cross. The struggle in the wilderness may well be described "the decisions in the wilderness" as well as the temptations in the wilderness. This was a decisive moment in his life. When he "set his face steadfastly" to go to Jerusalem, the choice of direction was evident in the ascendant rulership of this intention in the "sets" of his attitudes. There was no turning back. His direction had been chosen. The word for "set" here carries many connotations in the New Testament. It implies the fixing, setting fast, placing firmly, and making stable of one's mind. The word implies the flow of calm that comes into a life when the wrestle of decision is past and a direction has been chosen.

Furthermore, the New Testament word is used negatively also to describe medical conditions in which a disease is said to "set," to become chronic, to be determined. Colloquial speech today gets this in the saying that a person is "set in his ways." Another side of the need for direction is also portrayed in common speech, and especially that of disturbed, wondering, lost people. Counselors are likely to hear them say, "I don't know where I am going." "I am just beating around from one thing to another." "Where is it all going to lead to?" "Where does that kind of stuff get you?" "I can't seem to be getting anywhere." "Everyday is like the one before, I just don't seem to be anywhere else than I was the day before." Polly Adler, the little Jewish girl sent to this country alone when she was twelve, later found a hectic existence as a procuress in the prostitution circles of New York City. As she came to a dramatic turning of direction in her life she said:

> And suddenly it seemed to me that was no direction to my life at all. I had been rocking back and forth for years over the same waters, running before the storm in bad weather and hoving to when it was calm. Yes, I had been wrecked and in dry dock and refitted. I'd even learned the compass and a star or two, but I was just keeping afloat; I wasn't going anywhere.[11]

We have seen that the goodness and badness of innate desires is evaluated in terms of the direction in which they take the whole personality. In a sense, evil may be said to be good going in the wrong direction. This is the basic meaning of sin as perversion, the deflection of good from its legitimate goal and aim. As Buber says, "without setting off upon and keeping to one direction, man may have *quantum satis* of everything but existence, there is none for him without it." [12] When we interpret the Christian life as a *way of life*, we have a basis for interpreting many of the strange and unacceptable doings of people as aimlessness, directionlessness, threshing about for direction. The compass quivers in its box as it is magnetically thrust into a search for the north pole. The bee circles his hive madly as he springs upward and outward, searching for his true direction. The child, the college student, and the errant church member may actually collide with his fellows as he finds his true sense of direction in life. Thomas Wolfe expresses the importance of direction in the shaping of a human personality:

> My whole effort for years might be described as an effort to fathom my own design, to explore my own channels, to discover my own ways. . . . I think I know my way. And I shall wreak out my vision

of this life, this way, this world and this America to the top of my bent, to the height of my ability, but with an unswerving devotion, integrity and purity of purpose that shall not be menaced, altered or weakened by any one.[13]

In another place he repeats the refrain as he again writes to his editor:

Restrain my adjectives by all means, discipline my adverbs, moderate the technical extravagances of my incondite exuberance, but don't derail the train, don't take the Pacific Limited and switch it down the siding towards Hogwart Junction.[14]

Balance as a Spiritual Goal of Life

Another goal of man's becoming is that of balance, or "getting a firm footing" in life. The search for the meaning of life is a pilgrimage. The choice of a direction implies decision. The implementation of both calls for the capacity to "walk" in a certain way. This walking, just as surely as the semicircular canals establish the balance of the physical walk, calls for balancing the tensions of life and pointing them in the chosen direction of a given personality. It was Angyal who pointed out that

discordances . . . (in the setting of the direction of a person's life) may be well balanced or even disappear in a higher synthesis; but they may also remain "unbalanced," a term by which one often designates, not quite without justification, personality disorder in general.[15]

Homeostasis. Walter B. Cannon observed the ways in which the psychophysiological organism balances itself in response to stress situations as well as to the routine maintenance of itself. He devised the concept of "homeostasis." This means that the highly complex physiological processes "peculiar to living beings" are co-ordinated and balanced in a harmonious relationship to each other. The word homeostasis, says Cannon, "does not imply something set and immobile, a stagnation. It means a condition— a condition which may vary, but which is relatively constant." [16]

This constancy of the inner environment applies to the fluid matrix of the body, the water and salt content in the blood, blood sugar, proteins, fat, calcium, the balance of the body temperature, and the like. Illness represents a disruption of the homeostatic balance and an attempt of the organism to "right itself up."

Neurosis and "one-sidedness." Carl G. Jung applies the concept of imbalance to the meaning of neurosis. The neurosis represents a failure of adaptation, the appearance of a condition of "one-sidedness." The mechanism of projection is an example. The marriage partner loads his partner with blame "because that partner possesses those qualities" which he does not see in himself. The imbalance that exists in marriages between extroverted and introverted types of personality are cases in point, also. Furthermore, Jung says that the unconscious splitting off of unrealized or unacceptable parts of the psyche throws the whole personality out of balance. He draws the distinction between conscious one-sidedness and involuntary one-sidedness, that is, "the inability to be anything but one-sided." The former is a sign of highest culture, but the latter is a sign of barbarism, he says.[17]

Smiley Blanton, in his book, *Love or Perish,* points out that the psychological ailments of our lives arise out of an imbalance between the forces of love and aggression within our natures. "A proper balance is the only remedy which goes to the very source of the evil. It is the key to life itself, and hence the one victory we must gain in order to assure all others." [18] Emotional imbalance, observed by the clinicians as the spawning ground of the interpersonal difficulties of children and adults, is the negative after-image of the spiritual goal of the balanced personality. Balance is one of the goals of personality upon which religious and psychological insights are agreed.

Balance and the Christian life. In the New Testament, man is portrayed as being a contradictory being, filled with opposite but legitimate needs. The sacrifice of either side of the personality for the other always leads to unrighteousness. For instance, Paul speaks of the necessity of members of "the household of faith" bearing one another's burdens and so fulfilling the law of Christ. In the same breath he says that each man is to bear his own burden, thereby balancing up the need of a person for both the security that comes from the loving understanding of others and the security that comes from a healthy sense of personal responsibility (Galatians 6:1-11). Also, in another place (Ephesians 4:26, 32), Paul takes in consideration the aggressive-hostile needs of man by saying, "Be angry and sin not." In the same paragraph, however, he balances this exhortation by saying that his readers are to be kind, tenderhearted, and forgiving each other. The hostile aggressive need is legitimate. It can get out of balance. It may become paranoid apart from a quickness on the part of everyone to forgive. And, in Revelation 6:5, the Lord himself is symbolized as one who carries a set of balances in his hand.

In the history of religion, and especially Christianity as we know it, distortions of religious experience often represent heavy imbalances in the lives of religious people. The bacchanalian gorges of those who partook unfittingly of the Lord's Supper, the antinomian excesses of those who "sinned all the more" in order that the grace of Christ might abound (Romans 6:1 ff.), the strict legalism of the Galatians (Galatians 4:1-11), and the asceticism of the Cathari, the Shakers, and so on, are examples of the ways in which religion itself may symbolize deep personality imbalances in believers.

The Responsible Balance of Authority and Freedom

These imbalances of personality, seen from the perspective of the spiritual goals of personality, tend to appear repeatedly at the point of man's paradoxical needs for both authority and freedom. Striking a balance between these two needs is a necessary goal of personality. The New Testament struggle between those who interpreted the Christian doctrine of grace as a license to do as they pleased and those who dared not venture beyond Jewish legalism is an historical example of this tension. Present-day "half-turning of the psychological cake" of "directiveness" versus "nondirectiveness" is another example. The almost moralistic taint which some psychological authorities give the word "authority" is matched only by the compulsiveness of some religious personages who turn red in the face as they insist upon the absolute authority of the preacher in the pulpit.

Anxiety, authority, and freedom. Careful observation reveals that anxiety is directly related to authority and freedom in both instances. In fact, it might be said that wherever the responsible balance between authority and freedom is destroyed the anxiety quotient of individuals and groups goes up. *Anxiety and failures of communication increase in direct proportion to the degree which irresponsible individuals throw the balance between authority and responsibility out of kilter.* The major premise of this discussion is that the acceptance of responsibility is the balancing factor between man's paradoxical needs for authority and freedom. The compulsive demand for either authority or freedom to the exclusion of the other is in both instances, a symptom of irresponsibility.

Søren Kierkegaard, who has often been considered to have had little or no social consciousness, offsets such criticism in his book, *On Authority and Revelation.* He became deeply concerned with the imbalance of authority and freedom in the State Church's handling of the case of one Magister Adler. Adler had been deposed after having claimed to have had an authoritative, new, and special revelation from God which was given uniquely to him and not to others. He set his own teaching over against that of the church and Bishop Myster defrocked him for his religious insubordination. Kierkegaard writes his whole book as a commentary on the nature of religious authority and freedom, using this case as an occasion for the discussion. He could enter sympathetically into Adler's plight. He knew that Adler had been called by a revelation, and that he "must exert authority in the strength of the fact that he was called by a revelation." As Kierkegaard said,

> . . . he who is called by a revelation and to communicate a revelation, or the fact that he had a revelation . . . should proclaim this, appeal to it, exert authority.[19]

Apostles and prophets have been called to this ministry in all generations.

However, the mistake that Adler made, according to Kierkegaard, was to transpose his revelation into reflection and thereby to render it incomprehensible. He converted it into a system of philosophical impenetrables. This kept the revelation isolated and hidden. Thereby Adler avoided the direct communication of the truth that had come to him from God, "shuddering at the responsibility." In doing this he gave up his authority and made himself "presumptuously into a genius, whereas God had called him to be an apostle." [20]

In just this way, through the minutiae of exegesis, the "second parenthesis" of religious experience known as philosophy, and the so-called scientific study of the Scriptures, says Kierkegaard, the authentic demands of the Gospel are irresponsibly sloughed off by both the church and the priesthood. In a sense, then, both the static authoritarianism of the church and the irresponsible prophecy of Adler were symptoms of "the misfortune of our age," which, according to Kierkegaard, is "disobedience, unwillingness to obey." [21] In other words, unbalanced conformity to or rebellion against divine authority are both disorders of the spirit.

The authoritarian personality. Erich Fromm is a discerning modern analyst of the imbalance between authority and freedom in personality and society. Man "becomes more independent, self-reliant, and critical, and he becomes more isolated, alone, and afraid." Once a person faces the world outside himself as "a completely separate entity," he has to overcome his "unbearable state of powerlessness and aloneness." Two paths are open to him: he can "relate himself spontaneously to the world in love and work," or, he can "fall back, . . . give up his freedom, and . . . try to overcome his aloneness by eliminating the gap that has arisen between his individual self and the world." This latter path is what Fromm calls the "escape from freedom." [22] Authoritarianism is one of the ways man escapes his true freedom. As such, the authoritarian personality is considered by Fromm to be a truly sick person, one whose flight from freedom has unbalanced him.

T. W. Adorno and his associates produced a massive research volume on the characteristics of the authoritarian personality. Through questionnaires, clinical interviews, and psychological tests they concluded that the following salient features marked the person who is unbalanced in the direction of authority:

1. In childhood, he had, as a rule, highly ambivalent relationships to a domineering father. He himself became a mixture of latent rebellion and overt submission. As an adult, he denies his own passivity and weakness by attacking and hating the weaknesses of others.
2. In politics, he shows extreme prejudice toward minority groups and usually expresses it in the form of a pseudoconservatism.
3. In relation to the opposite sex, he or she is likely to have a depreciation reaction.
4. In relation to conventions, taboos, social appearances, he is likely to submit slavishly to "what folks will say."
5. In relation to the community as a whole, he is more concerned with his own power and his power group than he is with a total contribution to society.
6. In relation to religion, he is concerned with the externals and formalities of religion more than he is with the inner, personal insights of religion.
7. He perceives himself to be a "practical" man of action and rejects cultural and abstract interests.[23]

In evaluating religious experience, Fromm identifies two types of religious experience in terms of the "authoritarian" and the "humanitarian" religions. He rejects the overdependency, the conformity, and the irresponsibility of authoritarian religions. Fromm reflects little insight into the unbalanced personality and religion in which freedom is thrown into irresponsible rejection of man's inseparable need to belong to a meaningful fellowship of "those whose approval he considers most worthwhile." [24] Psychologists have been less discerning here than have the theologians.

O. H. Mowrer has helped us to see that man may really repress his need for social conformity until his very liberty itself becomes a kind of bondage. He says that one aspect of man's neurotic condition is due to his false sense of freedom and his lack of social feeling. He criticizes the psychoanalytic overemphasis upon the repression of unacceptable drives. He reasserts the fact that the finer and more distinctly co-operative drives of man may also be repressed.[25]

Community as a Spiritual Goal of Man's Becoming

The balance between authority and freedom in man's responsible life with his fellows usually expresses itself in his capacity to be related to without becoming enslaved by a community. Man must become a self in order to be free. He must be a self before being a part of a community of other selves in dialogic relationship can mean anything substantial. That community, as has already been pointed out, can become an idol of bondage in itself apart from faith in an ultimate God in whom love, power, and justice are in harmony. But when the faith fellowship, *the koinonia,* is established it becomes a "gathered community." This community is the first fruits of the active power, love, and justice of God. To use Augustine's name for it, it becomes "the city of God." The New Testament, especially the Letter to the Hebrews, takes great care to point out that this community is "not made with hands." The institutions of man are "no sure dwelling places." We are, in a vital sense, always "strangers and pilgrims," who are looking for the city of God which is always just beyond the horizon of our farthest vision.

The loneliness and social feeling of man. Thomas Wolfe considered himself at times "a mad fellow who made loneliness his mistress," and felt that "naked and alone, do we come into life, and alone, a stranger, each to each, we live upon it." Yet he could also say: "Something in me hates being alone like death, and something in me cherishes it. . . ."[26] Man's restless search for an accepting community is vigorously portrayed in Wolfe's letters. Hope for such a community causes man's heart to sink with anticipation beneath the contemplation of the "new Jerusalem." All the sons of God "stand on tiptoe," as J. B. Phillips puts it, in search for a fresh glimpse of that community. The "nobodies" of earth become "the people of God" in this royal priesthood of all believers.

Alfred Adler, probably more than other theorists of personality, has accented the importance of "social feeling" as a goal of the spiritual striving of human personality, antidote to the loneliness of man. He maintained that "the power of social interest lies at the base of all social products." In addition to the striving for individuality and superiority is the basic principle of social interest that "permeates all human evolution," and is "inherent in every human society." In commenting on religious movements, Adler says that "the one guiding thought which embraces and unites them all is expressed in the most exalted ideal purpose: "Love thy neighbor."[27] In fact, the point at which psychological and religious interpretations of personality are most helpful to each other is in plumbing the depths and assaying the quality of the motives people have for loving each other. One of the basic contributions of the psychological sciences has been both to point up the indispensable character of man's spiritual goal of community and at the same time to describe empirically the spiritual laws for evaluating his motives for relating himself to his fellows.

However, quite independently of the psychological sciences, theologians have made primary contributions to psychology itself in their penetrating understanding of the spiritual community. Martin Buber, for instance, sees into the heart of man's motive for belonging to a community. He distinguishes between collectively "bundling" people together and effectively relating them to each other in love. The community itself can "use" its members as means rather than as ends in themselves. Likewise, Dietrich Bonhoeffer, the Christian martyr of World War II, sharply demarcated between the spiritual community, created by the Holy Spirit through the Lordship of Jesus Christ, on the one hand, and the "psychic" or "human" community, on the other hand, which is created by the common miseries and hungers that people feel.[28]

Reinhold Niebuhr has in his own right contributed to the psychology of personality. In his book, *The Self and the Dramas of History*, he talks about the dialogic relationship within the self itself and talks of the inner community of the person. But this self, all the while it is "a unique center of life," is also "indeterminately 'open' to other selves." He says that "there are no geographic or temporal limits for the self's dialogue with others." Niebuhr speaks of the twofold relationship of the individual to the community, the horizontal through which he is a participant in the community, and the vertical through which he "looks down upon the community because he is, as it were, higher than it." From this point of vantage, the self as an individual "is embarrassed by the difference between the moral standards of the community and his own." In this sense, "the community will always remain both the fulfilment and the frustration of the individual." [29]

The ambiguities of the self in community have been apparent in the previous discussion of the imbalances of authority and freedom. For authority and freedom may, in a sense, be simply cognate terms for community and individuality. The tension between these two paradoxical realities has been evident in every chapter in this book. The resolution of this tension to higher and higher levels of expression calls for increasing maturity in the individual and the community. Different levels of maturity have been expressed in historical types of religion. These types of religion have taken some form or other within Christendom.

Maturity-in-Love as a Spiritual Goal of Man's Becoming

Love: the supreme psychological value. Man's ambiguous relationship to his community tests his capacity for love. Among the psychologists of personality, this capacity has become *the* criterion of maturity. Adulthood, or maturity, says Harry Stack Sullivan, is ushered into a person's development when he can "establish relationships of love for some other person, in which relationship the other person is as significant, or nearly as significant, as one's self." [30]

This capacity does not stop at a certain time in the healthy growth of a person, but it "goes on developing in depth" and in "scope of interest" until old age. The mature religious sentiment, according to Allport, is marked by comprehensiveness of affection, an awareness of one's own partial grasp of the love and knowledge of God, and "seems never satisfied unless it is dealing with matters central to all existence." [31] The importance of maturity for the religious dimensions of life and personality cannot be overestimated. As Allport says,

> To feel oneself meaningfully linked to the whole of Being is not possible before puberty. This fact helps to explain the one-sided emphasis we encounter in many psychological discussions of religion. Becoming has been much more thoroughly studied for the years preceding puberty than for adolescent and adult years.[32]

This is one of the reasons discussions of religion by psychologists have been more concerned with dependency, Familism, regression, and so on than with maturity. Also it explains why the value judgments of the psychologists often appear distorted to the mature adult who is not acquainted with the intricacies of psychopathology.

Psychology and value-judgments. Sensing this latter inadequacy, the psychologist like Lawrence E. Cole says that when the psychologist undertakes to assess personality as a whole, he "reveals *his* values." Psychologists must move out of their relativisms and run the risk of such participant observation of how human beings *ought* to act. Cole insists that normalcy and maturity should be interpreted in something more than just a statistical and relativistic way. "The curse of relativism," he says, "is that it so completely devaluates the inflated certainties of our own moral currency." [33] In the same context, Cole insists that *"normal* ought to be *normal in any culture. . . .* It ought to be no mere statistical mode: *normal* is something good, sound, healthy, *right.*" This psychologist's appeal for a universally valid criterion of the mature person, the normal person, has a two-edged effect on religious interpretations of the goals of life: it challenges the provincialism of religious persons, and at the same time confirms the need for a more absolute criterion of the mature and healthy person. In fact, it calls for a *comprehensive* religious sentiment which, says Allport, is one of the main characteristics of the religion of the mature person.

Stages of religious maturity. As has already been pointed out, the degrees of social and individual maturity are apparent in different types of religion which have emerged in history. These types of religion have appeared in Christendom. A brief description of the stages of religious maturity would appear somewhat as follows:

1. The religion of desire. Communities of religious living have been built upon the basic psychic desires of man. They are the kind of community to which Bonhoeffer refers as the "psychic communities." The agricultural religions, the healing cults, the mother cults, the fertility cults—all are shaped about the dominance of one or more of the desires of man. Much of this kind of religion also resides in contemporary forms of the Christian religion as it is practiced. Magical interpretations of prayer, the shaping of Christian holidays along the cycle of seed-time, harvest, winter, and so on and the identification of faith with success all point tellingly in this direction.

This is not to say that the Christian God is unconcerned with man's desires, however. He opens his hand and satisfies the desires of man with good things. It is simply to say that this is the infantile level of religious development. The religion of desire is represented in what Søren Kierkegaard called "aesthetics." Here man becomes the measure of all things, and his desire is omnipotent. Unfailingly the community roots of this kind of religion are very shallow. The hot sun of frustration causes such religious concern to wither.

2. *The religion of verbal interplay.* On the next higher level of religious maturity is the religion of articulation, of verbal interplay. Here religious people become concerned with the *thrill of communication.* An example of it, apparent in most forms of religious history, is "speaking in tongues." Another is the preoccupation with oratory and forms of rhetoric. Some religious groups have institutionalized preaching to the point that it has almost sacramental efficacy in their values. The apostle Paul encountered this kind of religion in the glossolalia and the silver-tongued oratory of his day. He chose to speak a few words with understanding more than thousands without it and said that if he spoke with the tongues of men and angels, and had not love, he was as sounding brass and clanging symbols (I Corinthians 13:1). However, he did not despise speaking in tongues. Rather he said: "Brethren, be not children in understanding: howbeit in malice be ye children, but in understanding be of ripe age" (I Corinthians 14:20).

3. *The religion of definition and exclusion.* The third level or

type of religion concentrates heavily upon the development of a peer group and a hierarchy. However, the establishment of a fixed community and its leaders depends upon the definition of terms of membership and statements of faith. Religion becomes a form of faith for accomplishing certain tasks, a kind of "gnosis" by which the inner group can tacitly understand one another without too much verbalization and discussion. In other words, at this stage of religious development certain things begin to be taken for granted and many questions are no longer asked. The very asking of these questions may be a form of disloyalty and a challenge of the covenant. Orthodoxy and heterodoxy, then, are primal preoccupations of this stage of religious maturity. In essence this stage is a "half-way house" between the religion of desire and the religion of love.

4. *The religion of the rules.* Desires, verbal interplay, definition and exclusion—all these efforts must be consolidated and conserved. They are codified into rules of action. In time these rules in themselves become less meaningful to the group that formed them, because the original threat which gave birth to them exists no more. Likewise, a new generation arises to whom the rules are meaningless, whether the threat still exists or not. They must be transmitted through teaching and other forms of discipline. They may become a substitute for experience itself, but at best they are the crystallized experience of the race.

5. *The religion of rebellion.* A distinctly adolescent level of religious experience is the religion of rebellion. Baron Von Hugel calls this "the stage of question and argument, Youth's mode of approaching religion." [34] This is not merely a chronological youthfulness, either. Religion at this stage breaks out of the molds of words, exclusions, rules, and institutions. The outburst of energy comes when the rules are so far out of keeping with the "lived-life," as Buber calls it, that life itself reasserts itself. The starving person rebels against even the Sabbath and his desires are expressed. That which is fixed is subjected to

change. At this point regressive types of behavior may appear, and the cycle of religious immaturity may be set in motion again. This is how many denominations get started. On the other hand, the rebellion may take a creative thrust into a deeper source of spiritual sustenance and a new level of maturity will be reached. The rebel, instead of ministering to his own need for freedom, may minister unto the whole community's need for redemption. Isolation thus may be *on behalf of the* community. Such was the suffering of Christ, who suffered on the "outside of the camp" in behalf of those within.

6. *The religion of mature love.* The New Testament discussions of maturity, or "perfection" to use the King James word for it, tend to be set within the context of the discussion of this kind of redemptive, unstimulated love. This is *agape*, Christian love. Paul's great hymn of love refers to "putting away childish things and becoming a man." The fulfillment or the equipment of the saints demands "speaking the truth in love and growing up into him who is the head," even Christ. Being children, tossed to and fro by every wind of doctrine, is to be put behind the mature Christian. Therefore, the religion of mature love represents the highest level of spiritual living. This religion has several characteristics. It is a religion of grace and acceptance, rather than works and achieved merit. It is a religion of inner perception and insight, which are the nourishing forces of love, rather than verbal statement and pronouncement. It is a religion of a total outreach and all-inclusiveness rather than exclusiveness and separation. This in turn is the basis of its missionary concern and comprehensive endeavor at relatedness to all men everywhere. Consequently, the religion of maturity is a religion of a universal God beside whom there is no other, who lays claim on the totality of the person.

John Wick Bowman has aptly said that religions of what he calls "altar, book, and throne" all fundamentally lack one thing: they absorb "but a portion of the talents and attention of the disciple." Their claim is always a "partial one," and "the result on personality is in each case the same . . . the production of a self-assertive or arrogant attitude." Then he says:

> The religion of maturity never makes this mistake. It demands every ounce of simon-pure energy the individual possesses—*all* of his emotional or love life, *all* of his intellectual powers, *all* of his will. . . .[35]

Integration as a Spiritual Goal of Man's Becoming

Such unified loyalty as Bowman describes, however, requires a high measure of integration. Personality is unified around the central loyalty to which persons give themselves most wholeheartedly. Josiah Royce perceived the relationship between the nature of loyalty and the organization of personality. It was he who defined loyalty as

> The willing and thoroughgoing devotion of a person to a cause, . . . something that unifies many human lives in one. The will to manifest, so far as is possible, the Eternal, that is, the conscious and superhuman unity of life, in the form of the acts of an individual self.[36]

Andras Angyal recognizes, as a scientist of personality, that "the problem of integration of part processes in the total organism is the most important and at the same time the most difficult problem for a science of personality." He assumes that the integration of personality cannot be dealt with merely from the individual, subjectivistic point of view: it involves the total biosphere of life itself. He says that the integration can be too rigid, or "tight," and that it can be too diffused or "loose." [37] As some psychiatrists have designated a "law of reversed effect," we could also say that integration of personality "is often hindered by direct, grimly determined effort." Tension needs relaxation, the psychologists say. Therefore, integration is a by-product of the other goals of life discussed here, not an end intention.[38]

The basic religious dimensions of personality integration have

been set forth by Allport when he says that the religious sentiment "is capable of conferring marked integration upon personality, engendering meaning and peace in the face of the tragedy
and confusion of life." [39] However, Allport also notes that the
integration of personality can be a self-centered integration and
that the religious sentiment can be merely rudimentary in the
personality. Something makes the difference. What is it?

Just at this point the theologian has something to offer the
psychologist of personality. As Cole has said, the psychologist
runs "head on" into his own values when he begins articulating
his conception of maturity, normalcy, and integration. The theologian always asks about the integration of personality: "Yes,
that is needed, but around *what* and *whom* is the personality
being integrated? The distinction needs to be made, as did Pascal, between God and god!" This necessarily must be answered
by evaluative rather than statistical and psychometric means,
although the pragmatic expression of various centers of integration can be tested. Henry N. Wieman sought to evaluate the
central objectives of man's personality organization when he
said that the maturity and integration of religion and personality
could be measured by the worthfulness, the completeness, the
efficiency, the sensitivity, the progression, and the social effec-
tiveness of the supreme loyalty of a person's life. He interpreted
conversion in terms of the limitedness, the reality, and the supremacy of the reorganization of personality when the sins of
incompleteness of loyalty, disloyalty, conflicting loyalty, loyalty-
lessness, and idolatry were broken through by an all-inclusive
loyalty.[40]

The integration of personality, the completeness of a loyalty,
and the durability of a loyalty are the main criteria for measuring the mature integration of a person. However, even completeness and durability can be but spatial and temporal abstractions
apart from a personal incarnation of them both that is "from
everlasting to everlasting." *For the final test of personality inte-*

gration is what the person does in the encounter with the reality of death and how he moves from the integrations of time and space to the coherences of the Eternal. When, therefore, I use the word durable, I do not use it in any finite sense. Consequently the theological dimension of the problem of personality integration emerges when he asks the question Job asked: "If a man die, shall he live again?"

Christian eschatology and the integration of personality. Revelational theology has always approached the spiritual goals of man's becoming in terms of the gift and the expectation of the Kingdom of God. The psychological realities in the biblical doctrine of the Kingdom of God are both wide and deep.[41] This transversal biblical teaching involves the sovereign rule of God, the covenant relationship existing between the people of God by reason of their having been brought into a conscious relationship to the sovereign God, the antithesis of this Kingdom to the idolatrous and demonic distortions of life-in-distance from the Kingdom, and the ultimate triumph of the Kingdom in the consummation of the ages.

The Kingdom of God is set forth as the ultimate meaning for which men are to seek. They are to turn from all other directions and seek first the Kingdom of God and his righteousness. This turning is repentance. If men ask for the Kingdom, it will be given to them; if they seek for the Kingdom, they shall find it; and if they knock at the door of the Kingdom, they may enter it. This is the good news of God enunciated in Christ. This is forgiveness. Apart from the supreme loyalty that God's forgiveness and gift of the Kingdom creates, men's lives are thrown out of balance by their distorted and misguided idolatry of family, church, state, philosophical system, and domineering teachers. The impinging power of the Kingdom of God separates the children of darkness from the children of light, weans them from their idols, and frees them from the possessive power of the demonic. The demonic is the finite parading itself as the ultimate.

The freedom of the Kingdom also balances itself with the ultimate authority of obedience to God. From singlehearted devotion to him comes purity of heart, the willing of one thing, the unification and integration of the Christian life in Christ. God moves the life of the individual through the set ends of his existence, and the Kingdom of God breaks through in the *kairoi* of each given stage of his life. The whole creation groans and travails in the breath-shortening anxiety of finitude, also, and the ultimate triumph of the Kingdom of God in the eschaton pronounces doom upon all Utopian schemes for the humanistic perfection of the world. At the same time, the consummation of the Kingdom fills the community of the believers with the lively hope of the resurrection and the motivating power for ethical action in the moment without being a slave to the moment.

The Kingdom of God is not the end result of man's treadmill action whereby he seeks to "bring the Kingdom in." Nor is it a kingdom he builds by his own efforts and presents to God as a basis for his salvation. To the contrary, it is the Father's good pleasure to give the Kingdom to his children. This is the quintessence of acceptance of the person who by faith believes that he is accepted, though in his immaturity and imperfection of achievement of his own highest goals for himself, he feels unacceptable. The beginning of maturity is not when men set themselves to the task of "becoming mature." Rather, it is when men begin to believe in an ultimate Love that has already been perfected on their behalf. Such is the Love of Christ, upon which the Kingdom stands, already having been perfected through his suffering on the cross. Then the "tasks" of life become "works of Love."

NOTES FOR CHAPTER XI

1. Gordon W. Allport, *Becoming: Basic Considerations for a Psychology of Personality* (New Haven, Conn.: Yale University Press, 1955), p. 98.
2. *Ibid.*, p. 76.
3. Nicolas Berdyaev, *Solitude and Society* (London: The Centenary Press, 1938), p. 128.
4. Seward Hiltner, *Self-Understanding* (New York: Charles Scribner's Sons, 1951), p. 150.
5. *Ibid.*
6. *The Church and Mental Health*, ed. Paul Maves (New York: Charles Scribner's Sons, 1952), p. 15.
7. Viktor Frankl, *The Doctor and the Soul* (New York: Alfred A. Knopf, Inc., 1955), pp. 64-65. Note needs to be made that Frankl does not substitute this kind of therapy for all other types of therapy; but, in the absence of clinical evidence for a psychopathological basis for motivation, this method, which he calls "logotherapy," should be used. Used by permission.
8. *Ibid.*, p. 5.
9. C. MacFie Campbell, *Human Personality and the Environment* (New York: The Macmillan Company, 1934), p. 131.
10. Andras Angyal, *Foundations for a Science of Personality* (New York: The Commonwealth Fund, 1941), p. 146.
11. Polly Adler, *A House Is Not a Home* (New York: Popular Library, 1953), p. 273. Used by permission of Rinehart & Co., Inc., publisher.
12. Martin Buber, *Good and Evil* (New York: Charles Scribner's Sons, 1953), p. 143.
13. *The Letters of Thomas Wolfe*, ed. Elizabeth Nowell (New York: Charles Scribner's Sons, 1956), Frontispiece.
14. *Ibid.*, p. 588.
15. Angyal, *op. cit.*, p. 146.
16. Walter B. Cannon, *The Wisdom of the Body* (New York: W. W. Norton & Company, Inc., 1932), p. 24.
17. C. G. Jung, *Psychological Types*, trans. H. G. Baynes (New York: Harcourt, Brace & Company, Inc., 1938), pp. 255, 597. Also see Jolan Jacobi, *The Psychology of Jung*, trans. K. W. Bash (New Haven, Conn.: Yale University Press, 1943), pp. 24, 39, 98.
18. Smiley Blanton, *Love or Perish* (New York: Simon & Schuster, Inc., 1956), pp. 42-43.
19. Søren Kierkegaard, *On Authority and Revelation*, trans. Walter Lowrie (Princeton, N. J.: Princeton University Press, 1955), p. 24.
20. *Ibid.*
21. *Ibid.*, xviii.
22. Erich Fromm, *Escape from Freedom* (New York: Farrar and Rinehart, 1941), pp. 104, 140-141.

23. T. W. Adorno, *The Authoritarian Personality* (New York: Harper & Brothers, 1950).
24. Erich Fromm, *Psychoanalysis and Religion* (New Haven, Conn.: Yale University Press, 1950), pp. 36-64.
25. O. H. Mowrer, *Learning Theory and Personality Dynamics* (New York: Ronald Press Company, 1950), pp. 531, 537.
26. *The Letters of Thomas Wolfe, op. cit.,* pp. 103, 707, and 241.
27. *The Individual Psychology of Alfred Adler,* eds. Heinz and Rowena Ansbacher (New York: Basic Books, Inc., 1956), p. 449.
28. Dietrich Bonhoeffer, *Life Together* (London: S. C. M. Press, 1949), p. 21.
29. Reinhold Niebuhr, *The Self and the Dramas of History* (New York: Charles Scribner's Sons, 1955), pp. 33, 35, 36.
30. Harry Stack Sullivan, *The Interpersonal Theory of Psychiatry* (New York: W. W. Norton & Company, Inc., 1953), p. 34.
31. Gordon W. Allport, *The Individual and His Religion* (New York: The Macmillan Company, 1950), pp. 67-69.
32. Allport, *Becoming, op. cit.,* pp. 94-95.
33. Lawrence E. Cole, *Human Behavior: Psychology as a Biosocial Science* (Yonkers-on-the-Hudson, N. Y.: World Book Company, 1953), pp. 816-821.
34. *The Mystical Element in Religion,* Vol. I (London: J. M. Dent and Sons, Ltd., 1923), p. 51.
35. John Wick Bowman, *The Religion of Maturity* (New York: Abingdon Press, 1948), pp. 311-312.
36. Josiah Royce, *The Philosophy of Loyalty* (New York: The Macmillan Company, 1916), pp. 351, 357.
37. Angyal, *op. cit.,* p. 243.
38. Allport, *The Individual and His Religion, op. cit.,* pp. 93-94.
39. *Ibid.,* p. 142.
40 Henry Nelson and Regina Westcott Wieman, *Normative Psychology of Religion* (New York: Thomas Y. Crowell Company, 1935), pp. 51-52, 147-149, 160 ff.
41. Wayne E. Oates, "Some Psychological Implications of the Doctrine of the Kingdom of God," *The Covenant Quarterly,* Vol. XVI, No. 1, February, 1956, pp. 3-12.

CHAPTER XII

THE CHRISTIAN UNDERSTANDING
OF PERSONALITY

THE MODERN UNDERSTANDING OF PERSONALITY, and particularly
the Christian understanding of personality, is a cultural tapestry
in which, as Goethe says:

> One treadle sets a thousand threads in motion,
> The shuttles shoot to and fro,
> Unperceived the threads flow.* [1]

Descriptive, naturalistic, supernaturalistic, and revelational perspectives of personality are inextricably interwoven in the Western Christian tradition. Therefore, historical wisdom is necessary
for a Christian understanding of personality which is at the same
time both related to and different from modern psychological
estimates of man.

THE HISTORICAL CONTEXT OF PERSONALITY PERSPECTIVES

The modern Christian in Western culture understands personality best when he identifies the various threads of culture that

* Notes and credits for this chapter are found on page 305.

have been woven into his understanding. These threads have been woven against each other in the warp and woof of action and reaction in theological and philosophical debate, controversy, and assimilation. They lie now in cross-woven support and contradiction of each other. The dialogic encounter between psychology and theology today is the end-product of the antagonisms and assimilations, the reformations and the conversations of Christian history.

Hebrew Versus Greek Culture

The biblical writers knew nothing of the modern distinction between "psychology" and "religion." They lived in one world. That world was in encounter with God. God unveiled himself, offering himself in a fellowship of holiness. God, in his divine self-disclosure "opened men's eyes to their deep need [and] at the same time . . . showed them how that need could be met." [2] However, the devout Jew joined battle with the Hellenizers who would bring their pantheon into the Holy of Holies of the one true and living God. The Christian missionary of first and second century also was in combat with the Greek Gnostics who would "objectivate" the revelation of God in Christ, making it a static knowledge for the "initiated" rather than a personal encounter between man as a sinner and God as redemptive love in the historical person of Jesus Christ.

Earlier Greek thought had sharply demarcated between "ideas" and phenomena. The understanding of man as a fallen creature in need of redemption from God in Christ was exchanged for the understanding of him as the pre-existently perfect person who can by reason lay hold of his own divinity if he becomes wise enough. Aristotle saw the world as the prime object of knowledge, a realm of cause and effect that can be known, of which God is the ultimate but impersonal cause. The ark of the covenant of the Christian faith was, through many a war of

minds, periodically lifted from the direct revelation of God in
Jesus Christ and placed on the wagon of Greek idealism.

Augustine, more than others, recaptured the lost radiance of
Christianity for the Western Christian tradition. He brought
about a rebirth of biblical theology. He shifted the emphasis
away from the categories and systems of the Greeks and re-
affirmed the despair of man as a sinner. However, he remained
in many respects a child of Greek philosophy in his understanding of personality. Thomas Aquinas canalized the two streams
of influence—Hebrew and Greek—into two types of approach to
man: the natural and revealed. The bifurcation of the Christian
understanding of man was a foregone certainty after Thomas
Aquinas.

The Enlightenment and Scientific Approaches to Reli-
gion and Personality

The Protestant Reformation initiated a renascence of biblical
theology. The categories and systems of the Aristotelian modes
of thinking were thrust aside. The mighty acts of God in Jesus
Christ redeeming fallen man from sin were vigorously preached.
The depth psychology of Augustine was affirmed, and his psychological dependence upon Neoplatonic estimates of personality
was sloughed off.

However, the Reformation and the Counter-Reformation were
so intense that the scientific movements of the later eighteenth
and nineteenth centuries were left to create revolutions of their
own. Sigmund Freud and other psychologists wrote their version of the great reformations in man's thinking about the world
and himself but they did not refer to justification by faith, the
sovereignty of God, and the Person of Jesus Christ. They listed
the discovery of the Copernican view of the universe, the Dar-
winian formulation of the origin of man, and the psychotherapeutic "discovery" of the unconscious. Like a rebellious child,
modern science broke loose from its parental relationship to the

Christian faith while the elders of the churches quarreled among themselves. This break with authority and tradition was a part of the rebellion of the Enlightenment which provided philosophical atmosphere in which the empirical study of personality gained its main momentum.

Charles Gray Shaw says that "in spite of its blind faith in what is called 'Nature,' the Enlightenment had the advantage and performed the service of emancipating the human spirit from authority and tradition." [3] Yet another dogma took precedence: the dogma of objectivity, absolute verifiability, and as Ernst Troeltsch has said,

> The spirit of the 18th Century . . . became atomistic, analytical, mechanistic, and practical; entirely on the side of the known and the evident. . . .[4]

Scientific students of personality have been enchanted by this spirit. Protestant theologians after the Reformation began talking only to themselves. In great numbers they failed even to notice that while they celebrated battles won by Luther, Calvin, and Zwingli, whole segments of culture were being secularized through empirical methodologies of science. Medicine, education, social work, and now *Seelsorge*, or the care of souls, to say nothing of the secularization of the family (and even of death itself by the morticians) have undergone a reinterpretation in their *apartness* from the encounter with God-in-relation. Some revelational, biblical theologians never established communication with the empirical scientists in their evaluation of man. They held themselves away in disdain of these practical matters. Others approached the conversation with a dearth of scientific knowledge and a plethora of speculation. Others simply exploded with insecurity and impatience. In the latter instance, obscurantist forms of fundamentalism pronounced noisy doom for any approach to human personality and its salvation other than their own literalism afforded.

Theological Liberalism and Scientific Estimates of Personality

A certain wing of Protestantism, however, took the findings of empirical study of personality seriously. Schleiermacher set the pattern by resting his theology neither on authoritarian dogma nor on speculative reason, but upon the religious consciousness, as such. In the tradition of Schleiermacher, the empirical theologians and the psychologists of religion have continued the conversation with the empirical students of personality. From Bushnell forward, too, the religious education movement also represents a "buffer state" between the sciences and what today is restrictively defined as "theology." The fundamentalist-modernist controversy may be said to have been precipitated by the scientific study of religion itself, especially of the sacred books of the faith.

Neo-Orthodox theology arose as a corrective of modernism and reasserted the essential content of the revelation of God in Christ without losing the major gains that came from the scientific study of the Bible and Christian history. In a sense, Neo-Orthodoxy is ambivalently related to modernism. It may be simply a restatement of a softened fundamentalism, rather than the helpful antidote to liberalism it was historically devised to be. Harry Emerson Fosdick says that some men whom he has heard preach did not arrive at Neo-Orthodox conclusions *via* liberalism. They are filled with "homiletical arrogance, such take-or-leave-it assumption of finality, such cancellation of the life and words of the historic Jesus by the substitution of a dogmatic Christ." [5] In fact, the easy rejection of the responsibility for conversation with the "naturalistic" scientists in the *kosher* attitudes of closed corporations of coffee-club theologians may well produce another theological drouth like unto that of the years between World War I and World War II. The either-or distinctions between the "practical" and the "theological" aspects of seminary education are rather noisy portents of the bifurcation of the totality of life still going on in theological circles.

Theological education today and the study of personality. However, the contemporary teacher of theological students cannot assume that students are aware of the essential content of the Christian revelation when he teaches the psychology of religion. Nor can he assume that students are intelligently concerned about the challenge of secular views of man expounded today. The varied patterns of thinking discussed thus far are a part of their unconscious confusion. They have been educated in public schools and state owned and supported colleges and universities. The empirical, naturalistic understanding of personality has been given them from the first grade. The revelation of God is discreetly avoided by legal necessity. They hold their previous education and their theological education in neatly airtight compartments. If they have been educated in a church-related school, they are often totally unaware of the scientific crisis in process as to the nature and destiny of man.

Consequently, at every point possible this book has dramatized the encounter of theological with empirical perspectives of personality. Often the same problems of personality emerge in different contexts and different terminology. No easy equations have been made to leave the impression that this is a soliloquy of one point of view among persons who "mean the same thing, but use different words." No. It is a dialogue. The Christian revelation itself both corresponds with and contradicts the naturalistic understanding of personality. The correspondence lies both in the questions asked and in the answers given. The contradiction usually lies at the shallowness, depth, and extent of both the questions and the answers. More than this, though, the Christian revelation both raises questions and offers answers about the nature and destiny of man which contemporary psychologies of personality have only recently begun to ask. For instance, the role that decision plays in personality integration as well as the creative interpretation of vocation and suffering are subjects which, as yet, have not been assessed in empirical approaches to personality.

CONTINUITIES BETWEEN THE SCIENTIFIC AND THE
CHRISTIAN UNDERSTANDINGS OF PERSONALITY

Even though the empirical study of personality has in large measure been cut adrift by biblical theologians, two remarkable results have been evident in the research of the preceding chapters. First, psychologists of personality are arriving at some of the same conceptions of man which are inherent in the Hebrew-Christian insights of the Old and New Testaments. Second, biblical theologians in revitalized examination of the conceptions of personality implicit in the biblical accounts have come to some of the same conclusions as to the Hebrew-Christian understanding of personality as have leading psychologists of personality. The psychologists and theologians, regrettably enough, have often done this in isolation from each other. Nevertheless, the overlapping of emphases is too obvious to overlook. The word studies found in the synoptic definitions of personality and religion are cases in point. The apostle Paul said that

> Ever since the creation of the world [God's] invisible nature, namely, his eternal power and deity, has been clearly perceived in the things that have been made.[6]

This has been true not only of God, but also of man; for in the study of man, man as the student of himself has often taken the slower route to learn for himself what has been clearly set forth in biblical revelation. Several of these confirmations of the biblical view of man in contemporary psychology can be spelled out here.

Types of Psychological Emphasis and the Christian Understanding of Personality

Anyone beyond a sophomoric smattering of psychological knowledge knows that the word "psychology" is like the words "religion" and "love": it covers a multitude of sins, as well as many other things! There are innumerable types of psychology, because of the relative youth of the field, the comparative geographical isolation in which psychologists work, and the language barriers between European and American psychologists. Some specific things can be said, however, as to *which* of these types of psychology of personality are most compatible and have the most in common with the distinctly Christian understanding of personality.

The wholeness of man. The Christian understanding of personality is most compatible with those types of psychology which emphasize the totality or wholeness of personality. The Christian understanding of personality is set over against any psychology which would attempt to explain personality by dividing it into its real or supposed component parts. As John Oman says, "the nature of a person is such and the grace which succours it is such that they cannot be divided. . . ." [7]

An instructive exploration of the Sermon on the Mount reveals the importance of the wholeness of personality, opposed to its division and adulteration. Jesus uses the symbolism of the function of the human eye as a basis for his teaching. In Matthew 6:22-23 he says: "The eye is the lamp of the body. So, if your eye is sound, your whole body is full of light; but if your eye is not sound, your whole body will be full of darkness. If then the light in you is darkness, how great is the darkness!" The eye is the instrument of insight and guidance for the whole body. If it is light, the *whole body* is filled with light. If it is dark, the whole body is greatly darkened. The part has no meaning apart from the whole organism, and the whole organism is dependent on the part.

Jesus makes a specific application of this to the psychosexual behavior of the individual. He says:

> You have heard that it was said, "You shall not commit adultery." But I say to you that everyone who looks at a woman lustfully has already committed adultery with her in his heart. If your right eye causes you to sin, pluck it out and throw it away; it is better that you lose one of your members than that your whole body be thrown into hell. And if your right hand causes you to sin, cut it off and throw it away; it is better that you lose one of your members than that your whole body go to hell.[8]

The eye is portrayed as one of the media of sexual stimulation, as well as the hand, symbolic of the sexual need of an individual. Sex may become the organizing center and consuming concern of a person, dominating all other needs, the part ruling the whole life. Jesus used a surgical figure here, to the effect that it is better that the part be sacrificed, even though the whole is crippled without it than that the part destroy the whole. The way of the total ascetic is better than that the whole life be subordinated to a part of the life, the worship of sex.

This concept of the totality of personality stands in contradistinction to the compartmentalization, fragmentation, and disjointedness of earlier research in the psychology of personality. These types of psychology are still being taught in colleges and universities now by professors who were trained in the first quarter of this century. An example of this is found in the "elementary psychology" of the German psychologist Wilhelm Wundt and his American disciple, E. B. Titchener. They reduced personality—or mind, as they preferred to say—to its constituent elements—sensation, image, and affection—and "compounded" these into the compound, perception-and-emotion. This psychology was decried by William James as a "brick-and-mortar" psychology.

Since the early 1890's, when Wilhelm Dilthey attacked all psychology which sought to "atomize" mental activity, there has been an increasing scientific insistence upon the wholeness of the human person. Further developments in the research of *Gestalt* psychologists such as Wertheimer, Koffa, and Kohler forcefully demonstrated the reality and unity of the whole as over against an additive meaning of the parts. With such wholeness in mind Leslie Paul says,

> It was inevitable that from the examination of the power of the mind to grasp wholes sooner or later psychologists would come forward with the intention of interpreting the peculiar mind-body whole which is the *person*. There arose the personalistic psychology of Stern. For him . . . there is not on the one hand *consciousness*, and on the other *behaviour*, there is only person. The person is an undivided totality. What we perceive as a person is not a consciousness joined to a body like a flag to a pole, but a purposive, individual unity seeking certain ends. The whole person, the only really perceived unit of psychology seeks one whole to pursue certain ends. The encountered whole person of daily life must be the basis of psychology.[9]

The works of John Pederson, A. R. Johnson, H. Wheeler Robinson, Eric Rust, J. A. T. Robinson, and Rudolf Bultmann—all biblical theologians—have been alluded to in the previous chapters. They have said virtually the same thing about personality wholeness as does Leslie Paul's succinct summary of a prevailing emphasis in modern psychologies of personality.

Man in struggle and conflict. The Christian understanding of personality abides at home, in the second place, with psychologists who take the basic conflicts of men seriously. Whereas personality is essentially a totality, both biblical and psychological estimates in increasing number of his nature portray him existentially in conflict with himself. In the biblical perspective man as a sinner struggles for redemption; in certain psychological perspectives of today, man in conflict seeks for integration and self-consistency. This conflict has been apparent in the paradoxical definitions of personality and religion as they fluctuated between man's finitude, his individuality and loneliness, his "outer" and "inner" selves.

Mary Thelan, as was seen in the discussion of the structure personality, described psychoanalytic and Marxian interpretations of man as "secular theories of man as a sinner." The main lines of description of "man in sin," as Zilboorg says, as set forth by evangelical theology and psychotherapeutic hypotheses of personality are remarkably continuous with each other. Divergences begin when the path of redemption is marked out. Even here the answers often move in the same direction, but the psychotherapist tends to stop at the "city limits" of naturalism as over against the wider country of religion.

The fact of struggle was recognized early by Darwin. It was taken as axiomatic that the organism will struggle for survival. But it remained for the psychologists of personality to try to define the meaning and direction of that struggle, rather than merely to take it as a fact. And, as Leslie Paul again says, "the organism is complete and whole: that is its very nature. But it is also . . . incomplete and unfinished," [10] and out of this basic capacity to struggle come purpose, direction, and the goals of man's becoming. This has been the signal contribution of Gordon Allport as he has evaluated the "propriate strivings" of man. He, more than other psychologists, has sought to define the essentially religious nature of these strivings. The point at which he stops is the city limits of "religion" as over against that more comprehensive plan of redemption of the Christian faith. But it needs to be said that he stops *as a psychologist,* and that his personal world-view apart from the psychological method might be quite different.

Man in relation. The Christian understanding of personality is most compatible with those psychologies of personality which see man in a realm of interpersonal relationships between dynamically interacting persons. The Hebrew-Christian view of personality has always been marked by its distinctly relational quality. Man is not only a totality; he is a whole person in relation to other persons. The person is both "self-contained" and yet "open to the world about him." He is both individually responsible to and socially involved in the "covenant relationship" of the people of God. As Martin Buber defines the Spirit, he says: "The Spirit is not in the *I*, but between the *I* and *Thou*. It is not like the blood that circulates in you, but like the air you breathe. Man lives in the Spirit if he is able to respond with his Thou. He is able to, if he enters into relation with his whole being." [11] The relational quality of Hebrew thought has been underscored all the way through these pages. The Christian theologians have perceived the Kingdom of God as the ultimate community which gives meaning to all the separated communities of men. The conflictual polarity between authority and responsibility has been encompassed in the ultimate meanings of man in relation to himself, to his neighbor, and to God.

Christians are powerfully related to each other in the covenant into which they have been born by faith in Christ. The ground of their existence is their relationship to Christ. They are bound together by the Holy Spirit. The Holy Spirit is the source of their energy and the fountain of their personal and corporate renewal, the sustaining power of their communication, and the revealing agent of deception and distortion in their interpersonal relationships. From the book of The Acts we are aware that "all who believed were together" (Acts 2:44), they tarried until they were endued with power (Acts 1:8), and each understood the other apart from the binding necessities of language (Acts 2:6).

A Christian understanding of personality, therefore, gives careful attention to nature and quality of fellowship between persons and to the disruptive disharmonies within personality and between personalities. From the vantage point of a Christian understanding of personality, the demonic effect of the "dividing walls of hostility" that separate people from their better selves and from each other are always taken seriously. The primary concern of the person who values personality above all other considerations is to see that both individuals and groups are at their best when they have adequate emotional access to their total sphere of interpersonal relationships. Spiritual growth is perceived by such a person in terms of the constant expansion of that sphere; that is, the removal of barriers of childish needs for omnipotence, family constrictions, cultural idolatry, and every other "high thing" of temporal status that separates, isolates, and insulates individuals and groups from the "largest family of mankind." Such barriers are simply signs of those points at which growth has ceased and death has set in. This, it seems to me, is the core of the thought of Paul in this passage:

> . . . remember that you were at that time separated from Christ, alienated from the commonwealth of Israel, and strangers to the covenants of promise, having no hope and without God in the world. But now in Christ Jesus you who once were far off have been brought near in the blood of Christ. For he is our peace, who has made us both one, and has broken down the dividing wall of hostility, by abolishing in his flesh the law of commandments and ordinances, that he might create in himself one new man in place of the two, so making peace, and might reconcile us both to God in one body through the cross, thereby bringing the hostility to an end.[12]

Probing further, we obviously discover that the substance of these dividing walls of hostility is fear. Persons and groups obviously are hostile toward that which they fear. To relate oneself to other people in a responsible way takes the courage to be a person in one's own right and the courage to provide and permit this privilege in others. To relate oneself to other people is to take the risk of investing love, time, energy, and money in other people. In short, it means to love them. Therefore, a dividing wall of hostility between people represents their fear of each other—the "erect defense against love's violence," to use Emily

Dickinson's phrase. These defenses are erected against the spiritual risk involved in loving one another in such a way as to be maturely and enduringly responsible to God for each other. Hence the icy walls of deception, hostility, and fear grow and separate, isolate and insulate people from the reciprocal interchange of energy, inspiration, and resourcefulness. Lines of communication are severed, actions and words are distorted as to their meaning, and the "increase of imagination" makes mountains out of molehills, and strains at gnats and swallows camels.

Oscar Pfister ably demonstrates in his book, *Christianity and Fear*,[13] that these barriers of fear are essentially "inhibitions in the capacity to love." As such, fear is seen not merely as the parent of hate, but the antithesis of love, and the deterrent to spiritual maturity. The First Letter of John clarifies these related emotions:

> There is no fear in love, but perfect love casts out fear. For fear has to do with punishment, and he who fears is not perfected in love. We love, because he first loved us. If any one says, "I love God," and hates his brother, he is a liar; for he who does not love his brother whom he has seen, cannot love God whom he has not seen. And this commandment we have from him, that he who loves God should love his brother also.[14]

Love is seen in all its perfection and maturity as the power which casts out, overcomes, and melts completely the demonic distortions of fear. It does so by re-establishing faith at the core of a man's being and extending it to the periphery of his total sphere of interpersonal relationships.

The "casting out" or "exorcistic" power of love is most vividly seen in the healing strength of the courageous love of Jesus in relation to the Gadarene demoniac. This man feared and was feared by his whole community. They consigned him to a graveyard without the benefit of a funeral. His was a living death of disruption, isolation, and separation. He was even divided within himself. The most dramatic fact in Jesus' relationship was that his perfect love cast out the man's fear and made him whole, "reclothing him" in his rightful mind.

This focuses attention on the ministry of reconciliation. Persons who are inhibited by fear and hindered in love need salvation not so much in terms of a morbid sense of guilt, as in terms of a morbid feeling of conflict and the need for peace that comes from a direct reconciliation of their conflicts. Their concern for their own salvation, egocentric as it can be, is evident in the gnawing emptiness, loneliness, and estrangement that they feel. Their boredom, ennui, and inner sourness with the world reflect the tattered meaninglessness of their lives. Found as "dead end" children, with "no exit," they break forth in the symptoms of "an age of anxiety": alcoholism, the need for a constant variety of sexual experimentation, the chronic need for counsel as an anxiety-allaying procedure, *ad infinitum* introspection, religious fads and dogmatism, and character assassination of one kind or another, both political and religious.

American theories of personality have emphasized social interaction more than European views. Nevertheless, persons like Sullivan, Horney, and others have had deep roots in European culture. The psychologists of America, such as James, Mead, and Dewey and the social psychologists such as Parsons, Allport, and Murphy, all have emphasized heavily man in relation to his total field of interpersonal involvements. Psychologists of personality who emphasize the interpersonal interaction of man have interpreted the relational qualities of his existence in horizontal and time-bound terms. The vertical relationship of man to God and to his own ultimate destiny and durable relations is dimly sensed. The severing of psychology in this century from philosophy and the earlier rupture between philosophy and theology in the age of the Enlightenment has aided and abetted this. Here again, the psychologist *as a psychologist,* afflicted as the rest of us are by overspecialization in the social sciences, stops at the city limits of his own methodological restrictions in his understanding of personality. Encouragingly enough, however, the work of Paul Tillich, David Roberts, Albert Outler, and others has done much to reopen conversation with psychologists at this point. Likewise, Frankl, Braceland, and others are taking initiative on their own to ask the transcendental questions about the depth and ultimacy of man's relationship to God.

Man as the Behaving Person Versus Behavior as the Man

The logical and psychological corrollary of the concept of personality as a struggling for wholeness is this: human behavior manifests either the order or the disorder of interpersonal relationships. Bad behavior is a symptom, not a thing-in-itself: it is a symptom of insecure interpersonal relationships and of the disrupted unity of personality. Behavior—bad or good—is a means of symbolizing and communicating "the state of our being," who we are, essentially. The Christian understanding of personality is most compatible with this kind of psychology. Therefore, the personality cannot be "added up" as a sum total of the outward acts of people. Behavior is a manifestation of the selfhood of a person. It is important in terms of the way it alters, directs, and redirects the selfhood of a person in his total interaction with his field of interpersonal relationships. The most classic example of this is the child who becomes a behavior problem in his group because of his self-rejecting alienation from others.

Some psychologists, however, have described behavior as an end within itself. John B. Watson saw human personality as the sum total of conditioned acts of an individual.[15] He drew upon the research of a greater and "clearer-headed" psychologist than himself, I. B. Pavlov, who did the basic work on conditioned reflex. Also certain neuropsychiatrists of today consider all mental disorders and behavior disorders to be direct results of chemical or mechanical imbalances or deviations within the body. They tend to depend entirely upon medical, mechanical, and surgical procedures for the treatment of patients.

Curiously enough, similarly contrasting concepts of personality appear in the biblical approaches to personality. The legalists of the Old and New Testament tended to fall into the priestly tradition of scribes who perpetuated a fixed law for all behavior. A child was to be conditioned in every detail of his growing life to depend upon the exactitudes of the law. Safety from all harm was to be found in conformity to all established law. It was a morality to be obeyed, strictly adhered to, and the traits the law gave were to be sought with diligence. Long life, prosperity, freedom from disease, and the favor of God and man were the sure rewards. It was epitomized in the scribes and Pharisees and has been called "religion at a low temperature."

Even in the Christian tradition this type of psychology took root as early as the work of the Judaizers, and was firmly established by the time of Tertullian who developed rules of behavior that he aptly called "molds" for Christian lives. Today this type of behaviorism is seen in the confusion of morality with spirituality which characterizes much of both Catholic and Protestant fundamentalism.

On the other hand, another biblical psychology presents life as the pilgrimage of faith in God which has as its goal self-discovery, self-direction, and self-dedication to a high calling of God in Jesus Christ. At its core this psychology is held together by a prophetic awareness of finitude, weakness, limitation, and sin, the acute need for reconciliation and fellowship with God and all of mankind. The realistic sense of personhood set in motion by such an awareness results in a sense of anointing, of having been sent. A sense of personal identity becomes the main determinant of behavior. The binding, covenant relationship of grace and love nourishes this personal identity with the fellowship to which the person belongs. The covenant relationship, as depicted in both the Old and New Testament, is the concrete biblical equivalent of what we have hitherto called "interpersonal relationships." The self-concept is cast in the devising dynamics of the covenant-situation between man and God in the Christian community. The Christian's sense of mission is the declaration of the fellowship of the forgiven.

Such a sense of mission creates a dynamic rather than a static morality. This morality becomes anxious over alienation and separation; when this anxiety is creative, it drives the individual constructively toward freedom through reconciliation and forgiveness. It does not become all the more anxious by adding more minutiae of the law. Such compulsion draws the individual more and more away from people as he seeks to devise new ways of atoning for his personal guilt apart from love. Self-atonement produces a compulsive fear of bondage unto death. But the distinctly Christian behavior springs from a covenant of love, not an institution that works automatically for its own good rather than personally for those for whom it exists. As Jesus said about the Sabbath, so it can be said about all human institutions: they were made for men, not men for them.

Otherwise, men become related to each other and to themselves as instruments and means rather than as ends within themselves. Men become tools of the Sabbath. Even divorce was made for men and not men for divorce. Men can become chattels and commodities to each other to be sold in job lots on the bargain counters of institutions: mass religion, mass education, mass states, mass pressure groups. Thus the demonic enters the sphere of interpersonal relationships. The glory of the incorruptible God is changed into the image of corruptible man, the worship of the Creator is exchanged for the worship of the creature, and the truth of God is exchanged for a lie.

Unconditional Love Versus Man as a Means, or Tool

The distinctly Christian understanding of personality is founded upon an unconditional love for rather than an instrumental use of persons. Therefore, it joins forces with psychologists who see men as persons rather than as things. Martin Buber says that there are two kinds of relationship: an I-Thou relationship and an I-It relationship. The I-Thou relationship can only be expressed by the whole being in relation to another whole person. The I-It can never express the whole being, but only a part responding to a part, although these may be quite legitimate responses.

He says, further, that the I-It relation is one in which we enjoy and use people as objects and things. The I-Thou relation is one in which we participate sacrificially with and without ulterior ends with people as persons. In the I-Thou encounter with God

> Every real relation with a being or life in the world is exclusive. Its *Thou* is freed, steps forth, is single, and confronts you. It fills the heavens. This does not mean that nothing else exists; but all else lives in *its* light. As long as the presence of the relation continues, this its cosmic range is inviolable. But as soon as a *Thou* becomes *It,* the cosmic range of the relation appears as an offense to the world, its exclusiveness as an exclusion of the universe.
>
> In the relation with God unconditional exclusiveness and unconditional inclusiveness are one. He who enters on the absolute relation is concerned with nothing isolated any more, neither things nor beings, neither earth nor heaven; but everything is gathered up in the relation. For to step into pure relation is not to disregard everything but to see everything in the Thou, not to renounce the world but to establish it on its true basis. To look away from the world, or to stare at it, does not help a man to reach God: but he who sees the world in Him stands in His presence. "Here world, there God" is the language of *It;* "God in the world" is another language of *It;* but to eliminate or leave behind nothing at all, to include the whole world in the *Thou,* to give the world its due and its truth, to include nothing beside God but everything in Him— this is the full and complete relation.[16]

Then also as Tillich has said:

> Our everyday tools are not merely things. Everything resists the fate of being considered or treated as a mere thing, as an object that has no subjectivity.[17]

Conversely this concept of an I-Thou relationship to God gives us some insight into his relation to us. We are not simply tools in his hands whereby he manipulates us toward his chosen ends, disregarding the creative power with which he endowed us. To believe that he does so makes magic of religion in that men "turn the tables" and begin to try to manipulate and manage God! Rather, as Kunkel puts it, creation continues. That which is wrought out in fellowship with God in participation toward eternal meaning in our ultimate concerns is truly "the finishing of his *new* creation."

Spiritual maturity and the capacity for love. The Christian understanding of personality is at one with those psychologies of personality which accord to the capacity for love the highest place in measuring of the mature person. Andras Angyal has declared, "Love . . . is the very crux of the entire problem of personality." [18] The capacity for love, says Erich Fromm, is not an automatically "given" reality into which one "falls." It is the culmination of the growth of a person.

Karl Menninger places love at the center of his conception of personality, describing it as "the transformer" of "the impulse to fight into the impulse to work or play, as the native strength of growth, as the power of reconciliation, and as the pre-eminent value in our scale of values." [19]

The Christian interpretation of personality has great compatibility with such thinking. The apostle Paul places love as the most excellent spiritual gift, and the supreme test of "those who walk by the Spirit of Christ." In I Corinthians 13 he rejected false criteria of spiritual excellence—silver-tongued oratory, cultic knowledge, fanatical faith, and compulsive religious service. He recorded the symptoms of immaturity—impatience and irritability, jealousy and hypercompetitiveness, and delight in evil tidings. He spelled out the characteristics of mature faith—humility of utterance, knowing that we know in part and prophesy in part, and accepting limitations in ourselves and others. In Ephesians also, we find the wedding of truth and love in the maturity that is in Christ:

Rather, speaking the truth in love, we are to grow up in every way into him who is the head, into Christ, from whom the whole body, joined and knit together by every joint, with which it is supplied, when each part is working properly, makes bodily growth and upbuilds itself in love.[20]

The continuities between certain types of personality psychology and the Christian understanding of personality are many and important, then. Likewise, the common concerns are obvious, even though the approach to these concerns is different. However, the unique contribution of the Christian faith to the understanding of personality does not appear until we recognize the unique manner in which the theologian approaches the problem of personality and until we assess the radical importance of faith in Jesus Christ for the understanding of personality.

UNIQUENESS IN THE CHRISTIAN UNDERSTANDING OF PERSONALITY

A Unique Relationship

The Christian deals with many of the same problems as does any other psychologist of personality. However, he approaches these problems in a unique manner, by reason of his relationship to God in Christ through the Holy Spirit. For example, the origin of religion, the development of personality, the structure of personality, the destruction of personality, and the spiritual goals of man's becoming are faced by both the Christian and the non-Christian psychologist.

However, the Christian faces these problems with the consciousness of a unique relationship. The results of his thinking may occasionally be the same. The spiritual motivation for the results and the meaning they have for the person involved may be quite different. For instance, to say: "I am trying to grow up, and therefore I have decided to do thus and so," is one thing. To say, "The Holy Spirit revealed my sin to me and I have decided to have done with this way of life," is quite another thing. The results in behavior may be the same, but the relationship in the one instance is to the self only, but in the other instance the relationship involves an I-Thou encounter with God. However, one must hasten to say that the two statements *may* mean exactly the same thing in our religiously shy generation. The former person may feel exactly as does the latter person, but does not want to appear "religious"!

So it is with the discussions of common concerns of psychologists and theologians at many points. The psychologist as a Christian may be perfectly willing, for example, to interpret personality development in terms of the Christian concept of sanctification, as does Ernest White in his book, *The Christian Life and the Unconscious*. But many of them probably would not want to be "caught dead" using such "archaic" thought forms with their colleagues in the American Psychological Association. However, this religious shyness does not prevent many theological problems from corresponding closely with those to which the psychologist gives his energies in study.

A Review of the Overlapping of the Psychological and the Christian Understanding of Personality

As has been pointed out in the preceding chapters, the psychology of personality represents a real secularization of the religious life of man. The discussion of the origin of religion, for instance, is really an effort to reduce the doctrine of the creation of man to phenomenological terms. Nevertheless, the theologian continues to discuss the same problem with equal concern in terms of the ultimate responsibility man has to God for his existence and in terms of the biblical and poetic insights which reveal his nature. The development of personality as a concern of psychologists is being dealt with eschatologically by the Christian theologian in terms of man's ultimate destiny as it affects the course of his Christian life, the given *kairoi* of his existence. The structure of personality as it is being dealt with by psychologists is also considered by theologians in terms of a man's fleshly nature in his distance from God and the spiritual nature of the same man in his relationship to God. The theologian talks of Christian ethics, and the psychologist describes the intracommunication of the self with itself and the bases of its communication with the larger community of selves.

The destruction of the personality is considered by theologians such as Tillich in the light of the threat of ultimate destruction, the threat of meaninglessness, and the threat of condemnation. In more biblical frames of reference, the whole issue of idolatry and demonism also conceptually overlaps with the psychological estimates of the disintegrated person. Furthermore, the mechanisms of personality have been intuitively identified, although not systematically classified, by the seers and spiritual "witnesses" since the writings of the eighth-century prophets and of the Genesis accounts. We also saw how vividly in the preceding chapters the Christian conception of revelation interplays with the functional descriptions of the psychological mechanisms of personality. Finally, we saw the whole problem of conflict and integration in relation to the spiritual goals of man's becoming as being intimately involved with the biblical doctrine of the Kingdom of God.

The Unique Personality of Jesus Christ

The fretful searches of both the empirical psychologist and the dogmatic theologian themselves seem to be quests for redemption. Together they represent the common frustration of a twofold movement. On the one hand, the dogmatic theologian, moving upon man's situation with an objective, authoritative, once-and-for-all revelation, has often tacitly left the impression that God "uses humanity only as a means of facilitating his stay here." On the other hand, the psychologists of personality, taking the lusty naturalism of the Enlightenment as their cue, have moved from the human angle, their method has been *ab homine* and, God, if he enters the convention at all, is an invited guest from another specialty.

The theologians come to the city limits of man's finitude on one side of the line, and the psychologists come to the same limits on the other side of the line. Apart from some unique Person before whom both are caused to accept the fact that psychologists and theologians, too, are weak and sinful men with hope in this Person, the conversation between them may become impossible. They both will remain strangers to each other. The confusion of tongues will continue to arise in the Babel of man's towerlike "systems" and "sciences." (Let it be noted here that "specialized" theologians today also often speak of themselves as "scientists.")

Both these methods, with no relation to each other are mere abstractions, and, in the phraseology of Surjit Singh,

> when the world of our knowledge is investigated under conditioned circumstances they are valid. But when an attempt is made to catch a glimpse of the oneness of the world they are useless tools.[21]

The claim to uniqueness of the Christian understanding of personality resides wholly in the Person of Jesus Christ. The experiential movement of man to God and the dogmatic thrust of God's dicta to man are overcome in the fact that Christ himself is the Word. As Singh says, in Christ

> we start neither from man nor from God. These two starting points are not at our disposal. We do not have God as such. He is the God of the world and man. He is related to his creation. It is this God we deal with and come in contact with, but God as such we never know. So also we do not know man as such. He is an abstraction. The man of our acquaintance is a man in relation. He is an evaluated person. He is either the bondservant of sin and the world, or the bondservant of Christ and the free man of the world.[22]

The unique factor in the Christian understanding of personality is that the origin of man has no meaning apart from his redemption in Christ. The development of man is a "wandering" apart from the relationship to Christ which endows that development with both motive and pattern of action, goals for living, and the hope to wait patiently upon their achievement. The structure of personality has no real form unless Christ be formed in man. Man's struggle with the demonic and for the ultimate ends of his becoming are lonely and pointless apart from the comradeship of the One who through the Resurrection is "with him to the end of the ages."

P. T. Forsyth is right when he says:

> God and man meet in humanity, not as two entities or natures which coexist, but as two movements in mutual interplay, struggle, and reciprocal communion. We have these two movements permeating the whole life of historic humanity, and founding its spiritual psychology. If we leave Christ out of the view for the moment, we recognize such a strife, such a "Lord's controversy," not in Israel only, but in the great psychology of the race.[23]

The early Christians did not see themselves as being persons related to each other because of their maturity, nor their inalienable rights as citizens of any created order, nor because of their God-given divinity in creation. They perceived themselves as persons by reason of their having met and received the gift of life from the Living Christ. In fact, they spoke in at least one place (I Peter 2:10) of having been "no people" before having met Christ and become the people of God by the call from darkness to light. This meeting was a decisive moment. Lines of continuity lay between their new lives and the lives they lived before having met Christ; they were not completely different. But the dramatic sense of identity and personhood they shared together by being "in Christ" marked a radical discontinuity between the "new creation" and the "old things" that had passed away; they would never be completely the same again. This meeting with Christ called for a decision.

Confronted with the uniqueness of the Person of Christ, we

can say, then, that the uniqueness of the Christian understanding of man involves five basic affirmations about human personality:

1. Man is a creature under the Lordship of Christ. Man's finitude is taken for granted in the Christian understanding of man. The bounds of his habitation are set, for it is God that has created him and not he himself. *Ab homine* approaches to psychology tend to perceive man as a creator rather than as a creature; the Christian understanding of personality adopts the fact of man's creaturehood forthrightly. He is the creature, the chief end of whom is to glorify God and to enjoy him forever. The fact of his creaturehood is consummated in the fact of death and overcome in the power of the resurrection through faith in Christ. Through the hope of the resurrection man is not shut up to the *no exits* of finitude. But he must come to terms with the fact of his creatureliness in the set end to his existence in death. At the risk of being misunderstood by all who do not like to face the fact of death, the Christian understanding of human personality begins with the fact of man's mortality, creaturehood, and finitude.

2. Man is a sinner, in need of redemption in Christ. Man's sinfulness does not arise merely from his finitude. His sin is something that he adds to his creaturehood by declaring himself independent of God and trying to be God. He infinitizes himself, even though the hard facts of reality are stacked against him. From the point of view of the insight gained in psychotherapy, a time comes when the patient either takes a stand with certain facts about himself and decides that these facts represent him as he really is, or he does not. He decides upon the nature of his resources for dealing with himself as he is, for getting himself off his own hands, that they may be free for creative effort. He turns to a redeemer. His therapist disavows the role if he is a good therapist for he, too, is a man of like passions with him. The patient has to call upon some name. The Christian faith affirms that this redemption comes through Christ and Christ alone.

Through the courage to affirm ourselves as sinners before God, we are faced with the possibility of redemptive acceptance in Christ. It is not that we accept Christ, but that he accepts us, though we know ourselves to be unacceptable. He encounters our chaotic distortions, lays bare our need to play God, and understands our desire to be an exception to the need for redemption by telling us of his own temptations in the wilderness. His love overwhelms us with a sure sense of lasting forgiveness and confronts us with a decision.

3. *Man and the power of decision.* The Christian understanding of personality leaves man at last "face to face with a choice and venture . . . actively in the sense of *a decision* . . . ." [24] as P. T. Forsyth has said. The Kingdom of God is at hand, and this day is the day of salvation. This is another way of saying that the issues are drawn and a decision is demanded. Kierkegaard has aptly described this as a leap of faith. Man does not move from stage to stage of personality development automatically. Nor is he kept from it by the plethora of circumstances, multiplied by the empirical descriptions. He moves as he decides to move or not to move. The role of decision in the making and remaking of personality is being brought to the fore by some of the existential psychologists of personality, but this is not yet being felt at the clinical level of treatment. The heart of the matter from the vantage point of a Christian understanding of personality is in both the freedom to make a decision and the necessity of making a decision, for redemption is a matter of life and death. In the presence of the Christ, a decision is unavoidable.

4. *Man's decision is to take up a cross, to suffer.* The redemptive character of suffering is unique to the Christian understanding of personality. Until recently the whole thrust of the psychological understanding of personality has been Aristotelian in that well-being, through the practice of the golden mean, is the

summum bonum of life. But today Viktor Frankl, Gordon Allport, and others are exploring the meaningful character of suffering. The death, burial, and resurrection of Christ present the
Christian hope in the context of meaningful and purposeful suffering. This suffering is consciously chosen in the decision of which
we have just spoken. Heidegger speaks of the "thrown situation"
into which man has been thrust. This is man's vocation. His suffering is his vocation. The decision facing man is not merely
what he will do with Jesus Christ, as was asked by Pilate, but
also what he will do about his own sufferings. He is faced as
were the sons of Zebedee of whom Jesus asked: "Are you able
to drink of the cup I am about to drink?" We are real persons if
we can answer as did they: "We are able!" This is the courage
to be, as Tillich calls it. Until this time this dimension of personality, being and becoming, is uniquely Christian.

5. *Man is called.* Whereas man's "thrown situation" is his
vocation, what he decides in Christ to do about it is *his calling.*
The New Testament speaks on almost every page of the calling
of persons forth to discipleship, on pilgrimages, not knowing
where they were to go, to be "saints," out of darkness into a
marvelous light, to be with Christ, to heal the sick, and so on.
This is a dimension of personality, both in its being and its becoming, to which almost no reference has been made in the empirical research which I have read. Gordon Allport is more explicit than others. Again, Viktor Frankl is helpful in his interpretation of suffering and work. But in the New Testament understanding of personhood in Christ this is the very atmosphere
which one breathes. John Knox maintained that a person is considered indestructible in the light of this calling. Neither life
nor death can touch this person, for he has received the love of
God in Christ, from everlasting to everlasting. He is called into
the durable relationships of the lasting fellowship of the resur-
rected community of suffering. To this end was he born and for
this purpose came he into the world.

NOTES FOR CHAPTER XII

1. Goethe, *Faust*, Part I, lines 1924-1926.
2. John Baillie, *The Idea of Revelation in Recent Thought* (New York: Columbia University Press, 1956), p. 43.
3. "The Enlightenment," *Encyclopaedia of Religion and Ethics*, Vol. V New York: Charles Scribner's Sons, 1912), p. 316.
4. "The Enlightenment," *The New Schaff-Herzogg Encyclopaedia of Religious Knowledge*, Vol. IV (New York: Funk & Wagnalls Company, 1909), p. 143.
5. *The Living of These Days* (New York: Harper & Brothers, 1956), p. 247.
6. Romans 1:20a.
7. John Oman, *Grace and Personality* (New York: The Macmillan Company, 1925), p. 26.
8. Matthew 5:27-30, RSV.
9. Leslie Paul, *The Meaning of Existence* (New York: J. B. Lippincott Company, 1950), p. 84. Used by permission.
10. *Ibid.*, p. 1.
11. Martin Buber, *I and Thou* (Edinburgh: T. & T. Clark, 1937), p. 39. By permission.
12. Ephesians 2:12-16, RSV.
13. The Macmillan Company, 1944.
14. I John 4:18-21, RSV.
15. See John B. Watson, *Psychology from the Standpoint of a Behaviorist* (Philadelphia: J. B. Lippincott Company, 1919).
16. Martin Buber, *I and Thou*, *op. cit.*, pp. 78-79.
17. Paul Tillich, *Systematic Theology*, Vol. I (Chicago: University of Chicago Press, 1952), p. 173.
18. Andras Angyal, "A Theoretical Model for Personality Studies," *The Journal of Personality*, Vol. 20, No. 1, September, 1951.
19. Karl Menninger, *Love Against Hate* (New York: Harcourt, Brace & Company, Inc., 1942), pp. 260-261, 272, 293-294.
20. Ephesians 4:15-16.
21. Surjit Singh, *Preface to Personality* (Madras, India: Christian Literature Society, 1952), p. 63. Used by permission.
22. *Ibid.*
23. P. T. Forsyth, *The Person and Place of Christ* (Boston: Pilgrim Press, 1909), p. 336. Used by permission.
24. *Ibid.*

BIBLIOGRAPHY

Abraham, Karl, *Selected Papers*, trans. Douglas Bryan and Alix Strachey (London: Hogarth Press, 1948).

Adler, Polly, *A House Is Not a Home* (New York: Popular Library, 1953). Copyright by Rinehart & Co., Inc.

Adorno, T. W., *The Authoritarian Personality* (New York: Harper & Brothers, 1950).

Allport, Gordon, *Becoming: Basic Considerations for a Psychology of Personality* (New Haven, Conn.: Yale University Press, 1955).

———, *The Individual and His Religion* (New York: The Macmillan Company, 1950).

———, "The Roots of Religion," *Pastoral Psychology* (May, 1954).

———, *Personality: A Psychological Interpretation* (New York: Henry Holt & Company, Inc., 1937).

Angyal, Andras, *Foundations for a Science of Personality* (New York: The Commonwealth Fund, 1941).

———, "A Theoretical Model for Personality Studies," *The Journal of Personality*, Vol. 20, No. 1 (Sept., 1951).

Ansbacher, Heinz and Rowena, eds., *The Individual Psychology of Alfred Adler* (New York: Basic Books, Inc., 1956).

Arey, Leslie B., *Developmental Anatomy: A Textbook and Laboratory Manual of Embryology* (Philadelphia: W. B. Saunders Company, 1947).

Bailey, Derrick Sherwin, *The Mystery of Love and Marriage* (New York: Harper & Brothers, 1952).

Baillie, John, *The Idea of Revelation in Recent Thought* (New York: Columbia University Press, 1956).

Barth, Karl, *Church Dogmatics*, trans. A. C. Cochrane (Philadelphia: Westminster Press, 1953).

———, *The Doctrine of the Word of God* (New York: Charles Scribner's Sons, 1936).

Berdyaev, Nikolas, *Solitude and Society* (London: The Centenary Press, 1938).

Bergsten, Göte, *Pastoral Psychology* (New York: The Macmillan Company, 1951).

Bergson, Henri, *The Two Sources of Morality and Religion* (New York: Doubleday & Company, Inc., 1954).

Berry, Brewton, *Race Relations: The Interaction of Ethnic and Racial Groups* (Boston: Houghton Mifflin Company, 1951).

Blanton, Smiley, *Love or Perish* (New York: Simon & Schuster, Inc., 1945).

Boisen, Anton, *The Exploration of the Inner World* (New York: Harper & Brothers, 1952).

———, *Religion in Crisis and Custom* (New York: Harper & Brothers, 1955).

Bonhoeffer, Dietrich, *Life Together* (London: S.C.M. Press, 1949).

Bowman, John Wick, *The Religion of Maturity* (New York: Abingdon Press, 1948).

Brunner, Emil, *The Christian Doctrine of Creation and Redemption: Dogmatics*, trans. Olive Wyon (Philadelphia: Westminster Press, 1952).

———, *Man in Revolt: A Christian Anthropology*, trans. Olive Wyon (Philadelphia: Westminster Press, 1947).

Buber, Martin, *Between Man and Man*, trans. R. G. Smith (London: Routledge and Kegan Paul, 1947). Copyright held by The Macmillan Company, New York.

———, *Good and Evil* (New York: Charles Scribner's Sons, 1953).

———, *I and Thou* (Edinburgh: T. & T. Clark, 1937).

Bull, N., "The Biological Basis of Value," *Science Monthly*, 1941, 53.

Bultmann, Rudolf, *New Testament and Mythology*, "Kerygma and Myth: A Theological Debate," ed. Hans W. Bartsch (London: S.P.C.K., 1953).

———, *Theology of the New Testament*, 2 vols. (New York: Charles Scribner's Sons, 1954).

Bunyan, John, *Grace Abounding*, Tercentenary edition.

Bushnell, Horace, *Christian Nurture* (New York: Charles Scribner's Sons, 1890).

Calvin, John, *Institutes of the Christian Religion*, trans. John Allen (Philadelphia: Presbyterian Board of Publication and Sabbath Work, 1902).

Calvin's Commentaries (Grand Rapids, Mich.: Wm. B. Eerdmans Publishing Company, 1948).

Campbell, C. MacFie, *Human Personality and the Environment* (New York: The Macmillan Company, 1934).

Cannon, Walter B., *The Wisdom of the Body* (New York: W. W. Norton & Company, Inc., 1932).

Cassirer, Ernst, *The Philosophy of the Enlightenment* (Princeton, N.J.: Princeton University Press, 1951).

Cattell, Raymond B., *An Introduction to Personality Study* (London: Hutchinson House, 1950).

Chamberlain, William D., *The Meaning of Repentance* (Philadelphia: Westminster Press, 1943).

Cochrane, C. N., *Christianity and Classical Culture* (New York: Oxford Press, 1944).

Cole, Lawrence E., *Human Behavior: Psychology as a Biosocial Science* (Yonkers-on-the-Hudson, New York: World Book Company, 1953).

Culler, E., "A Phobic Case," *British Journal of Medical Psychology*, 1930, 10.

Cullmann, Oscar, *Christ and Time: The Primitive Conception of Time and History* (Philadelphia: Westminster Press, 1950).

David, H. P., and Helmut Von Bracken, *Perspectives in Personality Theory* (New York: Basic Books, Inc., 1957).

Dewey, John, *A Common Faith* (New Haven, Conn.: Yale University Press, 1934).

Dobzhansky, Theodosius, *Evolution, Genetics and Man* (New York: John Wiley & Sons, Inc., 1955).

Dostoevsky, Fyodor, *The Idiot* (New York: Brentano's, 1887).

Dunlap, Knight, *Religion: Its Function in Human Life* (New York: McGraw-Hill Book Company, Inc., 1946).

Durkheim, Emile, *The Elementary Forms of the Religious Life* (London: G. Allen and Unwin, Ltd., 1915).

Eliot, T. S., *Collected Poems 1909–1935* (New York: Harcourt, Brace & Company, Inc., 1950).

English, O. Spurgeon, and G. H. J. Pearson, *Emotional Problems of Living: Avoiding the Neurotic Pattern,* revised and enlarged edition (New York: W. W. Norton & Company, Inc., 1955).

"The Enlightenment," *Encyclopaedia of Religion and Ethics* (New York: Charles Scribner's Sons, 1912).

"The Enlightenment," *The New Schaff-Herzogg Encyclopaedia of Religious Knowledge* (New York: Funk & Wagnalls, 1909).

Ferre, Nels F. S., *Evil and the Christian Faith* (New York: Harper & Brothers, 1947).

Fletcher, Joseph, *Morals and Medicine* (Princeton, N.J.: Princeton University Press, 1954).

Forsyth, P. T., *The Person and Place of Christ* (Boston: The Pilgrim Press, 1909).

Fosdick, Harry Emerson, *The Living of These Days* (New York: Harper & Brothers, 1956).

Frankl, Viktor, *The Doctor and the Soul* (New York: Alfred A. Knopf, Inc., 1955).

Freud, Sigmund, *The Complete Psychological Works*, trans. James Strachey (London: Hogarth Press, 1955).

———, "A Neurosis of Demoniacal Possession in the 17th Century," *Collected Papers*, Vol. IV, trans. Joanne Riviere (London: Hogarth Press, 1949), p. 70; "Repression," Vol. II; "Narcissism," Vol. IV.

———, *The Ego and the Id* (London: Hogarth Press, 1947).

———, *The Future of an Illusion* (London: Hogarth Press, 1943).

———, *Group Psychology and the Analysis of the Ego* (London: Hogarth Press, 1948).

———, *New Introductory Lectures on Psychoanalysis*, trans. W. H. J. Sprott (London: Hogarth Press, 1933).

———, *The Problem of Anxiety* (New York: W. W. Norton & Company, Inc., 1936).

———, *Three Contributions to the Theory of Sex*, trans. A. A. Brill (New York: Nervous and Mental Disease Monographs, 1930).

———, *Totem and Taboo* (New York: Modern Library Edition of the Basic Writings of Sigmund Freud, 1938).

Fromm, Erich, *Escape from Freedom* (New York: Farrar and Rinehart, 1941).

———, *The Forgotten Language* (New York: Rinehart & Company, Inc., 1951).

———, "Man Is Not a Thing," *Saturday Review of Literature* (March 16, 1957).

———, *Psychoanalysis and Religion* (New Haven, Conn.: Yale University Press, 1950).

Gardner, Edmund G., ed. and trans., *The Book of St. Bernard on the Love of God* (New York: E. P. Dutton & Co., Inc., 1915).

Gemelli, A., "The Nature and Genesis of Character," *Quarterly of Psychiatry*, 1930, 17.

Gesell, Arnold, Frances Ilg, and Louise Ames, *The Child from Five to Ten* (New York: Harper & Brothers).

————, *The First Five Years of Life: The Pre-School Years* (New York: Harper & Brothers, 1940).

————, *The Infant and Child in the Culture of Today* (New York: Harper & Brothers, 1944).

————, *Youth: The Years from Ten to Sixteen* (New York: Harper & Brothers, 1956).

Goethe, Johann Wolfgang von, *Faust* (New York: Random House, Inc., 1950).

Greenacre, Phyllis, "The Predisposition to Anxiety," *Psychoanalytic Quarterly*, 1941, 10.

Gruhl, Hans W., "Inheritance of Psychic Traits," *Deutsche Med. Wschr.*, 1947.

Hadfield, J. A., *Psychology and Morals: An Analysis of Character* (New York: R. H. McBride and Company, 1925).

Harding, M. Esther, *Journey into Self* (New York, Longmans, Green, & Co., 1956).

Harriman, Philip, ed., *The New Dictionary of Psychology* (New York: Philosophical Library, 1947).

Havighurst, Robert J., *Human Development and Education* (New York: Longmans, Green & Company, Inc., 1953).

Healy, William, Augusta F. Bronner and Anna Mae Bowers, *The Structure and Meaning of Psychoanalysis as Related to Personality and Behavior* (New York: Alfred A. Knopf, Inc., 1938).

Heraclitus, *Early Greek Philosophy*, trans. John Burnette (London: A. & C. Black, Ltd., 1930).

Hiltner, Seward, *Self-Understanding* (New York: Charles Scribner's Sons, 1951).

Hocking, William E., *Human Nature and Its Remaking* (New Haven: Yale University Press, 1923).

————, *The Meaning of God in Human Experience: A Philosophic Study of Religion* (New Haven, Conn.: Yale University Press, 1922).

Hoskins, R. G., *The Biology of Schizophrenia* (New York: W. W. Norton & Company, Inc., 1946).

Hugel, Baron Von, *The Mystical Element in Religion* (London: J. M. Dent and Sons, 1923).

Ilg, Frances, and Louise B. Ames, *Child Behavior* (New York: Harper & Brothers, 1955).

Jacobi, Jolan, *The Psychology of Jung*, trans. K. W. Bash (New Haven, Conn.: Yale University Press, 1943).
Jacobson, H. P., "Religion and the Fragmentation," *The Journal of Religion*, Vol. XXXII (January, 1952).
James, William, *Outlines of Psychology* (New York: Henry Holt & Company, Inc., 1950).
———, *The Varieties of Religious Experience* (New York: Modern Library, 1902).
Jastrow, Morris, *The Study of Religion* (New York: Charles Scribner's Sons, 1902).
Johnson, A. R., *The Vitality of the Individual in the Thought of Ancient Israel* (Cardiff: University of Wales Press, 1949).
Jolivet, Regis, *Introduction to Kierkegaard*, trans. W. H. Barber (London: Frederick Muller, Ltd., 1950).
Jowett, B. (trans.), *The Works of Plato* (New York: The Tudor Publishing Company).
Jung, C. G., *The Integration of Personality*, ed. Stanley Del (New York: Farrar and Rinehart, 1939). Copyright by Routledge & Kegan Paul, Ltd., 1948.
———, *Modern Man in Search of a Soul* (New York: Harcourt, Brace and Company, 1933).
———, *Psychological Types*, trans. H. G. Baynes (New York: Harcourt, Brace & Company, Inc., 1938).
———, *Psychology and Religion* (New Haven, Conn.: Yale University Press, 1938).

Kallman, Franz J., "The Genetic Theory of Schizophrenia," *Personality in Nature, Society, and Culture*, eds. Clyde Kluckhohn and Henry A. Murray (New York: Alfred A. Knopf, Inc., 1949).
Kant, Immanuel, *Gesemmelte Schriften* (Reimer-Verlag, 1908).
Kelley, T. L., "The Inheritance of Mental Traits," *Psychologies of 1930*, (Worcester, Mass.: Clark University Press, 1930).
Kierkegaard, Søren, *Either-Or*, trans. David and Lillian Swenson (Princeton, N. J.: Princeton University Press, 1949).
———, *On Authority and Revelation*, trans. Walter Lowrie (Princeton, N. J.: Princeton University Press, 1955).

————, *The Sickness unto Death* (Princeton, N. J.: Princeton University Press, 1941).

————, *Stages on Life's Ways*, trans. Walter Lowrie (Princeton, N. J.: Princeton University Press, 1945).

Kinsey, A. C., W. B. Pomeroy, and C. E. Martin, *Sexual Behavior in the Human Male* (Philadelphia: W. B. Saunders Company, 1948).

Kraemer, Hendrik, *The Communication of the Christian Faith* (Philadelphia: Westminster Press, 1956).

————, *Religion and the Christian Faith* (London: Lutterworth Press, 1956).

Kramer, Henry, and James Sprenger, *Malleus Maleficarum* (London: The Pushkin Press, 1948).

Lamprecht, Sterling P., *Our Philosophical Traditions: A Brief History of Philosophy in Western Civilization* (New York: Appleton-Century-Crofts, Inc., 1955).

Langton, Edward, *Essentials of Demonology: A Study of Jewish and Christian Doctrine, Its Origin and Development* (London: Eppleworth Press, 1945).

Lecky, Prescott, *Self-Consistency: A Theory of Personality* (New York: Island Press, 1945). Copyright by Kathryn Lecky.

Leroy and Medakovitch, "Mystical Delirium in Two Twins," *Annals of Medical Psychology*, 1929, 87 (II).

Leuba, James H., *The Psychological Study of Religion: Its Origin, Its Function, Its Future* (New York: The Macmillan Company, 1912).

Lewin, Kurt, *A Dynamic Theory of Personality* (New York: McGraw-Hill Book Company, Inc., 1955).

Lindbergh, Anne Morrow, *Gift from the Sea* (New York: Pantheon Books, Inc., 1955).

MacDougall, William, *Outline of Psychology* (New York: Charles Scribner's Sons, 1927).

Mainx, Felix, "Foundations of Biology," *International Encyclopedia of United Science* (Chicago: University of Chicago Press, 1955).

Marsh, John, "Time," *A Theological Word Book of the Bible*, ed. Alan Richardson (New York: The Macmillan Company, 1952).

Marx, Karl, *Capital: A Critique of Political Economy*, trans. Moore and Aveling (Chicago: Charles H. Kerr and Co., 1921).

Maves, Paul, *The Church and Mental Health* (New York: Charles Scribner's Sons, 1952).

McCasland, S. Vernon, *By the Finger of God: Demon Possession and Exorcism in Early Christianity in the Light of Modern Views of Mental Illness* (New York: The Macmillan Company, 1951).

McClanahan, John H. "The Psychology of the Self in the Writings of Augustine," unpublished doctoral thesis, Southern Baptist Theological Seminary, Louisville, Kentucky, 1957.

Mead, Margaret, *Male and Female: A Study of the Sexes in a Changing World* (New York: William Morrow & Company, Inc., 1949).

Meiburg, Albert L., "An Understanding of the Dream as a Means of Divine Revelation" (unpublished doctoral thesis, Southern Baptist Theological Seminary, Louisville, Kentucky, 1954).

Menninger, Karl, *The Human Mind* (New York: Alfred A. Knopf, Inc., 1945).

——, *Love Against Hate* (New York: Harcourt, Brace & Company, Inc., 1942).

——, *Man Against Himself* (New York: Harcourt, Brace & Company, Inc., 1938).

Moberly, R. C., *Atonement and Personality* (London: John Murray, 1904).

Mowrer, O. H., *Learning Theory and Personality Dynamics* (New York: Ronald Press Company, 1950).

Mullahy, Patrick, *Oedipus: Myth and Complex* (New York: Hermitage Press, 1948).

Muller, Max, *Lectures on the Origin and Growth of Religion* (London: Longmans, Green, & Co., Inc., 1878).

Murphy, Gardner, *Personality: A Biosocial Approach to Origins and Structure* (New York: Harper & Brothers, 1947).

Murray, Gilbert, *Five Stages of Greek Religion* (London: Oxford University Press, 1925). Copyright held by Beacon Press, Boston.

Niebuhr, H. Richard, *Christ and Culture* (New York: Harper & Brothers, 1951).

Niebuhr, Reinhold, *Christian Doctrine of Creation and Redemption* (Philadelphia: Westminster Press, 1952).

——, *The Self and the Dramas of History* (New York: Charles Scribner's Sons, 1955).

Notcutt, Bernard, *The Psychology of Personality* (London: Methuen and Co., Ltd., 1953).

Nowell, Elizabeth, ed., *The Letters of Thomas Wolfe* (New York: Charles Scribner's Sons, 1956).

Oates, Wayne E., *Anxiety in Christian Experience* (Philadelphia: Westminster Press, 1955).

————, "Some Psychological Implications of the Doctrine of the Kingdom of God," *The Covenant Quarterly*, Vol. XVI, No. 1 (February, 1956).

Oman, John, *Grace and Personality* (New York: The Macmillan Company, 1925).

Otto, Rudolf, *The Idea of the Holy: An Inquiry into the Non-Rational Factor in the Idea of the Divine and Its Relation to the Rational*, trans. John Harvey, second edition (London: Oxford University Press, 1950).

Overstreet, H. A., *The Great Enterprise* (New York: W. W. Norton & Company, Inc., 1952).

Pascal, Blaise, *Pensées* (New York: Modern Library, 1941).

Patten, Bradley M., *Human Embryology* (Philadelphia: The Blakiston Press, 1946).

Paul, Leslie, *The Meaning of Existence* (New York: J. B. Lippincott Company, 1950).

Pederson, Johannes, *Israel: Its Life and Culture* (London: Geoffrey Cumberledge, 1940). Copyright held by Oxford University Press, London.

Petry, Ray, *Christian Eschatology and Social Thought* (New York: Abingdon Press, 1956).

Pfister, Oscar, *Christianity and Fear* (New York: The Macmillan Company, 1944).

Pickett, Colin R., *Mental Affliction and Church Law* (Ottawa, Ontario: The University of Ottawa Press, 1952).

Pickford, R. W., "Ethics and Instincts," *Ethics*, Vol. L, No. 4 (July, 1940).

Prince, Morton, *The Dissociation of Personality* (New York: Longmans, Green & Co., Inc., 1913).

Pusey, E. B., trans., *The Confessions of St. Augustine* (Mt. Vernon, New York: The Peter Pauper Press, first published in 1838).

Rank, Otto, *The Trauma of Birth* (New York: Robert Brunner Publishers, 1952).

————, *Will Therapy* (New York: Alfred A. Knopf, Inc., 1945).

Richardson, Alan, ed., *A Theological Word Book of the Bible* (New York: The Macmillan Company, 1952).

Roberts, David, *Psychotherapy and a Christian View of Man* (New York: Charles Scribner's Sons, 1950).

Robinson, John A. T., *The Body: A Study in Pauline Theology* (Chicago: Henry Regnery Company, 1952).

Rogers, Carl R., Client-Centered Therapy (Boston: Houghton Mifflin Company, 1951).

Rogers, Spencer L., "Early Psychotherapy," *Ciba Symposia*. Vol. IX, No. 1, 2 (April-May, 1947).

————, "Psychotherapy in the Greek and Roman World," *Ciba Symposia*. Vol. IX 1, 2 (April-May, 1947).

Rose, Arnold and Caroline, *America Divided* (New York: Alfred A. Knopf, Inc., 1948).

Royce, Josiah, *The Philosophy of Loyalty* (New York: The Macmillan Company, 1916).

Ruesch, Jurgen, and Weldon Kees, *Nonverbal Communication: Notes on the Visual Perception of Human Relations* (Los Angeles: University of California Press, 1956).

Rust, Eric C., *Nature and Man in Biblical Thought* (London: Lutterworth Press, 1953).

Sass, H. R., "Mixed Schools and Mixed Blood," *Atlantic Monthly*, Vol. 198, No. 5 (November, 1956).

Saul, Leon, *Emotional Maturity* (Philadelphia: J. B. Lippincott Company, 1947).

Scherer, Paul, *For We Have This Treasure* (New York: Harper & Brothers, 1944).

Schleiermacher, Friedrich, *The Christian Faith* (Edinburgh: T. & T. Clark, 1928).

————, *Speeches on Religion: Its Cultured Despisers* (London: K. Paul, Trench, Trubner and Company, Ltd. 1893).

Schweitzer, Albert, *The Philosophy of Civilization: Civilization and Ethics* (London: A. & C. Black, Ltd., 1929). American edition copyrighted by The Macmillan Company, New York.

Shakespeare, William, *Richard III*.

Sheldon, W. H., *The Varieties of Temperament* (New York: Harper & Brothers, 1942).

Sherman, Mandel, "The Mental Defective," *An Introduction to Clinical Psychology*, eds. L. A. Pennington and Irwin Berg (New York: Ronald Press Company, 1948).

Sherrill, Lewis J., *The Struggle of the Soul* (New York: The Macmillan Company, 1951).

Simpson, George E., and J. Milton Yinger, *Racial and Cultural Minorities: An Analysis of Prejudice and Discrimination* (New York: Harper & Brothers, 1953).

Singh, Surjit, *Preface to Personality* (Madras, India: Christian Literature Society, 1952).

Sinnot, Edmund W., *The Biology of the Human Spirit* (New York: Viking Press, Inc., 1955).

Skard, Ase G., *Character and Personality*, VIII, No. 1.

Smith, H. Shelton, *Changing Conceptions of Original Sin: A Study in American Theology Since 1750* (New York: Charles Scribner's Sons, 1955).

Smith, W. Robertson, *Lectures on the Religion of the Semites* (London: A. & C. Black, Ltd., 1894).

Snygg, Donald, and Arthur W. Combs, *Individual Behavior: A New Frame of Reference for Psychology* (New York: Harper & Brothers, 1949).

Soper, Edmund Davison, *Racism: A World Issue* (New York: Abingdon Press, 1947).

Spencer, Herbert, *The Principles of Psychology* (New York: D. Appleton and Co., 1892).

Starbuck, Edwin D., *The Psychology of Religion: An Empirical Study of the Growth of Religious Consciousness* (New York: Charles Scribner's Sons, 1900).

Stockard, Charles R., *The Physical Basis of Personality* (New York: McGraw-Hill Book Company, Inc., 1948).

Sullivan, Harry Stack, *The Interpersonal Theory of Psychiatry*, eds. Helen Swick Perry and Mary Ladd Gawel (New York: W. W. Norton & Company, Inc., 1953).

———, "The Study of Psychiatry," *Psychiatry*, 10, 1947.

Swenson, David, *Something About Kierkegaard*, revised edition (Minneapolis, Minn.: Augsburg Publishing House, 1945).

Thelan, Mary, *Man as a Sinner* (New York: Kings Crown Press, 1946). Copyright held by Columbia University Press.

Tillich, Paul, *The Courage to Be* (New Haven, Conn.: Yale University Press, 1952).

———, *The Protestant Era* (Chicago: University of Chicago Press, 1948).

————, *Systematic Theology* (Chicago: University of Chicago Press, 1952).

Tylor, E. B., *Primitive Culture: Researches into the Development of Mythology, Philosophy, Religion, Language, Art and Custom* (New York: Henry Holt & Company, Inc., 1889).

Ueberweg, Friedrich, *A History of Philosophy from Thales to the Present Time*, trans. George S. Morris (New York: Scribner, Armstrong and Company, 1871).

Unger, Merrill, *Biblical Demonology* (Wheaton, Illinois: Van Kampen Press, 1952).

Ward, Lester F., *Psychic Factors of Civilization* (New York: Ginn and Company, 1906).

Watson, John B., *Psychology from the Standpoint of a Behaviorist* (Philadelphia: J. B. Lippincott, 1919).

Weatherhead, Leslie D., *Psychology, Religion, and Healing* (London: Hodder and Stoughton, Ltd., 1951).

Webster's New International Dictionary of the English Language (Springfield, Mass.: G. & C. Merriam Company, Publishers, 1948).

White, Victor, *God and the Unconscious*, Foreword by C. G. Jung (London: Harvill Press, 1952).

Whitehead, Albert North, *Religion in the Making* (New York: The Macmillan Company, 1926).

Wieman, Henry Nelson, and Regina Westcott, *Normative Psychology of Religion* (New York: Thomas Y. Crowell Company, 1935).

Williams, Daniel Day, *What Present-Day Theologians Are Thinking* (New York: Harper & Brothers, 1952).

Wundt, Wilhelm, *Ethics: An Investigation of the Facts and Laws of the Moral Life*, trans. E. B. Titchener (New York: Macmillan, 1892).

Zilboorg, Gregory, *A History of Medical Psychology* (New York: W. W. Norton & Company, Inc., 1941).

————, *Mind, Medicine, and Man* (New York: Harcourt, Brace & Company, Inc., 1943).

Zunini, G. E., "La Psicologia e L'Uomo," *Riv. Filosofia Neosc., Luglio,* 1940.

INDEX

318